This book is a unique exploration of the ways in which political belief is developed and sustained throughout a lifetime. It examines the lives of fifteen British men and women, aged between seventy and ninety, who have dedicated half a century or longer to working for social change and justice. Respondents discuss topics ranging from the importance of gender identity on their political activism to their perceptions of events in Eastern Europe. Dr Andrews combines an investigation of individual lifelong political commitment with a wider consideration of the formation of social identity, aging and the interplay between individuals and their environment.

Lifetimes of commitment

Lifetimes of commitment

Aging, politics, psychology

Molly Andrews

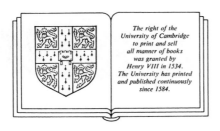

The right of the
University of Cambridge
to print and sell
all manner of books
was granted by
Henry VIII in 1534.
The University has printed
and published continuously
since 1584.

Cambridge University Press

Cambridge
New York   Port Chester
Melbourne   Sydney

Published by the Press Syndicate of the University of Cambridge
The Pitt Building, Trumpington Street, Cambridge CB2 1RP
40 West 20th Street, New York, NY 10011-4211, USA
10 Stamford Road, Oakleigh, Melbourne 3166, Australia

© Cambridge University Press 1991

First published 1991

Printed in Great Britain at the University Press, Cambridge

British Library cataloguing in publication data

Andrews, Molly
Lifetimes of commitment: aging, politics, psychology,
1. Great Britain. Political beliefs
I. Title
306.2

Library of Congress cataloguing in publication data

Andrews, Molly.
Lifetimes of commitment: aging, politics, psychology/Molly
Andrews.
    p.   cm.
Includes bibliographical references and index.
ISBN 0 521 40280 8. – ISBN 0 521 42249 3 (paperback)
1. Political participation – Great Britain – History – 20th century.
2. Social reformers – Great Britain – Interviews. I. Title.
JN1121.A84 1991
323′.042′0941 – dc20 90–24161 CIP

ISBN 0 521 40280 8 hardback
ISBN 0 521 42249 3 paperback

To my mother and father

Contents

Acknowledgements

I feel most fortunate to have been able to work on this project, not only because the research itself was so rewarding, but also because it is very heart-warming to experience the generosity of special people. I am filled with gratitude towards these people who have, in their various ways, helped to sustain me in my work.

First, I must mention the interviewees of the study. These men and women were so patient with me, as time and again I returned with yet more questions, more clarifications. Moreover, when I was tired, I drew inspiration from them which gave me the confidence and the determination I needed to carry on.

My work has benefited greatly from the feedback of several scholars. Colin Fraser, my Ph.D supervisor, sensitively combined patience with a pronounced critical perspective; he not only allowed me to pursue a project others might have rejected as too non-traditional, but he offered guidance when it was needed. I remember with great fondness Larry Kohlberg, under whose supervision I began the research which eventually led to this study. John Broughton read the whole thesis and offered me not only invaluable comments and advice but also enthusiasm and encouragement. I sent drafts of chapters to several people, and am thankful for their detailed comments: Sara Arber, Carol Gilligan, Chris Griffin, Chris Phillipson, Deborah Thom and Jay Winter.

I have made some very valuable friendships in my five years in England which have been most rewarding, emotionally and intellectually. Of the friends listed here, most have read and commented extensively upon chapters in this book, and I have had countless conversations with all of them about my work – conversations which were always stimulating while still supportive: José Alvaro, Anna Constantas, Willy Maley, Jeremy Roche, Richard Sparks and Arturo Trujillo. I have relied particularly on Shirin Rai for her unstinting support and friendship over many years. I am doubly privileged to have Marion Smith as a close friend and as my editor; I thank her for believing in this book. David Toze has had unwavering faith in me and in my work; his warmth and humour have strengthened me throughout my years in England. Finally, I thank my family who have always and everywhere been there for me.

I would like to thank the following publishers and authors for allowing me to use their copyright material at the openings of chapters: Editions Gallimard, Andre Deutsch Ltd and Weidenfeld and Nicolson Ltd for the quotation from Simone de Beauvoir's *Old Age*; Thomas Y. Cromwell and Co. for the quotation from Pope's *Poetical Works*; Transaction Publishers for the quotation from Becker's *Sociological Work: Method and Substance*; Center for Biographical Research for the quotation from Mark Harris in McCord's 'A Specter Viewed by a Specter', in *Biography* 9.3: 219–228; Faber and Faber Ltd for the quotation from Louis MacNeice's 'Autumn Journal' in Dodd's (ed.) *Collected Poems of Louis MacNeice*; Longman Group UK Ltd and Trevor Huddleston for the quotation from Caradon, Coulson and Huddleston's *Three Views on Commitment*; Methuen and Co. for the quotation from Jean-Paul Sartre's *Existentialism is Humanism* translated by P. Mairet; Unwin Hyman for the quotation from Bertrand Russell's *Portraits from Memory*; Macmillan Publishing Co. and Rhena Schweitzer Miller for the quotation from Albert Schweitzer's *Memories of Childhood and Youth*.

1 Defying the stereotype

There is only one solution if old age is not to be an absurd parody of our former life, and that is to go on pursuing ends that give our existence a meaning – devotion to individuals, to groups or to causes, social, political, intellectual or creative work. In spite of the moralists' opinion to the contrary, in old age we should wish still to have passions strong enough to prevent us turning in upon ourselves. One's life has value so long as one attributes value to the life of others, by means of love, friendship, indignation, compassion. When this is so, then there are still valid reasons for activity or speech.

Simone de Beauvoir (1970: 601)

This book tells the story of fifteen people who, for at least half a century, have dedicated themselves to working for progressive social change. It is the story of people who are both extraordinary and ordinary. The longevity of their sustained commitment marks them as extraordinary. But they are also ordinary: most are not particularly famous, although perhaps they are well known and respected in their own circles, and, apart from the fact of their long-term political activism, there is no immediately identifiable feature which sets them in an exclusive category. Finally, this is the story of a group of people who despite, or perhaps because of, their advanced years, still feel the urgency of social justice. It is this which has always inspired them and which still continues to fill them with a sense of purpose. These are lives of commitment.

Like the academic enquiries of many others, my interest in this area was initially sparked by personal experience. I was eighteen and had just begun college when I first became politically active. Frequently I encountered comments to the effect that my concern was age appropriate – that as I grew up, I would also grow out of my ideals. This was a most depressing message, and one which I intuitively rejected. Some of the faces I saw around me at political meetings and rallies bore many wrinkles indeed – a testament to the concomitant years of experience and wisdom. These were the faces of people who did not comply with the received version of the relationship between aging and activism. Years later, this was to be the subject of my doctoral study, and it is this study which forms the basis for the present book.

The project can be briefly described in the following way: between 1986 and 1988, I interviewed fifteen white[1] British socialist activists, who were between the ages of seventy and ninety. They were a heterogeneous group in terms of gender and class, and they were geographically dispersed throughout Britain. The ten 'core' respondents were interviewed for a minimum of six hours (three two-hour sessions), while most of the additional five I met on only one occasion (ranging from one to three hours). The interviews were semi-structured, bordering on open-ended. I am pleased and grateful to report that though my research for this particular study has concluded, the conversations are ongoing. The project has proven to be more longitudinal than I had anticipated.

A review of the academic terrain is most useful in assisting us in identifying and situating the major questions which have guided this work. In this chapter I shall examine how the construction of aging in the psychological literature mirrors dominant Western ideology regarding the measurement of purpose and productivity, and the relationship between the two. I shall then investigate some of the ways in which political activism has been understood and portrayed within so-called political psychology. Chapter 2 examines the potential usefulness of social identity theory for explaining the psychological make-up of elderly lifetime political activists.

Aging: the experience in Western capitalist societies

In Western capitalist democracies, elderly people tend to experience discrimination because of their age. Butler first introduced the word 'ageism' in 1968 in his description of the life of the elderly in America.

Ageism can be seen as a process of systematic stereotyping of and discrimination against people because they are old, just as racism and sexism accomplish this with skin colour and gender. Old people are categorized as senile, rigid in thought and manner, old-fashioned in morality and skills ... Ageism allows the younger generation to see old people as different from themselves; thus they subtly cease to identify with their elders as humans beings (quoted in Butler 1975: 12).

Even while some old people may have been victims of racial or sexual disrimination throughout their lives, being old introduces a new dimension of powerlessness and social marginalization. Arber and Ginn (1990) compare anti-sexist and anti-ageist arguments:

Both emphasise the socially constructed nature of their group's disadvantage ('biology is not destiny') and the ways discrimination, demeaning images and loaded language, rather than any natural differences, have all contributed to powerlessness and low self-esteem (p. 11).

However, there are also crucial differences between the two.

Most of us are socialised into our gender identity at an early age, and this gender is confirmed throughout adult life. We have never experienced being of the opposite gender, nor will we in the future. Age forms a quite different basis of stratification, since we have all been young, and expect to grow old (p. 12).

But the detrimental effects of ageism are not limited to the elderly. The not-old suffer from it in various ways, as they try to hide the physical signs of their own aging. The pressure, especially although not only for women, to remain forever youthful, is most pronounced in Western culture, and indeed very lucrative industries build their fortunes on this phenomenon. Western society as a whole is plagued by the same affliction which drove Oscar Wilde's Dorian Grey to his demise. Despite all this, however, the aging process is inevitable.

Moreover, everyone suffers from the existence of ageism because, at least in theory, everyone has their own old age to look forward to. Proust once wrote that 'Of all realities [old age] is perhaps that of which we retain a purely abstract notion longest in our lives' (quoted in de Beauvoir 1970: 10). Perhaps the not-old distance themselves from the old precisely because they see in them their future fate; in denying any identification with the elderly, they can somehow deny their own destiny. The thoughts of Martin, who is in his early teens, sum up the alienation of the young from the old:

We can't think of ourselves in that state. It is impossible. Nor can we think of the old as being like us. I suppose that if you really concentrated, you might be able to imagine the old folk you know as our age, but ordinarily you never conceive such a thing. They are old, *they are old*[2] – that is what you see and what you think. They are ill and ugly and their life is over (Blythe 1979: 93).

One older woman tells the tale from the other side:

The trouble is that old age is not interesting until one gets there, a foreign country with an unknown language to the young and even the middle-aged. I wish now that I had found out more about it (Ford & Sinclair 1987: 14).

The poet Philip Larkin begins his harrowing poem 'The Old Fools' with the question 'What do they think has happened, the old fools,/To make them like this?' His last stanza ends with a series of questions, and a final response which is both simple and resounding. 'Can they never tell/What is dragging them back, and how will it end? Not at night?/Not when the strangers come? Never, throughout/The whole hideous

inverted childhood? Well,/We shall find out.' We are all condemned to
the same fate. We all share a collective responsbility, therefore, to
redefine and rediscover meaning and purpose in later life.

Aging, like any other human phenomenon, is influenced by a variety
of factors, class, gender and ethnicity perhaps being the most salient.
Indeed, it would be wrong to speak of the elderly as a homogeneous
group: the only shared characteristic amongst them is that of increased
years. Moreover, the phrase 'old age' can indicate a period of thirty
years, or longer. As Ford and Sinclair aptly comment: 'For most of us
61 almost certainly differs in its implications from 80 or 90' (1987: 3).
Victor (1989) similarly comments: 'Few social researchers would
combine the 20–49 year olds in a single social category. Yet this is what
many do unthinkingly when they use the term "the elderly"' (p. 115).
Thus there are many ways in which the elderly represent a heterogeneous
segment of the population.

Class has a most considerable influence on an individual's experience
of their old age. Provided one enjoys reasonably good health, if one is
financially secure, this later stage of life might represent a time of great
liberation to relax and enjoy new experiences. Middle-class individuals
tend to have a higher life-expectancy, to have had an imput into the
terms of their retirement, and, in general, to suffer less from the many
problems associated with poverty. These people have been referred to as
'the retirement elite' (Bornat, Phillipson & Ward 1985: 18), and they are
'in a position to use retirement as an opportunity to develop and expand
a range of skills and activities'. This is not, however, the situation for the
majority of people for whom 'material deprivation ... is bound to limit
the range of activities they can undertake in retirement' (*ibid*).

In old age, gender, like class, continues to exercise great influence on
individuals' experiences, as it has done in all other phases of the life
cycle. Statistically, women tend to live longer than men, and yet

it is the male experience that tends to be taken as the norm, even though among
people aged 60 or more, women outnumber men by almost 50 per cent, and
among the very elderly (those aged over 75) women are 70 per cent of the total
(Bornat, Phillipson & Ward 1985: 15).

It is noteworthy, then, that elderly women have been systematically
excluded from most social-science research: 'we know very little about
how women reconstitute their lives following widowhood, how their
social relationships and relationships with kin change, and how the
material bases of their lives change (Arber & Ginn 1990: 7). After the
death of a spouse, many women fall back onto or below the poverty line:
48 per cent of all widows live at or below supplementary-benefit level
(Phillipson 1982: 11). Thus, for those women who have been married,

the death of a partner might mean the loss of economic security, as well as loneliness. However, if the marriage was not a particularly satisfying one, or if the husband needed to be constantly looked after, widowhood might also be associated with a new sort of freedom. Indeed, many women report the renewed existence of close female friendships following the loss of a partner.

Finally, the experience of old age varies significantly not only within, but across cultures. In Western capitalist societies, a premium is put on productivity, and in adult life much of one's sense of self is derived from one's professional identity, or that of one's partner. Thus, with enforced retirement at the age of sixty (for women), or sixty-five (for men), a primary source of purpose in one's life is taken away, often not to be replaced.

the dominant values within society stress productivity, a contribution to the wealth of society through work, achievement and competition. Even when people are no longer allowed to work (as with compulsory retirement), choose not to work, or are unable to work, they continue to be judged in terms of these values (Ford & Sinclair 1987: 2).

But, as Phillipson writes,

Older people do need improved health services, better pensions, different types of housing and a variety of aids when they become disabled. But they also need a reason for using these things. In our society the purpose of life in old age is often unclear...Old age is seen as a 'problem' with the elderly viewed as dependants; worse still, they are often described as a non-productive burden upon the economy (1982: 166).

In Western capitalist societies, once one is no longer in gainful employment, one is not perceived as making a significant contribution to society. Thus, the elderly become stigmatized as takers and not givers, people who must be provided for, but who in themselves no longer have anything of real value to contribute. Arber and Ginn describe a 'pathology model' of aging which has emerged in social-science research, which depicts the elderly 'in terms of disease, disability, poverty, bereavement, isolation, and role loss' (p. 3). They are 'welfareised' and 'ghettoized' into a 'largely social problem-focus' (p. 3). The authors refer to a 'well-intended "compassionate ageism" ...[which] has reinforced a prejudicial and discriminatory stereotype of elderly people as a "dependent" group, separate from and different from the rest of society' (p. 3). Jeffreys and Thane (1989) refer to this presentation of the elderly as 'perhaps useful for taxation purposes but bear[ing] little resemblance to the real world' (p. 15).

It is not surprising that the elderly experience isolation and alienation when they are denied access to the sources of meaning which are valued by the society in which they live. Indeed, Coleman (1986) reports that depression is one of the 'normal' characteristics of old age in Western societies. This contrasts with the experience of aging in other cultures:

In some societies age gives status, so that only those towards the end of their lives are regarded as having enough experience and wisdom to deal with the most important issues and crises in their societies. We, however, have successfully deprived age of authority and of interest (Ford & Sinclair 1981: 1).

Class, gender and ethnicity do not exist in isolation, and the experience of old age will be coloured by one's particular cluster of group memberships. 'Inequalities of class interact with those of sex to produce a further strand of differentiation in old age' (Phillipson 1982: 11). And, further, 'The disadvantaged position of women in terms of status, power and rewards is compounded for black women... The voice of older black women is rarely given a chance to be heard' (Ford & Sinclair 1987: 3). Questions of power and powerlessness continue to be shaped by the intersection of social, economic, political and historical forces. A person is not, for instance, simply an old woman, but an old woman of a particular class and race living in a particular country at a particular moment in history; all of these factors will contribute to the way in which she experiences her advanced years.

Theories of aging and life-span development

It is interesting that psychology, the study of the human mind, has tended to neglect the study of the whole of the life course. Concentrating on time-specific correlation between internal and external states, it has failed to incorporate a life-span perspective into the heart of the discipline. But without such a whole, the pieces cannot fully make sense. Thomae states that 'a study of development which excludes consideration of the entire life span is both incomplete and governed by misleading principles and hypotheses' (1979: 284). In order to understand even an aspect of human behaviour, one must have a perspective on the whole of human life. Other disciplines, perhaps most notably literature and philosophy, have grappled with questions of meaning across life. It was Hippocrates who first compared nature's four seasons with the stages of life, and this tradition has continued for centuries. The following passage is taken from Alan of Lille's twelfth-century natural philosophy:

See how the universe, with Proteus-like succession of changing seasons, now plays in the childhood of Spring, now grows up in the youth of Summer, now ripens in the manhood of Autumn, now grows heavy in the old age of Winter. Comparable changes of season and the same variations alter man's life. When the dawn of man's life comes up, man's early Spring morning is beginning. As he completes longer laps in the course of his life, man reaches the Summer-noon of his youth; when with longer life he had completed what may be called the ninth hour of his time, man passes into the manhood of Autumn. And when his day sinks to the West and old age gives notice of life's evening, the winter's cold forces man's head to turn white with the hoar frost of old age (quoted in E. Sears 1986: 36–7).

Despite widespread fascination with the whole of the human cycle throughout the centuries, it is only recently that psychology has taken up this interest. Charlotte Bühler conducted research in the 1930s on 'The Course of Human Life as a Psychological Problem', basing her study on the analysis of over two hundred biographical studies. Despite her pioneering work, it was not until the 1970s that life-span development became a popular field of study within psychology (Baltes & Brim 1979, 1980; Datan & Ginsberg 1975; Nesselroade & Reese 1973). However, Gergen (1980) identifies a crisis in life-span developmental psychology, and Freeman (1984) assesses that, 'despite noble intentions ... readily accessible, lawful propositions have not been forthcoming' (p. 1). Reviewing the literature of developmental psychology, Broughton (1987) protests that 'Unfortunately, the recent innovations ... turn out to be more public relations than substance', and using the example of research in the area of life-span development, he comments that it 'merely reruns traditional individualist and positivist psychology' (p. 7).

Much of the work that falls under the heading of life-span development, as in developmental psychology in general, still focuses on the early years of life. Perhaps this is because the changes during this time are at least physically more dramatic than at any other time in the life cycle. In addition, there is perhaps a more identifiable uniformity in the patterns of change and growth which occur during the early years of life as compared with those of the more advanced stages. Jennings and Niemi (1974) comment upon the lack of clarity regarding the 'extent and rate' of changes in adulthood, and conclude by saying that 'changes during adulthood are relatively small and of minor importance' (p. 252). Thomae (1979) casts aspersions on such a view:

The 'mature' person who remains changeless and motionless in the face of the different challenges, threats, and increasing opportunities of the adult years is a stereotype, having no psychological reality (p. 294).

Regardless of whether or not significant changes and development do occur in adulthood, the fact remains that most developmental theories concentrate on the early years of life. That literature which does examine the later stages of the life course often does so from an individualistic perspective, tending to perpetrate, rather than to challenge, traditional stereotypes of old people. One such theory of aging which has met with much criticism (R. Butler 1975; Itzin 1986; Coleman 1986), but which nonetheless continues to be debated, is that of disengagement. The phrase 'disengagement' was originally used by Cumming and Henry (1961), who based their theory upon the assumption that 'increased introversion with age is ubiquitous' (p. 20). This viewpoint was later reiterated by Bromley (1966) in his seminal work *The Psychology of Human Ageing*.[3] The section entitled 'The Individual and Society' is divided into three parts, each including the word 'disengagement' in its heading. Bromley refers to 'one of the more obvious features of maturity and old age' as a 'reduction in the amount of social interaction', but he does acknowledge that 'some elderly people stubbornly resist pressure put on them to reduce their commitments' (p. 68).

Disengagement, Bromley proposes, 'provides a solution to some of the problems of adjustment in old age... Normal disengagement seems to lessen the fear of death' (p. 68). In the third edition of this book, Bromley (1988) again proclaims that social disengagement is 'one of the more obvious features of maturity and old age' (p. 134), and later he expands this ostensibly descriptive statement into its prescriptive form: 'An older person who is inactive and isolated is likely at first to be bored and irritated, but this state of mind may pass as he or she becomes more passive, apathetic and inert' (p. 142). That older people who are inactive and isolated soon begin to disengage, and to become less fearful of death, is not in itself a surprising statement. What is more remarkable is Bromley's implicit message that this situation is as it should be.

Itzin (1986) comments on such attitudes towards the aging:

The stereotypes which portray old people as wanting to cut themselves off ('disengage') from society are really a rationalization of an ageist society's separation of itself from old people... Old people are often portrayed as inherently miserable, when in fact it is the oppressive conditions of their lives that make them miserable (on the occasions when they are) (p. 124).

Itzen, in her criticism of traditional stereotypes of the aging, highlights the importance of the interaction between individuals (in this case, the elderly) and their environment. Itzen successfully avoids two pitfalls: (1) she does not claim that all elderly people are miserable, and (2) when they are miserable, she does not assume that this is an inherent quality of biological aging. Unlike Bromley, who, seeing that disengagement exists amongst some of the elderly, then seems to promote disengagement as a panacea for problems in later life, Itzen locates the problem of alienation in its appropriate social and institutional context.

While Erik Erikson is described as holding 'pride of place when the whole life span is considered' (Sugarman 1986: 83), only two of his eight stages extend into the adult years. Moreover, his theory, written in the psychoanalytic tradition, emphasizes the individual life course and fails to substantively account for social influences, although he does acknowledge their existence. The last stage of the life course, according to Erikson's model, results in

the acceptance of one's own and only life cycles and of the people who have become significant to it as something that had to be and that, by necessity, permitted of no substitutions. It thus means... an acceptance of the fact that one's life is one's own responsibility (1959/1963: 98).

Buss (1979) criticizes the end goal of Erikson's theory:

Unqualified acceptance of one's total life history, and by implication of the external forces that have helped shape that life, is too heavy a price to pay for the comfort of integration (p. 329).

Throughout Erikson's works, the experience of living is effectively portrayed as an intra-individual phenomenon. The eight identity crises concern the ways in which individuals cope with the age-appropriate tasks with which society confronts them. There is no critical assessment of that society – it passes, rather, as an unchallenged given – nor of its generally socially accepted, developmental tasks (such as the implicit assumption that having children, 'generativity', not only can be, but should be, an integral part of the life process.) Thus his theory is essentially non-critical, lending psychological legitimacy to the *status quo*.

Erikson first described his theory of life-span development in 1950 with the publication of *Childhood and Society*. The eight stages which he outlined were continuous, in that each phase contained within it elements of the other seven. He explains that 'Each comes to its ascendance, meets its crisis, and finds its lasting solution during the stage indicated. But they all must exist from the beginning in some form, for every act calls for an integration of all' (1963: 263). Nearly thirty-five years later, when Erikson was himself an octogenarian, he concentrated his focus on the last stage of life. The result of his research, written in collaboration with his wife and one other person, is *Vital Involvement in Old Age* (1986). This work documents 'the eight psychosocial themes as they seem to "come to word" in the lifelong experiences, observations, and insights offered by the [twenty-nine] elders who took part in our study' (p. 54).

What is unusual and particularly satisfying about this work is that Erikson was himself elderly when he conducted this research, and this is evident in the sensitivity of the presentation. Describing the interviews, the authors write: 'The sessions lasted approximately two hours, although some of the older people (including the Eriksons) grew weary toward the end' (p. 22). Elsewhere, the authors write of their ability to empathize with the experiences related by the respondents.

Because they [the respondents] were born around the turn of the century, their experience encompasses the history of the twentieth century to date. We Eriksons were also children of the century. Our childhoods knew the wonder of the early years of the 1900s, when the world was different... We, too, had been close to real needs – simple bodily needs like food and clothes and the need not to waste materials and things... You could still sell door-to-door and peddle bunches of flowers and glasses of lemonade (in the shade). (p. 23).

In fact, researchers of aging are seldom themselves old at the time of their investigations. This has potentially problematic implications for their ability to comprehend the data they gather. Kohlberg and Shulik (1981) in their article 'The Aging Person as Philosopher: Moral Development in the Adult Years' identify one of the problems associated with conducting research on the aging:

if an aging person has developed some wisdom we do not have, it is hard for younger researchers to detect it. In reviewing [one particular case]... the authors had less a sense of fitting a person to a predetermined stage-category than of learning something from a person who has developed some wisdom or spiritual sense we do not have and may never attain. If some aging persons do attain a greater wisdom, then among the most important things a student of aging could do is to clarify and communicate that wisdom to others. This means that the student of aging needs to be not only a psychologist and a sociologist but also a philosopher (p. 72).

The work of the Eriksons clearly benefits from their ability to empathize with their respondents. Of course it is not always possible for a researcher to be a member of the group under study. In such cases, the social scientist who genuinely wishes to gain an understanding of what it means to be old must be able to listen to, and learn from, those who know.

A more recent statement of life-span development is D. J. Levinson's *Seasons of a Man's Life*[4] (1978), in which he constructs a life-cycle macrostructure consisting of five twenty-year stages. Although the theory extends itself across the life cycle, interestingly the data from which it was developed came from interviews with forty American men between the ages of thirty-five and forty-five, all of whom lived between Boston and New York at the time of the interviews. Levinson confesses that he had originally considered 'a more limited age range, say forty-three to forty-five' (p. 8) but even the focus he has adopted seems a rather narrow one for the purpose of building a theory of life-span development. Nonetheless the work has enjoyed widespread popularity.

Levinson concentrates almost exclusively on individual intrapsychic processes, failing to account adequately for social factors which might influence development. An example of this can be seen in his description of middle adulthood:

A man is by no means lacking in the youthful drives – in lustful passions, in the capacity for anger and moral indignation, in self-assertiveness and ambition, in the wish to be cared for and supported. But he suffers less from the tyranny of these drives (p. 25).

The language he employs here is most revealing. He characterizes the experience of moral indignation as tyrannical, and reduces it to the level of an instinctual drive, as opposed to, for instance, a reasoned or rational response to a situation or environment worthy of evoking outrage. Commenting on the ideology implicit in this quotation, Lichtman (1987) writes:

What is at work here is transparently clear: Levinson reifies the destructiveness of capitalism, its slow, insidious depletion of the human spirit, and presents the result of this socially induced decay as a natural decline. In some instances, such as the loss of moral indignation, he describes what is probably an actual occurrence and wholly misconstrues its cause (p. 139).

Lichtman argues that this misconstruction serves to accommodate individuals to the barrenness of their lives.

This criticism is equally applicable to other aspects of Levinson's theory, which is built upon the concept of the construction and alteration of life structures. 'Broadly speaking, a life structure is satisfactory to the extent that it is viable in society and suitable for the self' (Levinson 1978: 53). But Lichtman's incisive rejoinder underlines the theory's inherent *status quo* bias:

As we have no independent measure of what is suitable for the self, we are left with social viability as a guide. Since Levinson informs us that a transition period comes to an end 'when the tasks of questioning and exploring have lost their urgency' are we to conclude that the individual has outgrown the need to question this society or that it is not socially viable to continue the exploration? Our 'inner dreams and values' may not be 'workable in the world.' The burden lies with the individual to change in the face of this disparity (1987: 142).

The connections between the theory of disengagement discussed above and that of Levinson are most apparent in the latter's claim regarding the end of development:

What does development mean at the very end of the life cycle? It means that a man is coming to terms with the process of dying and preparing for his own death...he lives in its shadow, and at its call...Above all, he is reaching his ultimate involvement with the self (pp. 138–9).

While disengagement theory concerns itself with the end of the life cycle, Levinson's work attempts to provide a theory which can explain the whole of the life course. Both, however, adopt the same perspective on living in general and on aging in particular. Because this perspective conflates description (of aging in Western capitalist democracies) and prescription, it allows for no possibility other than the social alienation and estrangement which it observes. Thus, not surprisingly, psychological theories of aging have tended to reflect the values of the society in which they were constructed: disengagement is the appropriate response from someone who is past their productive years. The work of Levinson and the disengagement theorists contains an implicit message whose meaning is opposite to that expressed by Dylan Thomas in one of his most powerful poems:

> Do not go gentle into that good night
> Old age should burn and rave at close of day;
> Rage, rage against the dying of the light.

(Thomas 1974)

Engagement, or the active living-out and fighting for one's beliefs and principles – and thus involvement in an ongoing struggle to assert an essential connection between the self and society – is considered at least by some to be a desirable feature of the last stages of life.

All theories of life-span development must address, either implicitly or explicitly, questions regarding what constitutes development. Underlying such questions are, of course, assumptions relating to the grand philosophical issues of the meaning of life. There are some psychologists who challenge the very premises upon which mainstream developmental theories are built. One of the most recent and coherent statements expressing opposing views to those represented above can be found in a collection of essays, *Critical Theories of Psychological Development* (Broughton 1987a). The book opens with the statement that

Developmental psychology segments, classifies, orders, and coordinates the phases of our growth and even defines what is and is not to be taken as growth. It creates a developmental discourse that, like language itself, both engenders and preempts the range of conditions of possibility within which the human life course can make sense. Its interpretive function allows it to produce as well as consume meaning (p. 1).

Lichtman (1987), writing in the same collection, views the individualistic, socially decontextualized perspective of many developmental theories as a product of Western capitalist ideology: 'bourgeois individuation is an absolutely unique form of achieving social identity and has no counterpart among a large proportion of the world's cultures'

(p. 147). Such an environment codifies 'isolation, estrangement, and loneliness...as autonomy, independence and self-reliance' (p. 128). Lichtman's point is well founded: how individual development is measured, or whether even it is a meaningful category at all, are questions which are ultimately determined by the underlying political perspective of the researcher. In Western capitalist democracies, where most of the work on development originates, many researchers tend to ignore the importance of the society–individual dialectic, choosing to focus instead on more particularized elements, be they personality idiosyncrasies, parental relationships, or cognitive structures, as if such aspects of the individual's make-up could be neatly compartmentalized, existing in a contextual vacuum.

Yet, it would seem apparent that the context in which human lives are lived is central to the core of meaning in those lives. Researchers should not, therefore, feel at liberty to discuss or analyse how individuals perceive meaning in their lives and in the world around them, while ignoring the content and context of that meaning. Critical theorists such as Broughton argue that by omitting context as a crucial influence, developmental psychologists have succeeded only in binding themselves to the fundamental realities of human existence. Due to this crucial omission, the most salient achievement of developmental psychology is a 'qualitatively new stage of self-deception' (Broughton 1987: 10) as the forms of psychological inquiry, and the tools for its measurement, increase in apparent sophistication while the focus remains overly limited and thus essentially unbalanced.

Critical psychology, in contrast to mainstream psychological theories, takes as its primary task

the reconstruction of knowledge about human development in the light of a historical, social, and political understanding of the conditions under which that development takes form...It is not so much that developmental psychology is apolitical, asocial, or ahistorical, but rather that it is a discipline that has traditionally been political, social and historical in a presumptuous, self-deceptive, and oppressive way (Broughton 1987: 11).

Critical psychology has its roots in the dialectical psychology movement of the 1970s and early 1980s. Interestingly, Klaus Riegel, one of the leading figures of the movement in the English-speaking world, had come to developmental psychology through his work on gerontology, extending his criticisms of methodological problems in research on aging to wider questions of development in general. It is then a form of poetic justice that this critical approach should once again be applied to a study of elderly persons. The dialectical perspective which Riegel applied to psychology is encapsulated in a phrase which appears throughout his writings and which is the title of his two-volume work: 'the developing individual in a changing world'.

It is this movement between the coextensive circles of life history and social history which lies at the heart of life-span theory. Elder (1981) summarizes this:

Development across the life-span is contextual, multidimensional and transactional. Interacting processes (biological, psychological, social) characterize the dialectical relation between individual and social change, life history and social history (p. 78).

Let us turn now from our discussion of aging and life-span development to examine some of the existing debates regarding the way in which individuals come to think about politics, and how those thoughts are incorporated into their overall worldview.

The psychology of political activists

Thus far, we have examined several psychological theories of aging and life-span development, and have tried to situate the experience of growing old in the context of Western societies. We have seen the ways in which such theories mirror the dominant values of the culture, serving as a 'scientific' explanation of, and justification for, the state of alienation which many people past their working years experience. Now let us turn our attention to another dimension of the respondents' psychological make-up, namely, their political orientation.

Political psychology is the area of psychology which ostensibly has sought to grapple with questions regarding the intersection between psychology and politics. Unfortunately, however, it has failed to adopt a sufficiently political orientation, and thus has succeeded only in psychologizing politics, reducing political behaviour to a study of one psychological process or another. There has been a systematic neglect of the consideration of the social, political and historical influences which command an essential role in human development; by focusing exclusively on intrapsychic processes, behaviour which derives its very meaning from the context in which it exists or to which it is responding can instead be portrayed as idiosyncratic and/or irrational. Sadly there has been little evidence of the reverse effect, that is the politicization of psychology. As long as researchers are determined to limit the scope of investigation to the individual, this will continue to be the case. As Broughton (1985) writes:

The realm of politics is psychologized, being reduced to a set of cognitive exercises. It is subjectivized as a mere matter of rhetorics. It is relativized as a mere competition between ideologies...Political advocacy is trivialized by studies showing how superficial 'espoused' ideologies are, and how individuals switch preferences according to dictates of shifting tastes or fashions ... Last but not least, the realm of politics is individualized, distracting us from the existence of political discourses and political movements, and the historical meaning of resistance to the illegitimate authority of the state engendered by such discourses and movements (pp. 388–9).

A review of the discipline of political psychology during the past three decades lends much credence to Broughton's litany of criticisms.

Barber (1990) in his earnest piece entitled 'The Promise of Political Psychology' demonstrates some of the problems endemic to the discipline. He begins by asking, 'Political psychology – what has that to offer?' (p. 173). What his response to this question lacks in sophistication, it makes up for in enthusiasm:

The realities of politics are fascinating. As students we are lucky to live in a puzzling political world where the challenges to human coping are as enormous as they are bizarre. And the relevance of psychology to politics escalates daily ... (p. 173).

But it is not until later that his patriotic fervour reveals itself in all its splendour.

Democracy is blossoming in lands we thought could not grow it ... Democracy is 'on the roll,' fashionable these days. But the longterm hope may happen: that government by consent of the governed, committed to the protection of human rights, may actually be winning throughout the world ... The deeper psychological question is this: does democracy resonate with humanity? Is there a sense in which that linkage transcends culture? The needed answer is not some romantic ideal but an understanding of how and why democracy actually works ... We need studies of the psychology that makes democracy (p. 175).

This, then, is the 'promise of political psychology': it shall furnish the social sciences with the 'needed answer'. Notably, it is more the question than the answer which reveals the inherent bias of the discipline; by posing the critical questions of how and why democracy works, one has already assumed that it does indeed work, at least as it is practised in the Western capitalist world. That the realization of democracy in some countries is impaired by interference from the same Western capitalist world is not Barber's particular interest. Perhaps in order to answer Barber's question of what political psychology has to offer, we must first determine what is meant by political psychology.

The first eight pages of *Political Psychology: Contemporary Problems and Issues* (Hermann 1986 a) are, in fact, dedicated to the question 'What is political psychology?' Here, the author communicates to her readers that the discipline is experiencing an identity crisis, and is riddled with confusion regarding the very purpose of its existence. Hermann lists what she calls 'five apparent tenets of political psychology'; these are rather vague, ranging from the first tenet, that the 'focus is on the interaction of political and psychological phenomena' to the last, that 'there is a tolerance of multiple methods for gathering data' (p. 1), a claim which some might dispute. Hermann then follows this list by another one, which is equally vague but somewhat more interesting, in which she identifies five issues over which opinion in the field is divided. These problem areas do not appear to be insignificant. Her concluding paragraph in this section cites several works which have found that, 'there is no consensus on the topics, theories, and methods that should be emphasized' (p. 7) in the discipline. How much else is there left upon which to disagree? It appears that the opening sentence of the book, 'Political psychology is coming of age' (p. 1), is not a thoroughly accurate description of the current state of the discipline.

The identity crisis which now faces the discipline has its historical antecedents: the question whether political psychology was to be principally political or psychological was never sufficiently resolved. David Sears (1987) uncritically describes this history, with its orientation toward individual personality. Sears cites Wallas's *Human Nature in Politics*, originally published in 1908, as the first major work in political psychology. The first three decades of the discipline were marked by a distinctly psychoanalytic emphasis, and Wallas's book, typical for its time, emphasized human irrationality and its relationship to political behaviour. Effectively, the genesis of the psychological study of political behaviour was reduced to an investigation of personality predispositions and idiosyncracies. Charting progress in the field, Sears explains that 'political pscyhologists have more recently looked at a wider variety of personal predispositions, including attitudes, motives, decision style, modes of personal interaction, stress responses, and expertise' (p. 231). It is as if the only limitation of the earlier emphasis was the lack of variety of personal predispositions under investigation, rather than the limited nature of the orientation itself. Sears' claim that there has been a 'broadening of focus' in the field is thus quantitatively but not qualitatively well founded.

Another work which helps to plot the individualistic focus of the field is Harold Lasswell's *Psychopathology and Politics* (1930). The chapter 'Political agitators' opens with the statement: 'The essential mark of the agitator is the high value which he places on the emotional response of the public. Whether he attacks or defends social institutions is a secondary matter' (p. 78). It is the second of these sentences which reveals the crux of Lasswell's position: his analysis of political behaviour is entirely focused on its structure, to the complete exclusion of its content. Yet, how can such behaviour be understood if the very context from which it derives its meaning is ignored?

Klaus Riegel summarizes the effect of dichotomizing content and structure. While his comments are specifically directed toward experimentalists, they are equally applicable to political psychologists who attempt to analyse political thought and political behaviour while ignoring the political content.

But not even all the King's horses and all the King's men could put Humpty-Dumpty together again, and thus experimentalists were bound to fail in their attempts of putting meaning back into their psychology from which they had eliminated it so radically. Meaning is not something that can be added later to the system analysed; rather it is the most fundamental topic. Strictly speaking, it is the only topic for any inquiry by human beings of human beings (1979: 3).

Lasswell directs his efforts toward establishing a personality type which can be generalized, one which is characteristic of all political agitators of whatever persuasion. Through the presentation of a series of life histories, his 'findings' reflect the fascination with sexuality as an explanation for psychological dispositions which was so prevalent in his day. He describes 'a strong homosexual component' which is characteristic of agitators, who are 'as a class...strongly narcissistic types'. Their interest in things social can be easily explained: 'Repressed sadism is partly vented upon objects remote from the immediately given environment, and favours the cultivation of general social interests' (1930: 125). The guiding principle of Lasswell's theory is that through political activity, agitators displace homosexuality or fear of impotence (p. 126). It is clear why Broughton should describe this book as 'arguably the founding work for the psychopathology of rebellion' (1987: 20). Because Lasswell fails to take account of the social structure in which individuals become politicized, he effectively strips any social meaning from political behaviour. The very concept of rebellion is meaningless if there is nothing against which one is rebelling. People who engage in such activity are thus successfully portrayed as pathological.

The last four decades of mainstream political psychology have been characterized by a similar, if sometimes more subtle, approach. Arguably, the theories of political behaviour and activism which have enjoyed most prominence during that time are those of the following men: Adorno *et al.* (1950), Rokeach (1960), Eysenck (1954) and Keniston (1968). These theories all attempt to examine the structure of political beliefs while ignoring the content. Louw-Potgieter (1986) concludes that these approaches operate on an intra- and/or inter-individual level of analysis:

Adorno and his co-workers explained the origins of the personality type that is susceptible to anti-democratic ideas in terms of intra-individual, psychodynamic processes...For Eysenck, tough-mindedness can be traced back to intra-individual genetic origins. Rokeach was of the opinion that closed-mindedness originated from intra-personal, pre-ideological beliefs...Keniston and other researchers explained student activism in terms of intra-individual dispositions to activism, formed by family environment and specific child-rearing practices (inter-personal processes) (pp. 82–3).

Such reductionist theories can equate people occupying opposite ends of the political spectrum, as anything which deviates from the centrist ideological bias runs the risk of being portrayed as dogmatic, tough-minded, closed-minded, or authoritarian. One is reminded here of labelling theory (Becker 1963; Cohen 1972): political activists are collectively labelled as deviant. Becker's famous cry that 'Deviant behaviour is behaviour that people so label' (1963: 9) seems to apply here, even if its application elsewhere has been called into question.

What is interesting about deviance is not what it is, but what people think it is...Deviance, in general...is a creation of the public imagination (Becker 1976: 341).

Lasswell's theory of the 'psychopathology of rebellion' again comes to mind, and one is hard-pressed to locate the broadening of perspective in political psychology which Sears so readily identifies.

Louw-Potgieter summarizes the way in which psychologists have sought to explain political behaviour:

In examining political dissent, psychologists' main concern has been with the question 'Who, or what kind of person, becomes a political dissident?'...causal explanations of dissent are located firmly within the 'deviant' individual and the social context of the 'deviance' is ignored or uncritically accepted as a given. By neglecting societal variables such as the content and meaning of the political norms against which the political dissident is revolting...the existing *status quo* is rarely questioned or criticised. It could thus be argued that the kind of question which has been asked by psychologists as regards political dissent, has determined the answer and the level of analysis of the explanation (1986: 14–15).

Other examples of reductionist psychological theories of political activism include the psychoanalytic work of Davies (1980), which predictably focuses on individual irrationalities, and the plethora of reminiscence literature (Caute 1988; Cohn-Bendit 1986; Fraser 1988) and media events (including television documentaries and popular films) released on or near the twenty-year anniversary of 1968, the year of the height of international student activism. Such works exhibit an almost obsessional fasciation with the question 'Where are they now?', as if an entire movement could be reduced to, or retrospectively analysed by, a detailed summary of the lives of its more prominent individual members.

It should be noted that the elderly are excluded from most psychological literature on political behaviour – perhaps another manifestation of the general belief that the political arena is not an appropriate place for one who is meant to be disengaging from society. When the politics of the aging are considered, they are portrayed as inherently conservative. Again, one is reminded of the problems associated with presenting the elderly as a homogeneous group, for surely some are conservative, and some are not.

It is a common theme on the Left that the working-class movement is fragmented, with men and women, employed and unemployed, working in different groups with different aims and ideologies. But this works both vertically (i.e. across the life-cycle) as well as horizontally (i.e. among groups of similar age and status) (Phillipson 1982: 126).

While the problem of horizontal fragmentation has received much attention, the same is not true of vertical fragmentation. Works which do deal with politics of the aging, of which there are not many, tend to focus on 'social advocacy by and on behalf of the aging' (Nisbet 1984: 1). This description of senescent activism fails to encompass the breadth of political issues with which the respondents of this study are involved; they have a broader political agenda, which may include rights for the aging but is certainly not limited to this domain.

A review of the psychological literature on political activists reveals a very unsatisfactory picture; they are portrayed as sometimes pathological, usually irrational, and always deviant. Although some attempts at broadening perspectives are reported to have been made within the discipline of political psychology, the overall emphasis was and continues to be on individualistic personality traits. Political engagement has not been regarded as an enduring, lifetime activity: detailed studies have showed what motivates some people to become politically active, but none examine if or how such commitment is sustained. The only work on activism in old age documents a comparatively narrow political perspective. Political psychology has successfully, and unfortunately, reduced the role of the political, as it has heightened that of the psychological.

Political psychology, as a discipline, has not restricted its interests to the study of the psychology of political activists. Indeed, the work perhaps most commonly associated with the field is research on public voting behaviour. But even where it has ventured into questions of the psychology of the politically engaged, it has done so unsatisfactorily, seeking to explain political thought and behaviour as a predetermined product of a particular cluster of personality traits. In this way, all pronounced political behaviour has been grouped together, and stigmatized as extreme. There has been virtually no attempt to investigate the lives of political activists which incorporates both a political and psychological perspective. While this should be the business of political psychology, unfortunately it has not generally been the case. That is why I have not called this section political psychology – in order to distinguish this investigation from the kind of work which has been associated with the field.

When political psychology has taken to analysing the behaviour of political activists, it has tended to do so from a thoroughly external perspective. That is to say, that rarely have their thought processes been described, much less analysed, from their own point of view. Yet it is at least possible that a very good way to learn about the psychology of political activists is to listen to what they have to say about their own lives. These reflections are documented in a variety of ways. Auto-biographies, letters, diaries, collected essays, poetry, song, literature, painting, even novels: examples can be found in virtually all forms of human expression. One need not be a psychologist to understand the message of Picasso's *Guernica*. Nor could one argue very convincingly that the political content and context of such a work was irrelevant to its essential meaning. Through reading Nelson Mandela's concerned letters to his daughters, one gets a glimpse into his own psychological make-up, and of the personal resources that must have helped to sustain his political commitment during his long years in prison:

What you have every reason to do is to be angry with the fates for the setbacks you may have suffered from time to time, to vow that you will turn those misfortunes into victory. There are few misfortunes in this world that you cannot turn into a personal triumph if you have the iron will and the necessary skill... 'Count your blessings one by one' and your system will be immune against all forms of depression (Meer 1988).

Diana Russell's *Lives of Courage: Women for a New South Africa* (1989) is the testimony of sixty South African women who are engaged in the fight against apartheid. They represent a diverse group of women in terms of age, occupation, social class, and even race, but for all of them the political struggle is an integral part of their daily lives – it affects when and where they feed their children, and under what conditions, if any at all, they can see their partners. In story after story, the reader becomes acutely aware of the interconnections between politics and psychology, and of the undesirability as well as the impossibility of separating the two.

Examples such as this abound. *Women on War : Essential Voices for the Nuclear Age* (Gioseffi 1988) is an anthology of women's writings from around the world, focusing on questions of war and peace, and what these terms mean in daily life in the nuclear age. The American novelist and activist Lenore Marshall reflects:

Sometimes there is an agonizing conflict for the writer who takes part in a movement in which [she] believes... One wonders sometimes who one is when one feels torn limb from limb between the inner and outer lives, for one can't help it, if one believes passionately in a thing, one has to commit oneself to it. We hear about searching for our identities these days – identity crisis. Perhaps we now have to have more than one identity or perhaps the different sides really do compose into one. Who are we really? we ask. We would like to pursue a direction that is simple and clear and to arrive at our life's work (Gioseffi 1988: 56).

Surely this statement concerns itself with political psychology, for it is the musings of a woman who is trying to integrate her political convictions into her daily life. Michele Najilis from Nicaragua writes of her experience in a poem 'They Followed us into the Night':

> We were flogged and made to spit up blood.
> Our bodies were filled with electric shocks
> and our mouths with lime.
> For whole nights
> we were left out in the wild,
> or thrown into timeless cells.
> Our nails were torn out,
> our blood
> splattered on walls,
> even on their faces,
> but still,
> our hands
> are united with millions of hands.
>
> (Gioseffi 1988: 57–58)

The last line lifts the poem from the level of description to that of political consciousness, as the response to torture is that of organized resistance. This too, then, might fall under the discipline of political psychology if it were more broadly constructed. And why should it not be? 'The promise of political psychology' lies not in a reformulation of the same old questions, but in a reconceptionalization of the very discipline. If we wish to learn about the psychology of political activists, we must listen to what they have to say about their own lives: one way to put the politics back into psychology is to directly consider the lives of political activists.

2   The potential of social identity theory

All are but parts of one stupendous whole...
Alexander Pope, Essay on Man, 1.267

In recent years, there has been much criticism of psychology as being an essentially reductionist discipline which focuses almost exclusively on intra-individual psychological processes while ignoring the variety of contexts which influence the production of such processes (Bar-Tal & Kruglanski 1988; Broughton 1987; Parker 1989; Parker & Shotter 1990; Riegel 1976, 1979). Buss (1979) identifies elements of the individual–society debate as far back as Aristotle. Indeed, it is the ultimate relationship which any philosopher or student of human make-up must confront. Not surprisingly, it has been a central question of social psychology. Floyd Allport, one of the founders of modern social psychology, said that 'the problem of the individual and the group is really the master problem of social psychology (1962: 7). This was reiterated more recently by Turner and Oakes (1986):

> The raison d'être of social psychology is to solve scientifically a paradox. The paradox is to integrate two very different orders of phenomena: the *psychological* – to do with the mental properties of the individual – and the *social* – processes, properties and products deriving from the interrelatedness between individuals. The premises of the paradox are that, on the one hand, psychological processes belong only to individuals and not to any superordinate collective entity, and on the other, that social or even more so societal processes (political, cultural, economic, historical, etc...) [are]... distinct from and irreducible to... their elementary components, individuals... The issue is can there be and how can there be a *non-individualistic* science of the individual, a *social* psychology in the fullest sense? (p. 237).

Parker (1989) describes social psychology as being in 'permanent crisis... or racked by a number of intersecting *crises*' (p. 9). As a discipline, it 'excludes the crucial interconnected issues of ideology, power, and history... by denying developments in other academic areas, and by repressing its own past' (*ibid.*). Broughton (1987), in the tradition of critical psychology, argues that questions of human development must be considered 'in the light of a historical, social, and political understanding of the conditions under which that development takes form'. (p. 11) He documents an inherent bias in favour of the *status quo* which often characterizes psychology, observing 'a hidden advocacy of a specific and extreme kind: a trumpeting of the virtues of that which dominates' (p. 5).

Many have experienced frustration in their attempts to pursue research of socially relevant psychological questions, and have ultimately departed from the discipline: '"Left psychology" seemed a contradiction in terms, and so they left psychology' (p. 20). Others, however, have stayed, believing that there is room for, and indeed a dire need of, such work within the field; they decided that their task would be, rather than to psychologize politics, to politicize psychology. Brewster Smith makes the point that sound social psychological research must be built upon a dialectical model:

human beings in interaction and in action in the world produce themselves and history ... social psychology *must* be developmental *and* historical if it is to be adequately scientific (1977: 723).

The present work is a product of that tradition of thought.

To return, then, to the issue raised by Turner and Oakes: can there be, and how can there be, a non-individualistic science of the individual, a social psychology in the fullest sense? While there can be no single and final response to such a question, an initial step might be to advocate a greater acceptance of a variety of methods within social psychology. Bar-Tal and Bar-Tal (1988) observe that 'The foundation of social psychology is based on the positivistic approach as reflected especially in logical positivism' and that 'experimentation has become the hallmark of social psychology' (p. 84). George Allport (1968), in the first *Handbook of Social Psychology*, had warned against this tendency, pointing out that 'many contemporary studies seem to shed light on nothing more than a narrow phenomenon studied under specific conditions ... some current investigations seem to end up in elegantly polished triviality – snippets of empiricism, but nothing more' (p. 68). In contrast, when respondents are encouraged to speak about their lives in the way in which they actually perceive them, the constituent social influences are almost invariably highlighted. Most people when they speak about themselves, speak about others in their lives, groups to which they belong, and events which have been of particular importance in shaping their views or understanding of the dynamics of the social environment, or of the world at large. Thus, an insistence on experimental design, at the exclusion of all other methods of enquiry, is most unfortunate, in that such investigations are necessarily limited in the scope of their findings; few people experience themselves as living in a vacuum. Yet, when studied in a laboratory setting, from which social influences are systematically extracted, the psychology of individuals is necessarily individualized.

Traditional social psychology, like developmental and political psychology, has a long history of reductionism, which has taken one of two forms: individualism or the group mind thesis (Turner *et al.* 1987: 5–6). The first of these is epitomized by Floyd Allport's famous comment, 'There is no psychology of groups which is not essentially and entirely a psychology of individuals (1924: 24). (This is reminiscent of Mrs Thatcher's now famous comment, 'There is no such thing as society' – the hallmark of Conservative politics). A corollary of this premise is Allport's statement that 'There is likewise no consciousness except that belonging to individuals' (1924: 24). The group mind thesis can be traced back to Gustave LeBon's *The Crowd: A Study of the Popular Mind* (1896), which Allport once remarked was the most widely read psychology book of all time (Reicher 1987: 174). LeBon's thesis is built upon a separation of the individual and the social. While an individual, in isolation, is quite capable of rational behaviour, individuals in groups are characterized by

impulsivity, irritability, incapacity to reason, absence of judgment or critical spirit, exaggeration of emotions and more besides [which] are also observed amidst lower forms of evolution such as the savage and the child (LeBon 1896: 23).

Reicher refers to LeBon's

explicit ambition to use crowd psychology as a political tool. He was above all concerned to employ his ideas in combatting working class activism, and confessed himself proudest of his anti-socialist writing…LeBon's crowd psychology may be read as a sustained attack upon collective protest (1987: 174).

Reicher compares the work of LeBon and Allport, concluding that they share the same basic premises; they both have an antagonistic view of the group, dismissing the possibility of the existence of social consciousness and organization, and thus marginalizing if not patho-logizing any form of group protest. The only difference between the two theories is that

LeBon sees this [atavistic] universal [which is found in crowd behaviour] as in contradiction to and located outside the individual, [while] Allport sees it as the underlying essence of individuality and as located firmly within the individual (p. 176).

The views of both Allport and LeBon have modern expressions, most notably in the theories of social facilitation and de-individuation respectively, and Reicher argues that there has been 'more a shift of scope than of perspective... they [still] retain the disjunction between social and individual levels of explanation' (1987: 179). While there has also been a tradition of interactionism within social psychology, it has never enjoyed the predominance of either the group mind tradition, nor of the individualistic approach of Allport, and many others, which 'has come to dominate the mainstream of social psychology' (Reicher 1987: 179). Thus social psychology as a discipline has tended to segregate the social from the individual, never resolving the inherent paradox between the psychological and the social, identified by Turner and Oakes earlier.

In this chapter, I shall discuss one theory, that of social identity, which attempts to work within the tension posed by this paradox. I begin by describing the actual theory, emphasizing those aspects of it which are particularly relevant for our purposes here. It is a truism to state that human beings are social; they are members of society, and within that society they belong to various groups. The guiding premise of social identity theory is that 'People derive their identity (their sense of self, their self concept) in great part from the social categories to which they belong' (Hogg & Abrams 1988: 19). Whereas traditional social psychology has emphasized the individual in the group, the social identity approach 'turns the traditional perspective on its head and focuses on the group in the individual' (p. 3). The theory, then, has great potential for being both sufficiently psychological as well as social. For this reason, I have selected it as a base upon which to organize much of the theoretical discussion of this project. Following my general description of social identity theory, I explore its usefulness in explaining group consciousness and multiple group membership – areas to which we shall return in the presentation of the data – borrowing material from socialist and feminist debates to illuminate various points.

Social identity theory: the background

The European school of social psychology (Tajfel 1984) 'originated in a critique of such a desocialized view of the individual' (Reicher 1987: 180). 'The principle and explicit aim' of these psychologists

> was to forge a non-reductionist social psychology which would be able to deal with the dynamic relationship between individual and society without sociologizing or individualizing it: that is, to explore the *social* dimension of human behaviour... It is in this context that the social identity approach has developed as a spearhead of this attack on individualism in social psychology (Hogg & Abrams 1988: 13).

In the forefront of this movement was Henri Tajfel, who published his first paper on social identity theory in 1972. Since that time, the theory has been the focus of much research and speculation regarding the influence of social group membership on an individual's self-perception and perception of others.

Central to the theory is the concept of social categorization, which Tajfel describes as

the ordering of the social environment in terms of groupings of persons in a manner which makes sense to the individual. It helps to structure the causal understanding of the social environment and thus it helps as a guide for action (1978c: 61).

Social identification is the process by which the individual locates herself within that system of categorizations, and the sum total of an individual's social identifications is that person's social identity. Tajfel defines social identity as

that *part* of an individual's self-concept which derives from his knowledge of his membership of a social group (or groups) together with the value and emotional significance attached to that membership (1978c: 63).

Thus the concept has a very particular meaning; Tajfel makes explicit the fact that his theory addresses but one, albeit the most important, aspect of all that is embodied in the complex concept of identity.

While Tajfel does acknowledge – parenthetically – the obvious fact that people belong to more than one social group, he does not address the complex psychological dynamics that such multiple group membership involves. Social categorization includes the process by which individuals identify the salience of particular social groups which comprise their worldview. This 'sorting task' reveals the organization of an individual's social world, and consequently the way in which an individual perceives herself and others. However, before addressing the question of an individual's social and self-perception – which assumes a particular consciousness – it seems reasonable to attempt to differentiate between forms of actual group membership, regardless of such perception.

Social identity theory in general, and the concept of social categorization in particular, does not sufficiently differentiate between two kinds of group membership: involuntary and voluntary. However, this distinction is an important one, particularly in questions of consciousness. Involuntary membership encompasses those parts of oneself about which one has had no say – gender, race and the historical time of one's birth being the most obvious of these. Also relevant here is the background into which one was born, including religious affiliation, class and nationality. While one has no input into one's background, these three categories are more flexible (as enduring identifications) than the first three, in that individuals may be able to renounce their family's religion, alter their class status, and even change nationalities in the course of their lives. All of these identifications, however, are highly influential in shaping the way a person thinks about the world and about herself. The knowledge that one is a member of a particular group (the cognitive component) has no necessary direct correlation with either positive or negative feelings about that group or one's membership in it.

The second category, that of voluntary group membership, is, of course, more flexible. Given that one is born a particular gender, race, at a particular time, and into an entire network of familial background, one invariably has feelings, conscious or unconscious, regarding such affiliations. One can embrace, reject, or feel indifferent toward certain aspects of one's involuntary group membership (for instance, by becoming active in the women's movement or in the struggle against racial discrimination). These latter group memberships are voluntary, because people belong to them through choice. While there is a finite number of involuntary group memberships, those which do exist play an extremely important role in the formation of the individual's essential self-perception. In contrast, voluntary group memberships are virtually limitless, covering the whole range of human activities. The experience of membership has varying degrees of importance across groups: some groups are so vaguely defined that they fail to charge members with strong emotional affiliation. People belong to so many groups that ultimately they must prioritize their affiliations, as it is through these memberships that individuals communicate to themselves and to the rest of the world who they perceive themselves to be. For instance, it would be difficult to sustain an idea of oneself as a political activist if one never attended political meetings or had never engaged in the wide array of political activities available. Further, the concepts which one uses to identify oneself are not only a reflection of aspects of self-perception (both real and idealized), but are also themselves socially constructed.

Brunt (1989) wonders how it is that some people come to think of themselves as 'political animals', despite the often inhospitable environment for doing so:

It is not after all obvious why anyone, particularly in such an apolitical culture as Britain, should ever choose to define themselves as political. When politics is such a marginalised and minority activity, 'admitting' to being a 'political animal' of any sort, let alone a left one, is distinctly odd (p. 152).

It is only odd, however, if declaring oneself to be politically minded is perceived as an isolated, and isolating action. But indeed, it can have the opposite effect, as in so doing one is implicitly identifying a group of people with whom one feels one belongs, and which itself has a particular history. Thus, to identify oneself as a socialist is to make a statement which is not only political, but also social and historical. Reicher writes:

To define oneself as a 'socialist,' for example, is to say something fundamental about what one is as an individual; yet the meaning of 'socialism' is a social product that is irreducible to any one given person. Thus the concept avoids either defining a social mind independent of the individual or an individuality independent of society: it is capable of addressing the problem of social individuality (1987: 180).

Griffin (1989) makes a similar point regarding the identification of oneself as a feminist. 'Feminist identification is not simply an isolated individual phenomenon, but a product of specific social, political and historical conditions' (p. 189).

The concept of voluntary and involuntary group membership is useful in discussing the effects that political consciousness has on social identity. For instance, how one feels about one's own class membership – an involuntary group – might be strongly influenced by one's political orientation – a voluntary group. Working-class socialists would tend to strongly identify themselves with their class, and presumably would work to promote its interests. Non-working class socialists, however, would not identify their interests with those of their class, even while they would acknowledge the existence of class as a salient social grouping. We shall examine the question of class membership and class consciousness in more detail later. For the moment, suffice it to say that some voluntary group memberships are bound to reflect individuals' feelings about their involuntary group memberships. Members of the Afrikaner Weerstandsbeweging (AWB) in South Africa are not only white, but have very particular ideas about what membership in this race category entitles them to. Further, sometimes the very acknowledgement of particular involuntary groups might be a direct expression of a voluntary group membership, as with the example of class. Zandy (1990) comments, 'The British working-class has one advantage over the American: it is, at least, named ... Class identity is easier to obscure and deny than gender and race identity' (p. 2).

The question of group consciousness

Tajfel identifies three distinct components associated with group membership. These are:

cognitive ... in the sense of the knowledge that one belongs to a group; an evaluative one, in the sense that the notion of the group and/or of one's membership of it have a positive or a negative value connotation; and an emotional component in the sense that the cognitive and evaluative aspects of the group and one's membership of it may be accompanied by emotions...directed toward's one's own group and towards others which stand in certain relations to it (1978b: 28–9).

Moreover, 'the number and variety of social situations which an individual will perceive as being relevant in some ways to this group membership will increase as a function of' these constituent parts of group membership (p. 39). Thus, for one who is politicized, all situations, relationships and networks of relationships are understood to have important political dimensions. Central to social identity theory, then, is the role of consciousness: social identity is not only derived from the compilation of an individual's various group memberships, but is enhanced by the consciousness of, and the emotional and evaluative assessments of, those memberships. Thus knowledge of social group membership is an integral part of the awakening of political con-sciousness, as it is the foundation upon which social contrasts are made, just as the development of the awareness of one's self is related to the awareness of the existence of others. The concept of a group derives its meaning only when there is more than one group: 'us' implies the existence of 'them'. Identity is the product of difference.

Commenting on this, Tajfel writes:

The characteristics of one's group as a whole...achieve most of their significance in relation to perceived differences from other groups and the value connotation of these differences. For example, economic deprivation acquires its importance in social attitudes, intentions and actions mainly when it becomes 'relative deprivation'...the definition of a group...makes no sense unless there are other groups around (1978c: 66–7).

While Tajfel's point has its obvious merits, it is not unproblematic. By adopting a comparatively static and one-dimensional view of group membership, he fails to consider that one might simultaneously perceive oneself as relatively deprived (as a member of one group) and as relatively privileged (as a member of another), thereby reflecting the multifaceted nature of identity.

Gurin and Markus (1989) discuss identity centrality, or salience, and its effect on individuals' perceptions of the general relevance of a particular group membership:

Virtually all group members have some awareness of their group membership and thus have a group identity. Some group members seem to possess antennae that are tuned to receive group-relevant information that others miss. It is most often assumed that for these people group membership has become central to the self and thus the identity can be activated by minimal cues (p. 155).

The authors then relate this to gender identity and the feminist consciousness-raising groups of the 1970s. When women see themselves as having a shared fate with other women, 'gender functions as a social categorization and not merely as an individual characteristic' (p. 157). When Edwina Currie, one of the most prominent people in the Tory Party, comments 'I'm not a woman. I'm a Conservative' (Campbell 1987: 275), she intends not to deny the biological fact of her sex identity, but to indicate the value she attaches to that fact. Because of the parallel construction of the two sentences, she appears to replace 'woman' – an involuntary group membership – with 'Conservative' – a voluntary group membership – with stunning effect.

It is only when women realize that they are treated categorically that they will begin to engage in social comparison, contrasting the treatment of women as women with that of men as men. Through the process of comparing her group to that of others, the individual begins to develop a clearer idea of the nature of the social structure, and her position within it. Invariably such comparisons will reveal that some groups enjoy greater advantages than others, and that the distribution of social rewards often reflects this social hierarchy.

Whether this inequity is perceived as being unjust is influenced, but not directly determined by, the status of one's own social group(s). An individual's understanding of how and why intergroup relationships function as they do forms the basis of her political worldview. Regarding this issue, Tajfel writes:

The perceived illegitimacy of an intergroup relationship [in status, power, domination or any other differential] is thus socially and psychologically the accepted and acceptable lever for social action and social change in intergroup behaviour (1978c: 76).

Tajfel claims that individuals' understanding of the nature of intergroup relations can be identified on a social mobility/social change continuum. The crucial element distinguishing these two categories is that of perceived flexibility of the social structure. He argues that if an individual believes that movement within the hierarchy is possible, and thus that the boundaries of membership into more privileged groups are relatively permeable, this will affect the way she acts. Social mobility then consists of 'a subjective structuring of a social system' in which an individual believes that 'he can improve in important ways his position in a social situation, or more generally move from one social position to another, as an individual' (1978b: 52–3). Conversely, if such access is perceived as being blocked, one will identify oneself more as a member of her group, believing that 'the only way to change these conditions ... is together with his group as a whole, as a member of it rather than as someone who leaves it' (ibid.).

Tajfel then identifies variants of social conditions which determine the content of an individual's beliefs regarding the existing social structure and its potential for change. Only one of these is directly pertinent to our considerations here, namely that 'the structure of beliefs in "social change," if it exists, is not directly based on this perceived impossibility of individual mobility' (pp. 53–4). The implications of this statement are quite straightforward: a person's aspirations might extend beyond her perceived individual mobility. While it might be possible to move out of one's class – 'If you are born into the working class and are willing to change your speech, your gestures, your appearance – in essence, to deny the culture of your home and the working-class self of your childhood – then you might "pass" as a member of the dominant culture' (Zandy 1990: 2) – not everyone might choose to exercise this option. Instead, such movement might be regarded as token mobility – a key to the success of the maintenance of the *status quo*. If the whole of the social structure is perceived as being unjust, one might aim to alter the structure rather than operate as successfully as possible within it. While Tajfel makes a passing reference to this alternative, he does not explore it.

But the very complexity of the way in which individuals perceive their social and political environment, and where and how they place themselves within that structure, is crucial to the assessment of the social identity. If an individual is class conscious, the fact that some people have successfully risen out of their class (and thus that social boundaries have some degree of permeability, however small) need not alter her political convictions. The distinction which must be drawn here (and which Tajfel fails to adequately address) is between macro and micro social-perceptions. Without being logically inconsistent, one can simultaneously believe that one can 'move from one social position to another, as an individual' as well as that 'the only way to change his conditions of life [at a more general level] ... is together with his group as a whole'. The two viewpoints are not incompatible.

Tajfel further states that when the belief that a system consists of a rigid social stratification is accompanied by the belief that 'the system lacks legitimacy and that it is capable of change, the new psychological "problems" confronting these groups have a finite number of psychological solutions' (1978b: 53–4). The problems which Tajfel identifies are not merely psychological in nature, however, and nor are their solutions. Nevertheless, believing that a social system is both illegitimate and capable of change is sound psychological preparation for engagement in political activity.

Condor (1989) writes:

a careful re-reading of Tajfel's work suggests that this was never intended as a 'theory of social change.'...although Tajfel certainly *acknowledges* the occurrence of social change over macro-time, his 'dynamic' approach in fact focuses on social cognitive plasticity in micro-time (pp. 29–30).

She suggests that there has been a terminological confusion:

Tajfel often used this term 'social change,' in his writing but *not* (usually) in its sociological sense (i.e. pertaining to transformation in ideas and social structures over macro-time). Rather, he used the term to refer to a *belief in ascribed category membership* (p. 32).

The distinction which Condor makes is an important one. Tajfel appears to be concerned with self-perception and consciousness rather than the wider construction of ideology.

Locating one's own social group on the lower end of the social hierarchy can produce different effects upon different individuals. If one perceives the social structure as being just, then self-regard will be low. If, however, one views the social structure as fundamentally unjust, one is less likely to blame oneself or even one's group for the deprivation experienced. Ultimately, if one comes to adopt a politicized worldview, accurately locating one's position in the social structure, no matter how low that position might be, can itself be an act of empowerment.

Berkowitz (1972) states that it is only when individuals feel they have a strong sense of personal control over their environment that they will protest. What constitutes personal control is heavily influenced by one's worldview. If one believes, as socialists do, that through collective action, individuals can contribute to social and political outcomes, then one might experience a strong sense of control over one's environment, not as an isolated individual, but as a member of an organization. People experience some sense of control not only when they are in control, or members of a controlling group, but also, and perhaps more significantly, when they feel they understand the dynamics of power relationships within a society. Identifying forces of oppression, and subsequently embarking on a course of opposition to such forces, can be and often is experienced as regaining control over one's own life, and sometimes even over one's social environments. Elbers (1987) cites the work of Ute Osterkamp, which suggests that the individual's potential to develop cannot be separated from the collective means of influencing the course of society and the possibilities for associating with others to control social, and therefore individual, conditions of existence...in critical psychology 'being autonomous' has the meaning of associating with others to control and change the collective conditions of life (p. 162).

Through becoming politically conscious, individuals begin to develop a theory which explains the underlying reason for their relatively disadvantaged situation. If they are members of the oppressed class, their sense of membership is heightened. The advent of political consciousness for middle-class socialists, however, has quite the reverse effect. While acknowledging their class roots, which they are unable to change, they try to disassociate themselves from the interests of their class, and to realign themselves with those whose struggle they support. While they will never be of the working class, and these deprivations of others were never theirs, they can be with the working class.

Let us relate our discussion thus far to Marx's treatment of the relationship between class and class consciousness. There is both a subjective and an objective dimension of class membership; 'The point might be summarized by saying that, without consciousness, the working class is a mere mass: it becomes a class when it acquires consciousness' (Miliband 1977: 23). The difference between the objective and subjective dimensions become particularly clear in the following famous passage:

Economic conditions had first transformed the mass of the people of the country into workers. The combination of capital has created for this mass a common situation, common interests. This mass is thus already a class as against capital, but not yet for itself. In the struggle...this mass becomes united, and constitutes itself as a class for itself. The interests it defends become class interests (Marx, 'Materialist Conception of History', 1977: 214).

Oppositional identification, then, is not sufficient to produce class consciousness, although clearly it is an important component. Class consciousness, however, demands something more. In the terminology of social identity, the mere fact, and cognitive appreciation, of one's group membership cannot transcend 'class of itself' to 'class for itself'. The evaluative and emotional significance attached to the existence of this group and one's membership of it are pivotal.

Class consciousness is then the awareness which members of a class have of its 'true interest'. The raising of class consciousness is

least complicated in relation to the capitalist class and the bourgeoisie in general. Its true interests presumably consist in the maintenance and defense of capitalism; and its class consciousness is on this score very easy to achieve. As a matter of historical fact, privileged classes have always been perfectly class-conscious, at least in this sense (Miliband 1977: 31).

But the privileged class is falsely conscious in that it 'proclaims and believes that these partial and class interests have a universal and classless character' (p. 32). Their interests are, however, class-based, and they are only universal insofar as they coincide with capitalism. Still, there do exist some individual members of the bourgeoisie who betray the interests of their class. In the *Communist Manifesto* Marx describes 'a small section of the ruling class' which

cuts itself adrift, and joins the revolutionary class, the class that holds the future in its hands...a portion of the bourgeoisie goes over to the proletariat, and in particular, a portion of the bourgeois ideologists, who have raised themselves to the level of comprehending theoretically the historical movement as a whole (*Communist Manifesto*, 197: 229).

These are the revolutionary intelligensia, later identified by Lenin as the 'vanguard of the party'.

With these exceptions, under capitalism the class consciousness of the bourgeoisie is not revolutionary consciousness, which represents 'a certain understanding of the nature of the social order and of what needs to be done about it' (Miliband 1977: 35). Proletarian class consciousness, in contrast to that of the bourgeoisie,

may be taken to mean the achievement of an understanding that the emancipation of the proletariat and the liberation of society require the overthrow of capitalism; and this understanding may also be taken to entail the will to overthrow it (p. 33).

Class consciousness pertains to consciousness about one aspect of one's identity. To return to the language introduced earlier in this chapter, every individual is born into a particular class; class membership is thus one of several involuntary group memberships. But one is not only a member of a class; other involuntary group memberships include the categories of race and gender. Can the concept of consciousness incorporate the various, and sometimes competing, aspects of an individual's social identity? Does 'identity centrality' demand that one involuntary group membership be highlighted at the exclusion of all others? One of the problems with raising feminist consciousness, as identified by Gurin and Markus above, is women's 'interdependence with men in families, ethnic groups, and social classes [which] tend to inhibit women from comparing themselves with men' (Gurin & Markus 1989: 157). Is there not a way to accommodate simultaneously the multiple dimensions of identity difference? Need the boundaries of 'us' and 'them' be ever constant?

Multiple group membership: prioritizing difference

Hogg and Abrams (1988) make reference to the multiplicity of social categories:

The social identity approach rests upon certain assumptions concerning the nature of people and society, and their interrelationship. Specifically, it maintains that society comprises social categories which stand in power and status relations to one another. 'Social categories' refers to the division of people on the basis of nationality... race... class... occupation... sex... religion... and so forth, while 'power and status relations' refers to the fact that some categories in society have greater power, prestige, status, and so on than others. Categories do not exist in isolation. A category is only such in contrast with another... Any individual is at once a member of many different social categories... but is unlikely to be a member of mutually exclusive categories (p. 14).

One will notice here that once again the concept of social categories does not differentiate between voluntary and involuntary groups, so that one's chosen religious faith or occupation enjoys the same psychological import as sex, class, race and nationality. That categories do not exist in isolation is common sense. To say one is female if everyone is female is a meaningless statement; the category 'female' only has significance if there exists a category 'not-female'. Further, that individuals cannot belong to mutually exclusive categories (for example, one cannot be both female and not-female) also seems logical.

That 'any individual is at once a member of many different social categories' is an obvious truth, but one whose implications are far reaching. Social identity concerns itself with 'the group within the individual', but which group? Race? Gender? Class? The problem with the concept of social categorization is that it is additive and not integrative; it can account for serial group memberships, but it is not equipped to explore the ways in which these various group memberships inform each other. For instance, in the first chapter, we saw how race, gender and class influence the experience of aging.

Social identity theory, in its failure to consider multiple group memberships which exist in the same person at the same time, reflects a historical problem experienced by many oppressed groups, regarding how to deal with difference amongst their own members. Tajfel and others concentrate most of the discussion on ingroup–outgroup relations. Yet perhaps these very labels are misleading; the boundaries between 'us' and 'them' are forever changing, depending upon which aspect of social identity is being focused upon.

Debates over the prioritization of class, gender, or race as the dominant 'social category' of analysis – to borrow the language of social identity theory – have a long history. The classical socialist position on women's oppression is that it is a product of class oppression, and that when the latter is abolished, so too will the former disappear. The first well-known, coherent and influential statement of this position was in Frederich Engels' *The Origins of the Family, Private Property, and the State*. Here Engels

asserted that women's oppression was a problem of history and not a consequence of biology...[he] suggested that women's subordination was determined by the form of the family, which in turn was to be related to the level of development of the mode of production and class struggle. This analysis has provided the guiding light of socialist analysis of women's oppression for a hundred years (Kimble & Unterhalter 1982: 12).

Questions regarding the subordination of the 'women's question' to the primacy of class struggle have reappeared many times. Eleanor Marx drew a contrast between bourgeois feminists and socialist women. She speaks of:

the difference between the party of the 'women's rightsers' on the one side, who recognised no class struggle but only a struggle of sexes, who belong to the possessing class, and who want rights that would be an injustice against their working-class sisters, and on the other side, the real women's party, the socialist party, which has a basic understanding of the economic causes of the present adverse position of workingwomen and which calls on the workingwomen to wage a common fight hand-in-hand with the men of their class against the common enemy, vis. the men and women of the capitalist class (Draper & Lipow 1976: 180–81).

Elsewhere she elaborates upon this, saying that workingwomen see no more in common between Mrs Fawcett ('the star of the women's rights movement') and a laundress than 'between Rothschild and one of his employees. In short, for us there is only the working-class movement' (Draper & Lipow 1976: 225).

The argument regarding the role of separate women's organizations in the newly created Soviet system was rehearsed between Lenin and Clara Zetkin. Lenin made clear repeatedly that 'The proletariat cannot achieve complete liberty until it has won complete liberty for women' (Lenin, *Emancipation of Women*, 1985 [1934]: 83). Still, like Engels, he believed that this battle should not be fought separately but rather as part of the larger struggle. 'We want no separate organisations of communist women! She who is a Communist belongs as a member to the party, just as he who is a Communist' (Beall *et al.* 1989: 36). Zetkin, on the other hand, argued that 'the fight for changes in the relations between women and men [should be seen] as a task for the present, not for some indefinite socialist future' (p. 37).

The traditional socialist position has come under increasing scrutiny in more recent times – most particularly by Marxist and socialist feminists. One example of such a critique is an article on the struggle for a socialist South Africa, '"A Bit on the Side"?: Gender Struggles in the Politics of Transformation in South Africa' (Beall *et al.* 1989). Looking to a 'post-apartheid' future, the progressive movement in South Africa has adopted the position that

women's oppression will be eliminated in the course of the transition to socialism. In strategic terms, this involves women's concerns being subordinated to, rather than included *as part of* struggles to achieve socialism in SA (p. 30).

The debate regarding the 'women's question' has been cast along familiar lines. The authors speak of an artificial and unnecessary polarization between 'those who see the emancipation of women as being secondary to and contingent upon national liberation, and those who separate women's emancipation from broader concerns' (p. 31). As an alternative to this false dichotomy, they offer 'a socialist-feminist position which sees women's struggles as a legitimate and integral part of broader struggles which transform not only the form and content of those struggles, but also the type of development policy which flows from them' (pp. 30–1). The authors refer to the concept of triple oppression – the 'experiential unity of race, class and gender oppression' – and to the 'tendency at the level of formal politics and policy to separate and prioritize the three aspects of women's oppression' (p. 48).

Much of the debate within feminist discourse has become more sophisticated since Robin Morgan's rallying cry that 'Sisterhood is powerful' and then 'Sisterhood is Global'. Indeed, the very concept of sisterhood has proven to be quite problematic. Ramazanoglu (1989) states that 'Even a cursory look at the variety of women's experiences, around the world and through history, shows the limited extent to which women's experiences are shared' (p. 17). Other writers describe 'a pretense to a homogeneity of experience covered by the word *sisterhood* that does not in fact exist' (Audre Lorde, quoted in Spelman 1988: 1). While Morgan argues that 'class analysis is at best incomplete and at worst divisive of women... invented by patriarchy to divide and conquer' (quoted in Ramazanoglu 1989: 113), others hold that 'Sex is a Marxist Issue... [and] Class is a Feminist Issue' (Armstrong & Armstrong 1983: 27–9). As Thornton Dill (1983) summarizes:

the cry 'Sisterhood is powerful!' has engaged only a few segments of the female population in the United States. Black, Hispanic, Native American, and Asian

American women of all classes, as well as many working-class women, have not readily identified themselves as sisters of the white middle-class women who have been in the forefront of the movement (p. 131).

Thornton Dill describes the way in which black women, historically as well as currently, 'have felt called upon to choose between their commitments to feminism and to the struggle against racial injustice' and refers to the tendency of groups of blacks and groups of women battling over 'the dubious distinction of being the "most" oppressed' (p. 136).

Beall *et al.* also describe 'the tendency within national liberation movements to equate feminism with western bourgeois feminism' which 'results in a dismissal of the insights of feminism as being irrelevant to Third World women' (1989: 32–3). An article on the history of the ANC women's struggles (Kimble & Unterhalter 1982) addresses the problems which Western feminists have in understanding the South African women's struggles:

Western women cannot hear what third world women are saying. Thus, for example, when South African women clearly assert that 'Our struggle is not a women's struggle'; 'the enemy is not male chauvinism,' they are making two important points. Firstly, they do not want to fight for mere equality with their men, since black men are themselves still subject to all the oppressive and exploitative legislation of the apartheid system. Secondly, they want to maintain the dicipline of the political movement (p. 15).

The same article quotes a leading woman of the ANC expressing a virtual hierarchy of the various forms of oppression they experience:

In our country white racism and apartheid coupled with economic exploitation have degraded the African woman more than any male prejudices (p. 14).

But even in the West, feminism as a movement has been able to mobilize only a very select group of women; 'as an organized self-conscious movement [it] has been largely middle class and white' (Brenner 1989: 249). While in the last few decades women who did not fit this description have entered into politics and other spheres of influence, they 'spoke as women of an oppressed class, or race, or community, while the feminist movement spoke of Woman' (*ibid.*). Many women do not hear their own voice represented in this white middle-class feminism.

Black women, despite their sexual oppression, are correct in their belief that oppression is greater on the question of race, that along race lines white women participate with white men in creating this oppression, and that the division of the black community along sex lines can only weaken our already unenviable position and may, in fact, spell doom to all of our black people (quoted in Ramazanoglu 1989: 127).

But need such a hierarchy be established? Must feminists and blacks, in Thornton Dill's words, battle over the 'dubious distinction of being the "most" oppressed'?

Let us now return to our earlier consideration of the concepts of social categorization and social identification. Recall that social categorizations are 'discontinuous divisions of the social world into distinct classes or categories' (Turner 1982: 17–18), and that social identification is the process by which individuals locate themselves within such social categorizations. But herein lies the problem. 'Selves are not made up of separable units of identity strung together to constitute a whole person' (Spelman 1988: 158). The argument against what we shall call essentialism – the idea that a person's identity can be boiled down to an essence – is forceful and cogently presented by Elizabeth Spelman in her book *Inessential Woman: Problems of Exclusion in Feminist Thought*:

thinking about a person's identity as made up of neatly distinguishable 'parts' may be very misleading... in the case of such feminist thought we may get the impression that a woman's identity consists of a sum of parts neatly divisible from one another, parts defined in terms of her race, gender, class, and so on... This is a version of personal identity we might call tootsie roll metaphysics: each part of my identity is separable from every other part, and the significance of each part is unaffected by the other parts... As a woman, I'm like other women; my difference from other women is only along the other dimensions of my identity (p. 136).

Spelman illustrates her point with the example of herself. Is there a 'woman part' of her, she asks, which is distinct from the 'white part'? 'Any part of my body is part of a body that is, by prevailing criteria, female and white' (p. 134). She paints a hypothetical situation whereby she is standing on a stage next to James Baldwin: 'Is my difference from him as a woman separable from my difference from him as a white person?' (p. 135). To answer this question, she then brings Angela Davis up onto the same hypothetical platform: 'Is there some respect in which I am different from James Baldwin in just the same way Angela Davis is different from him?'

If it were possible to isolate a woman's 'womanness' from her racial identity, then we should have no trouble imagining that had I been Black I could have had just the same understanding of myself as a woman as I in fact do, and that no matter how differently people would have treated me had I been Black, nevertheless what it would have meant to them that I was a woman would have been just the same (*ibid.*).

It is then not only the social identifications which we ascribe to ourselves, but equally those we ascribe to others and which others ascribe to us which are profoundly influenced by the multiple and simultaneous dimensions of our identities. Each category in an individual's social categorization system exists in relation to all the other categories; the whole, that individual's social identity, is not reducible to the sum of its parts.

To speak of social identity, as Tajfel does, as being 'the sum total of social identifications used by a person to define him- or herself' is to ground the theory on a serial model of identity, Spelman's 'tootsie roll metaphysics'. Groups are not portrayed as coexisting in the same individual; the theory does not realize its full social potential. One woman comments: 'Women don't lead their lives like, "Well, this part is race, and this is class, and this part has to do with women's identities," so it's confusing' (quoted in Spelman 1988: 133). Thornton Dill makes the same point:

> most people view their lives as a whole and do not explain their daily experiences or world view in terms of the differential effects of their racial group, class position, or gender. Thus, we must examine on an analytical level the ways in which the structures of class, race, and gender intersect in any woman's or group of women's lives in order to grasp the concrete set of social relations that influence their behavior (1983: 138).

It is this integrative analysis which social identity theory must strive toward. Indeed, were it to do so, there would be much greater success in constructing a truly political psychology. For surely, it is not only in the fact, but in the variety of power differentials which people experience in their lives that they come to construct their ideas about the structure of the social system and their place within it – in short, their political ideology.

Amongst the stated aims of social identity theory are:

> to overcome the separation that has been wrought between the individual and society, and to find a way of relating psychological processes to historical, cultural, political and economic determinants of behaviour. It is central to the concept of social identity that it is viewed as being at the same time a social construct and an individual cognitive construct (Reicher 1987: 172).

If this is to be taken seriously, then a concerted attempt must be made to consider the interactions amongst and the synthesis of the multi-faceted aspects of identity; individuals stand in relation to society not first as members of a particular class, or race, or gender, but rather as whole people.

Let us adopt, then, a new rendition of Socrates' 'Virtue is one and its name is justice': Wickedness is one and its name is oppression. Individuals must sensitize themselves to oppression in all of its many forms. One manifestation of difference need not take priority over all others, since they coexist within the network of power relations of which the social structure is comprised. To say that one is oppressed as a woman is not to exculpate one from being an oppressor as a white member of the middle class. Similarly, the experience of one form of oppression does not offer a guarantee against the experience of another; many people experience double and triple oppression.

the claim that all women are oppressed is fully compatible with, and needs to be explicated in terms of, the many varieties of oppression that different populations of women have been subject to. After all, why should oppressors settle for uniform kinds of oppression, when to oppress their victims in many different ways – consciously or unconsciously – makes it more likely that the oppressed groups will not perceive it to be in their interest to work together (Spelman 1988: 132).

Even this statement needs a bit more clarification, for as it reads it seems as if there is but one, constant group of oppressors, and that there is not an overlap between members of oppressed and oppressing groups.

Rather, and this relates back again to social identity theory, individuals should acknowledge all parts of themselves (or, the consequences of their involuntary group memberships) – those which are oppressed, and those which are oppressing. Oppression, by its very nature, relies on hierarchy. By prioritizing one aspect of difference over another, are we not creating fertile grounds for oppression to reproduce itself? One is reminded here of the well-worn strategy: Divide and Conquer. Let us move away, then, from this dangerous essentialist construction of identity.

Later, when we listen to the way in which respondents speak about themselves and others in their lives, we shall see how problems of inconsistency can arise when individuals prioritize one dimension of difference over all others. Before that, however, let us first consider the methodology of the study. Following this, we shall meet the respondents, place them in their historical setting, and then hear what they have to say.

3 On the subject of subjectivity

Methodology is too important to be left to methodologists.

Howard Becker (1976: 3)

This chapter is not about method but methodology. The distinction between the two, for our purposes, is that method is about what we, as researchers, do, and methodology is about our reasons for doing it that way; one is a description of the nuts and bolts we use, the other the theory behind why some nuts and bolts are more appropriate to the task at hand than others. While it is difficult to speak of one without the other, the two are not synonymous.

I have described the essence of my method in the opening pages of this book.[1] My concern here is to explain why I did what I did. Given that I wished to learn about how lifetime socialist activists made sense of their lives, particularly in regards to their political commitment, why did I interview so few people? In fact, why did I interview at all? Why did I not construct a questionnaire (as was suggested to me), and distribute it as widely as possible, so that the size of my sample could give me confidence in the truthfulness of my findings? Why should people have to take note of what fifteen people say? Five hundred – now that's something else.

Indeed, I felt intuitively that it was something else, not that it was better or worse but merely different from the project I had envisaged. I did not, and do not regard generalizability as the sole legitimate goal of the study of human behaviour. And presumably others feel as I do, for if not, why are biographies such a popular form of narrative writing? One is reminded here of a quote of Samuel Johnson, who was himself the subject of a very famous biography:

there has rarely passed a life of which a judicious and faithful narrative would not be useful. For, not only every man has, in the mighty mass of the world, great numbers in the same condition with himself, to whom his mistakes and miscarriages, escapes and expedients, would be of immediate and apparent use; but there is such a uniformity in the state of man...that there is scarce any possibility of good or ill, but is common to human kind (1969: 320).

Jack Lindsay, who has written many biographies, describes himself as driven to uncover the deep universals in human experience: 'The effect should be simultaneously how like ourselves, how different' (Henderson 1990: 397).

A choice was to be made: did I wish to learn a lot about a small number of people, or a little about many people. Because there had been virtually no research conducted on lifetime activists, and hence strong presuppositions were unjustified, I chose the former course. Given what I saw to be my project, it was clear to me from the start that mine would be a qualitative study. The kind of information which I was seeking could not be revealed through a questionnaire survey. I felt then, as I do now, that if I wished to understand how commitment to working for social justice is sustained throughout a lifetime, who better to learn from than those whose existences were a living embodiment of that phenomenon? Some critics might feel that understanding fifteen people is a modest objective indeed for a researcher. My experience was quite the contrary. We have problems enough understanding ourselves, our motivations, our heartstrings; how then to understand another, much less fifteen others? Of course the end result, the findings as it were, are but my understanding of their understanding of themselves. But this is inevitable in the imperfect study of human lives. Aristotle wrote in *The Ethics*:

Our discussion will be adequate if it has as much clearness as the subject matter admits of, for precision is not to be sought for alike in all discussion ... it is the mark of an educated man to look for precision in each class of things just so far as the nature of the subject admits (quoted in Runyan 1982: 164).

The methodological debates in which I found myself engaged have a long history, and one from which we can learn. Particularly within sociology, there is a strong tradition of both qualitative and quantitative methodology, and perhaps the most forceful arguments for the complementarity of the two orientations can be found in this discipline. Academic psychology, on the other hand, from its inception in the second half of the nineteenth century, began as a laboratory experimental discipline, and its positivistic approach remains pre-eminent.

The history of the debates over qualitative and quantitative methodology extends back over two hundred years (Hammersley 1989), each vying for the claim of 'the most valid' form of research of human beings by human beings. But the polarization between qualitative and quantitative is not only unfortunate, but unnecessary, representing a false dichotomy. Qualitative methodology seeks to explore the depth and complexity of particular phenomena, while quantitative research is oriented toward determining prevalence. Qualitative and quantitative methods together provide the social sciences with a bifocal lens; they involve different 'ways of seeing' and 'observe different realities, or different aspects of the same reality' (McCracken 1988: 18).

During the past thirty years, there has been a tremendous growth in the use and acceptability of qualitative methods (Hammersley 1989: 1). Hammersley, in his stimulating book *The Dilemma of Qualitative Method: Herbert Blumer and the Chicago Tradition* (1989), gives a history of the emergence of qualitative methodology in the nineteenth and twentieth centuries. The University of Chicago, founded in 1892, quickly established itself in the forefront of American sociology; in the 1920s and 1930s its Department of Sociology was pre-eminent, and particularly associated with what we would now call qualitative methods.

However, even at this time, there existed both within the Chicago department and in wider academic circles, an ongoing debate about 'what were then regarded as the two main social research methods: case study and statistics' (Hammersley 1989: 92). Describing the difference between the two, E. W. Burgess in 1927 stated that 'quantitative methods deal in the main with cruder, more external aspects of human behavior, and... some other more sympathetic and discerning method is necessary to probe beneath the surface and to depict and analyze the inner life of the person' (quoted in Hammersley 1989: 94). He then illustrated this distinction:

How can the so-called intangible facts of life, its qualitative aspects, be apprehended by so crude an instrument as statistics? What figures will measure the degree of affection between husband and wife, or the nature and intensity of a father's pride in his children, or qualities of personality like charm, loyalty, and leadership? (*ibid.*).

Many leading intellectuals of the time, including Burgess, did not view the two methods as being in competition with each other, but rather as being complementary; statistical and case-study methods were to be distinguished 'on the basis that the former are concerned with the distribution of a particular trait, or a small number of traits, in a population, whereas the case study is concerned with the whole variety of traits to be found in a particular instance'. Both methods were seen as important and scientific; the difference was one of focus (Hammersley 1989: 95).

In the late nineteenth and early twentieth centuries German-speaking historians and sociologists, most notably Wilhelm Dilthey and Max Weber, mounted a hostile attack on 'the postivisitic social thought of France and England, represented by men like Auguste Comte and J. S.

Mill' (Outhwaite 1975: 1). They promoted the concept of *verstehen*, or interpretative understanding. Summarizing the debate, Outhwaite writes:

The concept of 'understanding'...is the nub of a long-standing theoretical controversy about the sort of method which is appropriate to a social science. On the one hand there are those who argue that social science should follow as closely as possible the well-tried methods of the natural sciences and look for general laws in social life... On the other hand are those who claim that the social sciences differ from the natural sciences either in the character of their subject matter or in their methods or both. The sociologist's or historian's understanding of the people he studied was variously conceived as following unproblematically from what they had in common as human beings, or as involving some imaginative act such as the 'reliving' of their experiences... (1975: 11–12).

These thinkers fought for a sociology of 'the inside', claiming that human action could not be sufficiently appreciated and analysed by exclusive focus on its observable components. *Verstehen*, whose origins lie in theological hermeneutics, 'consists of placing oneself in the position of other people to see what meaning they give to their actions, what their purposes are, or what ends they believe are served by their actions' (Abercrombie *et al.* 1988: 265). The major criticism of *verstehen* is also that which is lodged against hermeneutics: there is no ultimate arbitrator in the validation of interpretations. Again, as we shall later see, this question of validation continues to be paramount in more current criticisms of qualitative methodology.

It is quite striking how methodological arguments similar to those discussed above have, in more recent years, been reconstructed but not substantively reconceptualized. Moreover, it is interesting that these long-standing debates, well known to sociologists, rarely appear in the psychological literature, where it seems that qualitative methodology is being introduced as the new kid on the block. And yet, if we cannot learn from history, we are, as the cliché goes, doomed to repeat it, forever reinventing the wheel. In the remainder of this chapter I shall present some of the methodological debates in their current form, drawing on examples from my own data to illustrate various points. I conclude the chapter with a discussion on retrospective data, reintroducing in a slightly different form some of the issues presented in earlier sections.

Objectivity, subjectivity and the question of bias

Perhaps the most persistent criticism made of qualitative methodology is that it lacks the necessary objectivity of a proper scientific approach (Runyan 1982). Because, in the dominant view, the social sciences still seek to emulate the natural sciences; there exists a 'hierarchy of research methods' which follows a quantitative (having the most status)–qualitative continuum (Sherif 1987: 39–41). Sherif contests the grounds upon which that status is conferred: despite the language of objectivity employed by experimental psychologists, they cannot control for the fact that 'it was the researchers who selected the topics, presented them in certain orders, varied the contents of the screen, etc' (p. 46). At issue, then, is whether social-science research, regardless of the methodology employed, can ever be objective in any meaningful sense of the word.

It is my contention that questions of objectivity and subjectivity emerge at virtually every step of the research enterprise. Using the example of in-depth interviews, one can see the influence of the researcher in the conceptualization of the project; the construction of the interview schedule (on what basis does one judge certain questions to be relevant?); the selection of respondents (whose voices are to be heard, and, significantly, who is neglected, effectively silenced?); the interviewer/interviewee relationship (whom does each perceive the other to be and how does this feed into the construction of the data?); the actual interview (how is the field defined? What are considered data – only things said while the tape recorder is turned on, or also more informal exchanges?); the act of transcription (is it an interpretative process? Even if one writes in all the ums, ahs, moments of laughter and silence, is it ever possible to re-create the actual interview? Moreover, what is the effect of transforming the spoken word into its written form? Should respondents be allowed to change what they have said upon further reflection?); the analysis (how does the researcher make sense of what she had heard? Does she try to distance herself from the respondents or to enter into their point of view as much as possible? Is the analysis inductive or deductive?); and the final write-up (does the researcher acknowledge her own presence and its effect on the production of data; to whom does she feel responsible? How does she deal with any discrepancy between her own and respondents' interpretations of their words, even their lives?). It would be far too lengthy for me to give illustrations of each of these steps from my own research, so instead I shall select some of the more interesting examples.

The question of what was to be considered data was problematic for me simply because I spent so much time, over many months, with respondents. Were data only the transcribed words of the conversations we had while the tape recorder was turned on? This seemed to me an unnecessarily limited and simplistic definition, and not one which encompassed the variety of interactions between myself and the respondents. All interviews took place in respondents' homes. Meetings usually involved not only tape-recorded interviewing sessions, but sharing meals and other casual social interaction. Often I was introduced to family members and neighbours, and on occasion we would conclude our meetings by going to the local pub. In addition, because respondents were geographically dispersed around England, interviewing sometimes entailed staying overnight in respondents' homes. Thus, our encounters were not limited to our tape-recorded sessions. Sometimes over a meal, I would find the conversation directly relevant to my investigation. Attempts at reproducing the conversation when the tape recorder was on were not always successful. It occurred to me that what was and was not to be considered as data was almost arbitrary. My solution was instead to make notes of my thoughts following every meeting, and to regard interaction outside of the formal interview as adding perspective to our recorded discussions. In addition, participants would often write to me following a meeting, to elaborate upon a particular issue addressed in the interview, or to introduce a new, but relevant issue. Anything which directly related to the actual interview, I considered as an extended form of data.

For instance, I received a lengthy letter from one of the respondents elaborating upon something she had said in an interview. In this case, the respondent was motivated to write the letter after reading the transcript and feeling that a particular issue had been misrepresented. During our interview, she had described her feelings about starting work at the dentist's by saying:

I really loved it, because I was a person in my own right, you know, I wasn't classified. (MA: Do you think it was the job, or the people around you?) Both. It was a very high-class practice. They were all wealthy clients in the main...And the fact that you were on an equal – the man I worked for...he treated you as an equal, and it was always 'Will you do this? Thank you.' So that you really felt, a real person. The first time, I would think, in my life.

In her letter, the respondent clarified this, writing:

working at the Dentist looks as though I was happy moving out of my social class, not at all, but interesting looking at those people and hearing their views, but more important was the educative side, there were two newspapers I read every day. Liberal and Tory, we never had a book or newspaper in our house; there was a regular camping magazine, with encouragement from the Dentist I became interested in Camping, Climbing, Pot-holing and Motor cycling...He encouraged me to go on a walking holiday and said 'stay for the week if you're enjoying it,' that was my first holiday...[After a page of more examples] So working at the Dentist's opened my eyes to many enriching experiences.

It seemed to me that this elaboration on her original statement only deepened my understanding of her feelings regarding that situation.

Interestingly, independent from her, I too had thought that the typewritten form of her spoken word had conveyed a different sense to the one I had received during the interview. To have discounted the letter as legitimate data simply because those words had not been said when the tape recorder was on would have benefited no one.

Similarly, another respondent, dissatisfied with his responses to the questions on morality in the interview, wrote a long letter to me regarding his thoughts on this:

I am sorry that a number of your questions left me floundering. One of these (or rather, a number of these questions you put to me) was on the lines of what was my yardstick to measure and decide what was moral or what was immoral. How did I decide as each issue came up in the course of my life? I completely failed to produce any clear answer and yet it should have been reasonably easy to state that what benefits the majority in life is moral and which only benefits an individual or a class in the minority – at the expense of the majority – must be immoral and to be resisted.

Again, the contents of this letter only illuminated aspects of the original taped conversation. In this instance, the participant had thought about our discussions after my departure, and had wanted to elaborate upon his earlier responses. Both letters, therefore, seemed to me to be legitimate sources of supplementary data.

One important step in my research was sending copies of transcripts to the respondents. I asked respondents to check for factual inaccuracies such as misspellings, and, perhaps more importantly, for impressionistic inaccuracies. An example of the first was a typographical error, which reported the respondent as saying that 'God leads us' rather than what he really had said, which was 'God needs us'. Obviously the difference is significant. The example of the respondent's letter about working in the dentist's, cited above, illustrates the second kind of inaccuracy: the respondent felt her words, as they stood, misrepresented her feelings about her class. In other instances, respondents noted significant areas which we had not discussed. The respondents and I reviewed the transcripts first independently, and then together. I always began the next meeting by posing questions which had arisen from the transcripts, some concentrating on the intended meaning of a particular word, others on the meaning(s) underlying entire sections.

Briggs poses the question 'Is there no way of rechecking one's perceptions against the text, that is, asking the speakers if we have understood them?' He then answers his own question:

Taken literally, the notion is absurd. The researcher can, of course, go back to the interviewee and ask if the interpretation is correct. This can produce interesting data...but it hardly solves the problem. Human introspective capacities do not necessarily extend to recalling exactly what one was intending to say at some point in the past... What is needed is some means of rechecking one's perceptions against those of the participants at the time (1986: 107–8).

Briggs' suggestion of taking the transcript back to the participants is only absurd if what the researcher is seeking is specific information about how a participant felt during the course of the few hours in which the interview happened to be conducted. However, if the researcher believes, as I do, that respondents should be allowed to change their minds about a given issue (for instance, after having given it greater consideration), then contradicting an earlier statement should pose no problem. Moreover, the kind of information I was seeking was not of such a transient and shifty nature that there would be radical alterations in respondents' thoughts in the course of a relatively short period of time. My interest was not specifically centred on participants' thoughts at the precise moment of the interview, but rather on the more generalized construction of their enduring belief system.

Any form of communication which involves the use of words will be imperfect. Even if one wishes to explain an intended meaning of one word, one has still to resort to other words for elaboration, and there is no guarantee that speaker and listener share the same meanings even of the words being used for description. Still, within this inevitable limitation, certain precautions can be taken to check for mutual comprehension. I would suggest that this dialectical approach to data production and interpretation is one of the only means by which an interviewer can systematically check the foundation upon which her analysis will be based. In this way, researchers are more directly accountable to the original source of the data, i.e. the participants themselves.

The question of accountability and responsibility is particularly prevalent in the final write-up. Throughout this stage of the process, I tried to heed the advice of Gilligan (1985). She suggests that in writing up results, a researcher should imagine that she will be sitting beside her respondents as they read what is written about them. I do not interpret this to mean that a researcher should only be complementary about her participants, but rather that she respect her respondents' integrity, and carefully consider her words. She must not write what she knows to be untrue, but she need not write all that she knows. She must ask herself if she can justify her presentation of her participant's life to the most difficult audience: the participant whose life it is. In my own case, I chose not to include several accounts which might have been interesting for the reader but unnecessarily painful for the respondent. In no case did the omitted information contradict what I had written. Had I chosen to include such stories in my presentation, I do not think I would have been at ease with the respondents after I had given them their copies of the theses. These are just some of the many examples from my own work which illustrate the vulnerability, indeed the subjectivity, of the research endeavour.

The objectivity/subjectivity debate is not limited to comparisons between quantitative and qualitative methods. Within qualitative research, nowhere is the question of personal involvement more salient than in discussions of proper interview strategies. Many, though not all, qualitative researchers believe that objectivity is not only a desirable, but an achievable goal. They feel that a detached attitude can and should be maintained, and warn of the dangers of 'overrapport'. (Burgess (1984) summarizes this approach, saying:

> It would...appear that there are 'rules' about 'proper' interview behavior which should be friendly but not over-sociable in order to overcome problems associated with 'bias' (p. 101).

Much of the advice given in the name of objectivity is based on the concern that 'over-rapport' produces biased data. Consider the following 'words of advice' taken from a variety of texts on interviewing techniques and quoted in Oakley (1981):

> Never provide the interviewee with any formal indication of the interviewer's beliefs and values. If the informant poses a question...parry it. (Sjoberg & Nett 1968: 212) When asked what you mean and think, tell them you are here to learn, not to pass any judgment, that the situation is very complex. (Galtung 1967: 161) If he (the interviewer) should be asked for his views, he should laugh off the request with the remark that his job at the moment is to get opinions, not to have them. (Selling *et al.* 1965: 576) (Oakley 1981: 35–6).

Oakley summarizes the underlying message contained in the above statements: 'the reason why the interviewer must pretend not to have opinions...is because behaving otherwise might "bias" the interview' (p. 36). The implicit ideology that forms the foundation of this approach to methodology is that through the standardization of procedures, researchers can arrive at some form of objective truth, about an individual or group of individuals; if they perform their jobs professionally, this truth can be grasped in its pure form. Building on this set of assumptions, then, it is understandable why the researcher should try to remain distant, so as not to contaminate this truth or set of truths. The quest for scientific precision within the social sciences lives on.

Still, some qualitative researchers do not perceive their involvement with their participants as problematic. Indeed, many regard such contact as a source of enrichment. Cottle candidly discusses his experience as a researcher, and calls attention to the limitations of the claim to objectivity. He writes:

I make no pretence at objective assessments of these people's lives, the inquiry being subjective and dependent on my relationship with these families, and on paying attention to what is transpiring...what I observe and record is not only material experienced by me, it is, in part, generated by me (1982: 123–5).

Judi Marshall makes a similar claim: 'I am part of any social situation I explore, and always have attitudes, values, feelings and beliefs about it. I do not, therefore, believe in, or aspire to, objectivity' (1986: 195). Griffin echoes this sentiment: 'I did not try to adopt a pretence of objectivity or invisibility. The research perspective I employed would challenge the notion that objective research is ever possible (1989: 183). Oakley, too, endorses this view: 'personal involvement is more than dangerous bias – it is the condition under which people come to know each other and to admit others into their lives' (1981: 58). Bar-Tal and Bar-Tal (1988) state that 'Each individual...perceives, understands, and experiences the world in his own way. According to this view, there is no such thing as objectivity, since each person, including a scientist, is a captive of his own perspective' (p. 91). If researchers wish to grasp the meaning which individuals perceive in their own actions, they might be well-advised to utilize personal resources which are commonly employed in other contexts of human interaction. Briggs (1986) comments that

'Bias', meaning inter-respondent and inter-interviewer differences in the presentation of questions and the perception of responses, *is rather an interactional resource* that is used in accomplishing the task at hand (p. 24).

One is reminded here of a description of *verstehen* made by Herbert Blumer of the Chicago School of Sociology:

[sympathetic introspection] becomes the essential method for the understanding of contemporary problems and life. Wherever any event, individual act, social situation, or cultural phenomenon is to be understood in its full social significance, sympathetic introspection must obviously be employed (quoted in Hammersley 1989: 141).

Moreover, 'reliance on *verstehen* is not restricted to social science, [but] it is "a most common procedure in human association"' (p. 140).

It is through establishing rapport, or 'bias' as some may call it, that interviewers come to understand interviewees. Ideally, sympathetic understanding is a reciprocal process which aids mutual comprehension; as such, one would have thought that it also improved the quality of the data. Interviews are not, however, just conversations, they are conversations of a particular sort, 'conversations with a purpose' (Webb & Webb 1932: 130). Thus interviews can be understood as related to, though not identical with, other, more familiar forms of human communication; from this perspective, rapport is not regarded as something to be avoided, but rather as a resource which has potential to enhance the quality of the interview.

Interviewer and interviewee: the power of relationship

At the centre of the controversy regarding bias, then, is a dispute concerning the optimal relationship between interviewer and interviewee. Goffman's *The Presentation of Self in Everyday Life* (1959) is useful as a starting-point in this discussion. He posits that individuals, like actors, play certain roles in their lives, not only sequentially, but simultaneously. In some measure, how they act depends upon their reading of the situation.

Ordinarily the definitions of the situation projected by the several different participants are sufficiently attuned to one another, so that open contradiction will not occur... each participant is expected to suppress his immediate heartfelt feelings, conveying a view of the situation which he feels the others will be able to find at least temporarily acceptable (p. 20).

Goffman then proceeds to describe what he calls an 'interactional *modus vivendi*'.

Together the participants contribute to a single over-all definition of the situation which involves not so much a real agreement as to what exists but rather a real agreement as to whose claims concerning what issues will be temporarily honoured. Real agreement will also exist concerning the desirability of avoiding an open conflict of definitions of the situation (p. 21).

Exactly how the roles of interviewer and interviewee are negotiated in research settings is the focus of our discussion here. It is probable that both interviewer and interviewee share some rather vague expectations of what their encounter will entail; interviewers expect to interview, and interviewees expect to be interviewed. Equally, each expects the other to play their part. With that said, they might not share assumptions regarding the relationship between interviewer and interviewee, both in general and in their situation in particular. Moreover, the question of 'whose claims concerning what issues will be temporarily honoured' might be a complicated one, in that during the interview it may appear that the claims of the interviewee are being honoured, while in the write-up (the ultimate and often only representation of that meeting) the reverse may prove to be the case.

What is and what should be the relationship between interviewer and interviewee? In the past decade, much feminist literature, coming from different disciplines, has addressed this issue (Harding 1987b; Roberts 1981; Wilkinson 1986). Oakley states unequivocally that 'when a feminist interviews women...[the] use of prescribed interviewing practice is morally indefensible' as it is 'objectifying your sister' (1981: 41). Geiger claims that 'notions of objectivity themselves are andro-centric... the higher levels of abstraction assumed to present a "true" picture of "reality" often represent neither truth nor reality for women' (1986: 338). MacKinnon criticises 'objectivist epistemology that measures rationality by point-of-viewlessness' (1987: 135). The points raised in these criticisms, while specifically written by women about women, transcend issues of gender. The relationship between inter-viewer and interviewee, regardless of the presence or absence of shared group membership (in this case gender), is always a tenuous one which merits careful consideration.

However, problems arise when one realizes that the process of *verstehen*, however desirable (or not) one might regard it, has necessary limitations: to what extent is it ever fully possible to place oneself in the position of another, and thereby to comprehend that other's perception of their experiences and the meanings they attach to them? Outhwaite's description of *verstehen* was that understanding follows 'unproblemati-cally from what they [researcher and researched] had in common as human beings, or as involving some imaginative act such as the "reliving" of their experiences' (1975: 12). Indeed, it might be the case that the only thing the two persons involved have in common is that they are human beings. Regardless of how developed one's imaginative capacities are, an individual will invariably impose her own way of making sense onto the experiences of another. When one says 'If I were you...', the implicit assumption is that 'I am not you, and can never be you. Even if I were confronted with the same set of circumstances which you now encounter, I would still be me, and this is what I would do.'

As we have seen in the previous chapter, even (or perhaps particularly) within feminist discourse, there has been criticism of an approach which overemphasizes commonality – based solely on shared gender – at the expense of acknowledging difference. Whom the interviewer and the interviewee perceive each other to be, and whom they perceive themselves to be in relation to each other, is not only of theoretical but of methodological interest. The title of Oakley's article, 'Interviewing Women – A Contradiction in Terms', reveals the lack of a differentiated perspective of women's identities. The title of Riessman's (1987) rejoinder to Oakley, 'When Gender is Not Enough: Women Inter-viewing Women', highlights this point.

Bhavnani and Coulson state that

an assumption of automatic sisterhood from white women towards black women is ill-founded. Sisterhood can only be nurtured and developed when white women acknowledge the complex power relationships between white women and white men in relation to black women and black men (1986: 90).

They indicate the importance of 'recognizing that black women and white women have different histories and different relationships to present struggles, in Britain and internationally' (p. 82), and refer to the long-standing 'legacy of racism within feminism' (p. 82). Thus, while gender is important, so too are race and class (Bhavnani & Coulson 1986; Riessman 1987; Dill 1987). This perspective challenges

the tendency of white women to generalize from the situation of white, Western women to that of all women...criticiz[ing] the value of imagining a racially and culturally homogeneous 'woman' – one who is really a bourgeois, white, Western woman...(Harding (on Dill) 1987b: 97).

While acknowledging the legitimacy of these criticisms, the issues of interviewer–interviewee relationship which have been placed, primarily by feminists, on the agenda of debates regarding social science methodology are still worth pursuing. Indeed, the message of Riessman and Dill is more one of caution regarding over-identification. They express a more finely tuned sensitivity to interviewer–interviewee dynamics. Rather than denying the relational aspects of the interview identified by Oakley and others, they ask for the point to be developed further.

Riessman argues that when gender, class and cultural congruity exist between researcher and respondent, they share an 'assumptive world' (1987: 190). Perhaps it is useful here to recall the discussion on social identity theory presented in the previous chapter. While interviewer and interviewee may share certain group memberships (such as gender) they do not necessarily share others. It is important for the researcher to be sensitive to the way in which she is perceived by the participant, as this will also influence the dynamics between the two people. Additionally, the researcher interprets what is said to her through her own frameworks of understanding, which will invariably be influenced by her group memberships.

Consider the case of Janet Finch, who conducted her research on the lives of clergy women and mothers, a group to which she herself belonged at the time she initiated the project. Clearly her sensitivity not only to the problems these women faced, but also to the difficulty involved in discussing complications with 'outsiders', was heightened by her own personal familiarity with the situation. They seemed to welcome the opportunity to have someone with whom they felt they could speak candidly and confidentially. Finch writes that

Comments like 'fellas don't see it that way, do they?' and 'you can't ask your mother because it's an admission of defeat' indicate an identification between interviewer and interviewee which is gender specific (1984: 77–8).

Perhaps the point to be made here is slightly different from that which Finch suggests. While she interprets her respondent's comment to be gender-specific, it might be more accurate to describe it as an acknowledgement of a shared gender between the two speakers. Similarly, former athletes often become sports broadcasters and interview people who occupy positions which they themselves once had. The strategy is one of evoking shared group membership; the content of the comment will be determined by the particular group.

In my own research, there were many occasions in the interviews when respondents highlighted similarities between us. The following example is similar to Finch's account in that the speaker is overtly acknowledging a shared gender between us.

I thought a great deal of my father, and I think girls tend to think more of their fathers than their mothers, especially as my mother was the one who dealt out the punishments, and also exploited me to a great extent. But in later years you realise that what a woman or a mother comes through, and I think a girl then appreciates her mother more, but in the early days... I don't know about you, but I think most girls think more of their fathers than their mothers.

While this particular example addresses the issue of our shared gender, in fact this same respondent alluded to other similarities between us. We had established in our first meeting that not only did we both have a Jewish background, but that our ancestors had come from the same Russian village. She would often allude to various aspects of what she perceived to be a shared culture between us. In the following example, she draws a comparison between being Jewish and being a communist.

People had these prejudices, they would say to you just the same way as you know yourself, people who say 'Oh, my best friends are Jews,' or they say to you 'Oh, you're not like all the other communists.' ... They just wouldn't know you see.

On another occasion, I had just begun my first interview with one of the respondents, asking her questions about her early childhood, when she turned to me and asked where I had grown up. 'Buffalo, New York', I responded, 'very near to Niagara Falls'. I was quite surprised when she said that not only did she know Buffalo, but that she had a recent newspaper clipping from there, which she promised to show me during our coffee break. My interest was piqued, not only because she was one of the first British people whom I had met who knew Buffalo, but also because my family has been in the newspaper business there for generations. As she went into the back room to get the clipping, she called out to me 'Perhaps I should preface this by saying that my son is a bit of a rock n' roll star'. I had visions of an overgrown, unemployed, mediocre guitarist playing in a local pub. I was, therefore, quite taken by surprise when she emerged with the front page of a Buffalo newspaper with large headlines which read something to the effect 'Roger Waters Comes to Buffalo.' I was interviewing Pink Floyd's mother.

Respondents' efforts at establishing a similarity or connection between us were not, then, wholly dependent upon perception of a shared group membership. One respondent, with whom I shared neither class, religion, nationality, gender, nor age, continually emphasized the influence that Jewish people had had on him in his early life in East London. Indeed, throughout our time together, he would use Yiddish phrases.

I think when I look back, they [the Jewish people] had a great influence on my life. They taught me to be, I'm going to say it myself, they taught me to be a nice human being... I've been a real mensch.

Speaking of the importance of perseverance in fighting for a cause, he says:

I'm not cutting the cloth to suit the garment, but I have to use it. Let's take the struggles of the Jewish people... Look what they suffered, but they never gave up.

A similar effort at establishing connection was repeated when he learned that my paternal ancestors were Irish; he then taught me some Gaelic sayings.

In the case of Finch, she shares more than just gender with her respondents: there is a familiarity of life circumstances. The speaker might well have said 'women who aren't married to clergy men don't know these problems'. Connections between interviewers and interviewees can be made through affirming whatever characteristics one or both parties may perceive themselves to hold in common. While establishing a relationship between interviewer and respondent is clearly not the object of the interview, it is, in whatever form it takes, a by-product of it, and one which has much potential to enhance the quality of the data. Riessman concludes her article by stating that 'perfect congruence between interviewer, interviewee, and interpreter is probably not possible, not even always desirable'. What she does strongly advocate, however, is 'sensitive collaboration' between the parties concerned (1987: 191).

With none of the respondents in the study did I share either nationality or age, and sometimes differences between us also included gender, religion and class. While I did not think it was necessary or even appropriate to begin our meetings with an explicit statement regarding my identity, some aspects of it were obvious, and others became apparent during the course of our interviews. I did not hesitate to answer any question respondents asked of me, as it was clear that it was important to them to have some understanding of who I was, particularly as they were being asked to reveal so much of themselves to me.

In addition to the aspects of interpersonal identification discussed above, there is another dynamic to be addressed: embedded in the interview process, there are 'ideological assumptions ... tied to relationships of power and control' (Briggs 1986: 123). Reminiscent of Goffman, Briggs then states:

the interview presupposes a set of role relations, rules for turn-taking, canons for introducing new topics and judging the relevance of statements ... This effects a displacement of many of the norms that guide other speech events ... Even in the most 'unstructured,' 'open-ended' interviews, the interviewer has a great deal more control over the development of the discourse (p. 27).

Not only is the relationship between researcher and researched inherently unequal, but depending upon the various group memberships of the parties concerned, there is potential for this imbalance to be compounded. Thus, for instance, the situation in which a white person interviews a black person introduces a new set of power dynamics to be considered. Bhavnani observes

an implicit assumption that qualitative research ... [gives] a voice to the interviewees, and is therefore, empowering ... Empowerment and 'having a voice' are not, however, the same, although the two are often conflated (1990: 145–6).

The presentation of qualitative research can tend to create a semblance that the words of the respondents speak for themselves. However, as Bhavnani indicates, some qualitative research can, through 'masking the power inequalities within that research, be part of a disempowerment' (p. 145). Moreover, the words of respondents can never really speak for themselves, in that transcripts are invariably edited by the researcher, and the very processes of deciding which data are relevant, and how data will be analysed, are ones which guarantee the interviewer ultimate control over the interview, although, as discussed earlier, attempts can be made to share control.

Even when the interviewer and interviewee share most or all of their involuntary group memberships, however, there remains a basic inequality between them – which may be only situation-specific – which reveals itself at every stage of the enterprise. Mishler comments on this, stating that

In a standard interview respondents are presented with a predetermined scheme of relevances: topics, definitions of events, categories for response and evaluation are all introduced, framed, and specified by interviewers, who determine the adequacy and appropriateness of responses. Finally, researchers through their analyses and reports define the 'meaning' of responses and findings, whereas respondents have no opportunity to comment upon interpretations of their words and intentions. [In the language of Friere] this way of doing research takes away from respondents their right to 'name' their world (1986: 122).

Typically, it is the interviewer who exercises most power in the interview, for it is she who determines what questions are posed. Indeed, in the examples of textbook advice quoted earlier, researchers are specifically warned against answering questions which participants might ask them. Oakley comments on this, saying:

interviewers define the role of interviewees as subordinates; extracting information is more to be valued than yielding it; the convention of interviewer–interviewee hierarchy is a rationalisation of inequality (1981: 40).

Mishler, who is by profession a medical doctor, describes the way in which interviewers communicate to interviewees whether or not their response was 'adequate'. Thus, if a question is repeated, or if a response is met with silence, the speaker knows that the person who posed the question is somehow not fully satisfied with the answer provided. Mishler suggests that, as an alternative,

A question may more usefully be thought of as part of a circular process through which its meaning and that of its answer are created in the discourse between interviewer and respondent as they try to make continuing sense of what they are saying to each other (1986: 54).

If Mishler's suggestion is to be taken seriously, then interviewers must not view questions which are posed to themselves as threatening the research process, but rather as enhancing it, as it is only through the creation of genuine dialogue that any form of interpersonal understanding can be achieved. Oakley comments that 'one piece of behaviour that properly socialised respondents do not engage in is asking questions back' (1981: 35). And yet Oakley's respondents did ask her questions – which she quite happily answered – and very often. Burgess adopts the same approach as Oakley, answering questions in the same way as he poses them.

To have avoided these questions would have provided the 'sanitised' interview demanded by the textbook writers but would have ruined my relationship with teachers and pupils (1984: 105).

A similar situation arose in my study. On arrival at the house of the first person I was to interview, I was asked, before having passed the front hallway, what proof, if any, I had to show that I was not with the CIA. I hesitated, and then responded that I had none, other than my word. Moreover, I suggested that if I were able to produce a note on CIA letterhead stationery stating specifically that I was not with the CIA, she should be most suspicious. Thus it was made abundantly clear to me from the start that traditional textbook interviewing advice about personal non-disclosure did not apply in my situation. Had I not answered the question posed to me concerning the CIA, for instance, there would have been no possibility of an interview. I was, in a sense, being interviewed for the job of interviewer. When another respondent read of this encounter, he wrote to me:

No, it never occurred to me to wonder if you were a C.I.A. infiltrator... [quoting a former Battalion Commander] 'There is only one approach that any person can adopt – rely on your own common sense and judgment of the person who approaches you' – so now you know what was going through my mind that first day I met you at Grantham station; can I co-operate with this person or do I stay on my guard?

Fortunately for me, he decided in favour of the first option.

When participants are socialized not to challenge the hierarchy of the research setting, and thus only to answer questions which the interviewer asks them, the scope of the possible response is invariably predetermined. Respondents often asked me questions in the course of our interviews, which I always answered. The following exchange proved to be quite humorous.

Q: How would you describe yourself to yourself?[2]
A: Well, I'm an easy going fella, I'm easy going. I'm very outward, I'm very extrovert... I think if I'd been an American they would have named me Johnny Friendly (laughter).

. . .

Q: How do you think other people describe you, or would describe you?
A: Well, I mean I've overheard people say, it's like flattering yourself, 'well-loved person.' Of course amongst the boss class the reaction is that I'm a well-hated person, but nevertheless they always give me respect, 'cause I'm not what they call the usual loud-mouth what they expect from public orators like in industry...

Q: How do you think your good friends would describe you?... What's he like as a person, what's he really like?
A: What do you think of me as a person?

. . .

Q: I think you're great.

A: That's it, you gave me the answer, that's how they think.

It is not enough, however, for respondents to feel that they can pose questions and that they will be answered. It is the responsibility of the researcher to create an environment within the interview in which respondents feel free, and even encouraged, to challenge questions asked of them or assumptions which they perceive the researcher to be making. While both researcher and respondent probably share the idea that their interview will focus on the aspects of the latter's life that are relevant to the subject being investigated, considerations of what is relevant might vary significantly between these two people. Before any of my initial interviews I asked respondents to indicate to me if they found any question (1) too personal (or if, for any reason, they did not wish to respond to it), (2) answerable though irrelevant, or (3) not clear. The extent to which the interviewer determines the precise content of the interview – that is to say the extent to which her ideas of what is relevant prevail – depends in large part on the type of interview being conducted. It is probably fair to say that highly structured interviews tend to limit the possibility of the participant to communicate her concept of what is pertinent to the given subject.

Even when interviews are semi-structured, as was the case with my study, there are no guarantees against researchers imposing their own beliefs and styles of communication on their respondents. Briggs describes many research efforts as

fraught with the same contradictions inherent in more exploitative journeys to other lands...communicative hegemony is a rather more subtle and persistent form of scientific colonialism (1986: 121).

Embarrassingly, an example of this can be seen in the following exchange between myself and one of the respondents. Here I do not accept the respondent's answer to my question. Because I had strongly anticipated that there would be some differentiation between cognition and affect, I implicitly communicated to the respondent, through my repetition of the question, that his answer was inadequate (for the sole reason that it had not met my expectations). Fortunately in this situation the respondent was equally forceful in his persistence, until finally I relinquished my assumption.

Q: In your life, do you think you would describe yourself as someone whose decisions are generally guided by your feelings and emotions, or by more detached intellectual analysis?

A: Well, I never think with my heart, I think with my mind. Because the heart doesn't think...Pose me that question again. (Question repeated). My political education creates my emotions, they're integrated. I look at a thing, I act emotionally to something, it's from, the base of it is politics...

Q: Would you say that it's difficult to sort them out in the sense of your heart and mind?

A: As I say again, everything is through me mind, the heart you don't think with, nobody does. They say 'oh, it's from the heart.' It isn't, it's from the mind. Isn't it?

Q: Um, I don't know.

A: The heart is just the largest muscle in your body, pumping blood round, retaking it back and cleaning it. It doesn't think, it's the brain that thinks, and when the brain stops the heart stops.

.   .   .

Q: So do you often find that your heart and mind pull you in different directions?

A: No, because I dismiss that. I don't want to keep on saying it. No, everything is controlled by my mental process.

Q: So would you be able to describe a situation when you didn't agree intellectually with what in your heart you felt? Is there ever a time like that for you?

A: No, deep in my mind I feel it.

Q: So in other words there's never been a time like that?

.   .   .

A: All my emotions come from my thinking.

Q: So they're never in disagreement?

A: No, no, no.

While interviewers should be open to having their questions rejected by respondents – and indeed they should listen quite sensitively for any cues, verbal or non-verbal, which indicate this – the reality sometimes falls short of the ideal.

Briggs suggests that interviewers must be sensitive to the communicative norms of participants, and, equally important, that they must be aware of their own role in the production of data.

A mode of analysis that envisions interview data as, even ideally, a direct outpouring of the interviewees' thoughts or attitudes obscures the nature of the interview as a social interaction and a communicative event (1986: 102).

Rather, the researcher should view herself as a 'co-participant in the construction of a discourse' (p. 25). DeWaele and Harre advocate a similar approach in their method of 'assisted autobiography', which they refer to alternately as a 'collaborative model' and a 'participatory methodology' (1979: 180, 182).

Another aspect of the interview setting which will affect what is said in the course of interview is the question of how the interviewee perceives the wider situation, i.e. for whom does the respondent perceive herself as telling her story? What does the presence of the interviewer communicate to the participant? DeWaele and Harre write:

variations in the content and the form of an autobiography may… derive from the differences in the author's conception of the person to whom it is addressed… There is, for example, My History for Me, against My History for You, and My History for Anyone. Each of these will involve its own selection criteria and its own interpretative principles (1979: 188).

Respondents had different reasons for agreeing to participate in the study. At one level, they had consented simply to aid me in my research, and because they felt that the subject area had some inherent worth. However, they often said to me that they benefited from our discussions as well, and that it had provided them with an opportunity to reflect on the course of their lives in a way they most probably would not have done on their own.[3] After I had explained the project to one potential participant, she commented, 'In other words, you're asking me to make sense of my life.' She paused a moment, and then said that it was a challenge she could not resist. I heard several comments to this effect, most often just after finishing an interviewing session. Another reason people agreed to participate was to create a record of their life's story. Several respondents told me they had given copies of their transcripts to their children. One woman commented, 'these are the answers to the questions my daughter never asked me'. It was important for me to consider for whom it was that participants might have perceived themselves to be telling their story, although of course such knowledge was not ultimately available to me.

I have no doubt that the relationship which developed between myself and the respondents had considerable influence upon the actual data. Much of what was said in the course of the interviews was of a highly personal nature: the content was so humanly engaging that neither the possibility nor the desire to remain detached existed. It is doubtful that respondents would have spoken with the candour they did had there not been some form of established trust between us.[4] Over the eighteen months during which I conducted my research, I feel I came to know and be known by participants in the study. One woman wrote in a letter to me that her good friend who had put me in contact with her 'does not know me half as well as you do, nor does anyone else'. Several have lost their spouses in the time I have known them, others have undergone serious ailments themselves, and one of the most forthcoming participants has died. I entered their lives at a time when, for some, marked changes were happening. Thus, it is not surprising that we developed genuine relationships, and in most cases have stayed in contact even after our interviews were complete.

Reconstructed memory: invalid data?

Runyan states that 'critics of life history method argue that such studies are based on retrospective and introspective data of uncertain validity' (1982: 3–4). Questions of validity, however, depend upon the intent or purpose of the investigation. Life histories are not meant to be histories as such, but rather histories of a particular sort. The way in which a life is recalled by the person who lived it is as important as what actually happened during that life. As Thomas and Thomas (1928: 572–2) proclaim: 'If men define situations as real, they are real in their consequences.' The purpose of the present study was not to establish a factually accurate historical record of these fifteen lives, but rather to grasp what these lives have meant to the people who have lived them.

Debates within psychology regarding the nature of memory can be traced back a century, to Ebbinghaus's publication of his essay *Über das Gedächtniss* (1885). Ebbinghaus conducted laboratory experiments on what he considered to be pure memory, asking his participants to memorize nonsense syllables, and then testing the accuracy of their memory accordingly. It was in response to this form of memory testing that Bartlett conducted his own memory tests in the Laboratory of Experimental Psychology at the University of Cambridge opened in the spring of 1913. Bartlett's conclusion was that 'the description of memories as "fixed and lifeless" is merely an unpleasant fiction' (1932: 311). Rather, Bartlett argued, people remember things because they have particular significance for them, and the way in which they remember them reflects this significance. Thus, Ebbinghaus's participants, while able to recall strings of nonsense syllables, were only able to do so because of particular internal systems or tricks which they had devised to aid them in their recall.

The act of remembering, Bartlett stated,

is an imaginative reconstruction ... It is thus hardly ever really exact, even in the most rudimentary cases of rote recapitulation, and it is not at all important that it should be so (1932: 213).

In order to illustrate his point concerning the variability of interhuman and intrahuman memory regarding the recall of a particular event, Bartlett made the following analogy:

We may consider the old and familiar illustration of the landscape artist, the naturalist and the geologist who walk in the country together. The one is said to notice and recall the beauty of the scenery, the other details of the flora and fauna, and the third the formations of soils and rock. In this case, no doubt, the stimuli, being selected in each instance from what is present, are different for each observer, and obviously the records made in recall are different also ... If we were to put rock sections before all three people, the differences would still persist and might very likely be greatly exaggerated (p. 4).

The memories of the landscape artist, the naturalist, and the geologist are equally 'true' and yet they are divergent. Carmines defines reliability as 'the extent to which an experiment, test or measuring procedure yields the same results on repeated trials' (Carmines *et al.* 1979: 11). By this definition, memory is not completely reliable, but it is a sensitive indicator of an individual's internal construction of an external event. To illustrate this point, let us extend Bartlett's analogy of the three people on a country walk: not only would the recall of the walk vary among the three individuals, but, moreover, there is no certainty that an individual would experience and subsequently recall the walk in precisely the same way a second time, even if it were on the very same afternoon. While over time individuals might exhibit some form of overall consistency, this is not necessarily replicated on a situation-to-situation basis. Bartlett's point is twofold: (1) perceptions vary across individuals; thus, what is initially stored in memory varies similarly; (2) memory is not stored in pure form, but reflects temporal changes within the individual; thus 'Remembering is not the re-excitation of innumerable fixed, lifeless and fragmentary traces' (Bartlett 1932: 213). Writing for the *Encyclopaedia Britannica* in 1963, Bartlett reflected that the critical questions regarding the nature of memory remained the same as they had ever been (quoted in Robinson 1986: 23).

Gittins states that 'the very process of selection in recollection provides in itself important historical data ... what someone remembers can be a good indicator of what has been most important to that person over time' (1979: 85). Becker and Geer also call attention to the changes in perspective which result in alteration of memory:

Changes in the social environment and in the self inevitably produce transformation of perspective ... Reinterpreting things from his new perspective, he cannot give an accurate account of the past, for the concepts in which he thinks about it have changed and with them his perceptions and memories (1979: 141).

DeWaele and Harre make a more explicit connection between an individual's past and present and the way in which the transformation between the two is reflected in the transformation of memory:

the individual's past is not a relic ... Quite the contrary, it is part of the living present ... what is remembered of it is inevitably subject to continuous modification ... the past not only makes us, but we also make it by putting pieces together into a more or less coherent whole (1979: 180–1).

This view of memory represents a dialectical perspective on the passage of time. Individuals are constructed by their pasts, but at the same time they are constantly involved in reconstructing, reinterpreting, and re-membering that past. In such a way do persons make sense of their life as a whole. Berger and Luckman comment that if memory were not selective, 'the individual could not make sense of his biography' (1966: 103). Elder states that 'Memories of the past shape experience in the present, and the past may be restructured to fit the present' (1981: 110), and similarly Kohli comments that 'The reference to past events occurs in the context of the present situation, and under the criterion of their significance to it' (1981: 67).

It is clear that when an individual looks back over her life, she makes connections between events and situations which she would not have had the perspective to make at the time that she lived through them. The term 'life story' is useful; in a story it is not until the end, if at all, that the various aspects of the tale all come together, and connections are thus illuminated. In telling one's life story, one recalls feelings or thoughts one might have had at a particular moment. However, as already discussed, these recollections are not stored in pure form, and instead what the listener hears is how the speaker, in her present life, makes sense of her past. In this way reconstructed memory provides the rememberer with some sense of continuity in her life. 'Life memories', Robinson writes, 'tell us something about remembering and about the rememberer' (1986: 19).

Kohli remarks that even allowing for the reconstructive elements of memory 'there is at least some truth in what is being narrated... there is some specifiable relation between the narrative reconstruction and the events to which it refers' (1981: 69). Thus someone who listens to a life story can feel relatively confident that the content of what she is hearing has some degree of factual basis. It is significant that in the present study, there was no occasion in which a respondent's description of a past experience or event contradicted in any way a previous or subsequent account. Even on the one occasion when I thought that the respondent's recollection of the chronology of an event might have been inaccurate, this turned out not to be the case. While I would not claim that all accounts of the past were strictly accurate – only a longitudinal study could verify such information, particularly that which is not of a factual nature – at the very least, it is interesting that respondents' life stories have such a high level of internal consistency.

Moreover, it is possible that some individuals' retrieval systems, particularly in regard to things which are of interest to them, are extraordinarily accurate, even in relation to events in the distant past. Thomas Butler cites the example of Nirad Chaudhuri, an 'Indian nonagenarian and Oxford resident' who was asked how he could remember with such precision the details of things which happened seventy and eighty years ago. To this Chaudhuri responded, 'Memory is a product of life...I don't memorize. It comes. I'm interested' (1989: 14). In regard to the debate on the nature of memory between Ebbinghaus and Bartlett, it would seem that this case offers evidence in support of the latter. It is by virtue of the internal significance associated with the events described that they have been stored for so long in the memory bank of this man. Similarly, the events which played a crucial part in the lives of the respondents of this study also 'interested' them. This, too, then might account for the apparent high level of accuracy of the accounts they offered.

There is, of course, no way of controlling for purposeful fabrication, but this limitation is not a unique problem of retrospective data. Clearly listeners must be sensitive to whether or not the speaker may perceive a particular incentive to misrepresent her actual memory of an event. Thus, for instance, the findings of Hessing, Elffers and Weigel (1988) that individuals' self-reports tend to be erroneous when they are describing illegal actions (tax evasion) in which they had partaken in the past, should be in no way surprising. It would be wrong to extend these findings to other areas of self-report, however, as there are obvious reasons why individuals may not wish to describe their own socially proscribed behaviour.

The concept of memory is most fully understood when one considers it in relation to oblivion. Butler wonders why, even though every individual has 'a huge mnemonic system with 100 billion cells and a dual memory system', our retrieval systems are still faulty.

Why? Did God do an imperfect job? Has the evolutionary process lagged in this area of our development? Or is Forgetting, i.e. the nonretrieval of most of the information that is processed in a lifetime, somehow a part of the plan? (1989: 15).

Jay (1987) sensitively describes the relationship between remembering and forgetting. Discussing Wordsworth's *The Prelude*, he writes:

it is precisely 'forgetting' which allows for Wordsworth's imagination to creatively 'remember' his past which gives his past something like what Eliot called in *Four Quartets* 'another pattern' (pp. 47–8).

Thus, remembering and forgetting, rather than being definitional opposites, are instead conceived of as complementary processes, which together constitute the imaginative process of reconstruction, through which an individual, time and again, makes sense of her life.

Brewer identifies three types of autobiographical memory: (1) personal memory (mental images corresponding to particular episodes in a life); (2) autobiographical fact (recall of facts with no particular accompanying image); and (3) generic personal memory (an image from the past which does not appear to be of any specific moment) (1986: 26). In constructing a coherent story about one's past, these three strands conjoin to form a coherent story. It is, however, the first of these, personal memory, which tends to dominate in such reconstructions, as the past is often made sense of through a series of specific events.

Lillian Hellman's autobiography offers a particularly interesting example of a self-conscious attempt to reconstruct her past. She reflects on this process, noting that:

What I have written is the truth as I saw it, but the truth as I saw it, of course, doesn't have much to do with the truth. It's as if I have fitted parts of a picture puzzle and then a child overturned it and threw out some pieces (quoted in Brown 1985: 3).

Hellman makes a distinction between her personal truth and the truth. Presumably the latter corresponds to concrete reality, but, as Bartlett's example of the three persons on a walk illustrates, reality is perceived differently by different people. Brown comments, 'the truth revealed by critical probing of memory is more relevant to the structure of human personality and life than a bookkeeper's record, however adequate that might be to the historian' (1985: 2). What is most important for an interviewer, then, is the personal truth of the respondent. Luisa Passerini contends that 'All autobiographic memory is true. It is up to the interpreter to discover in which sense, where, for what purpose' (quoted in Personal Narratives Group 1989: 261). The American oral historian Studs Terkel echoes this sentiment:

I guess I believe more and more in this as I grow older...Fact is not always truth. Truth is something else...if it's their truth it's got to be my truth, it's their experience. Somebody lived through that time with a certain something he remembers: that scar left on him; the memory is true. It's there (Grele 1985: 13–14).

Terkel's attitude toward his interviewees inherently respects the way in which they make sense of their own lives. This contrasts sharply with the attitude of some researchers, epitomized in the advice offered by Schwartz and Jacobs (1979), who suggest: 'treat your own version...as [the] real objective life. Treat the subject's version of his life as "the member's point of view"' (p. 72). This statement is based on the assumption that there exists such a thing as an objective life, which can be constructed in pure form by putting together a series of factual data.

It is not original to state that in selecting the very facts to be presented, the objective life is transformed into a subjective representation of that life. Thus, the objective presentation, much less assessment, of a life, whether one's own or that of another, is an unrealizable goal.

The researcher can assist the interviewee in remembering the past by asking questions. Hindley (1979) claims that there are three processes involved in the production of retrospective data. Events have to be (1) perceived; (2) remembered or retained; and (3) recalled. It is in the last of these that the interviewer can be of particular service. Not all recall is spontaneous. Often in the course of interviews, memories emerge which respondents have not thought of in decades. Indeed, William James (1890) claims that 'the most frequent source of false memory is distortion introduced through the process of giving successive accounts of a particular personal memory episode' (quoted in Brewer 1986: 42). It is, thus, the challenge of the interviewer (1) to have enough knowledge about the subject area to be able to pose relevant questions, or even to challenge a particular account, and (2) to be able to move respondents away from mere retelling of an old story, and then to find a new entry into it.

In my attempt to meet the first of these challenges, I spent the better part of the first year of my Ph.D. studying British social history of the twentieth century. I felt that only in so doing would I be able to situate respondents and the stories they told into their appropriate context. Moreover, I felt that such knowledge would aid me in asking pertinent questions during our interviews. There was one notable occasion in which my general familiarity with historical dates aided me in discerning an inconsistency in one of the respondent's accounts. Early in our first interview, the participant had said that she had started to become politicized as a result of moving up North and seeing the harsh living conditions there. The headmistress of the private school where she worked had taken on a Jewish refugee student, and previously at her college 'two young Jews came who weren't going to go back'. I also knew from my research that starting in about 1933 – the year of the Reichstag Fire – the British newspapers were full of reports of the happenings in Germany. The respondent also said that she had been a member of the Left Book Club, and regularly attended its meetings. From this information, I surmised that by the mid-1930s she was aware of the political situation, not only domestically, but internationally as well.

I was, then, surprised to learn at the end of the same interview that she had gone to Germany for several skiing holidays approximately between the years of 1934 and 1937. She describes herself as being 'entirely starry eyed about Germany, in spite of being there in '36, '37' and even seeing, in the Cologne train station, Hitler's map of intended expansion. The following exchange was perhaps the most awkward I encountered during my interviewing.

Q: How did you sort of square those sort of feelings [of being anti-fascist] with going there?

A: I didn't. I went in '36 (I think one Easter, could have been '37)... I didn't go there after that... I suppose, (yes, I can see you could think), we certainly – I was in Munich and had tins shaken under my nose – I don't...

Q: What was that for?

A: Oh, collecting for the national socialist movement. We certainly never – of course we were in ski resorts – it's an interesting question. I don't know. We must have known from the children coming over that Jews were losing there rights.

Q: I suppose the question is one of chronology. In other words, if you knew before you went...

A: I think my going, which started in '34, '35, '36, certainly people were heiling Hitler. Not the first time. But I don't think there was any feel of concentration camps.

I returned to this question in our second interview. The respondent explained that she had been offered inexpensive ski holidays through the National Union of Students. She then proceeded to explain:

I think it would be around '37ish before one knew about the concentration camps and the burning of books and the wearing of the star. (MA: Yes, I'm not sure. I should look up the year of the Reichstag Fires.) They were about '33 I think.... (Several moments later, referring to the timing of her ski trip). But it was before any question of Jewish shops being stoned, or Jewish wearing the star of Judah, or Jewish children being turned out of schools. I think certainly the Jews were getting anxious and maybe some were already coming abroad. I'm not really sure.

The only point upon which the respondent is thoroughly consistent is the approximate time of her trips to Germany. The intersection of her personal biography with what she knew to be the events at that time causes her apparent unease, and thus her recall of the climate appears to fluctuate slightly in her account.

Finally, one distinct aspect of autobiographical memory (which is also exhibited in the example above) is the way in which individuals relate historical events through which they have lived to their recollection of their own lives (Brown et al. 1986; Frisch 1981; Kaufman 1986; Passerini 1987; Popular Memory Group 1982; Riegel 1973). Not surprisingly, individuals tend to remember those public events which had private significance for them, and such memories are stored in very personalized ways (Brown 1986). But the relationship between individual and collective, or social, memory is a dynamic one. Burke, in his thoughtful essay 'History as Social Memory', addresses this issue. He cites Maurice Halbwachs, a French sociologist of the 1920s, as 'the first serious explorer of the "social framework of memory"'.

Halbwachs argued that memories are constructed by social groups. Individuals remember, in the literal, physical sense. However, it is social groups which determine what is 'memorable' and also how it will be remembered (1989: 98).

Burke outlines the political dimensions of the process of social memory. 'It is important to ask the question, who wants whom to remember what, and why? Whose version of the past is recorded and preserved?' (p. 107). And social memory, like individual memory, is constructed not only from what is remembered, but also from what is forgotten, or erased. Throughout the centuries, those in power have often found the 'rewriting of history' to be a most effective tool in stripping another people of its identity. Vaclav Havel, in his open letter to the then President of Czechoslavakia Husak, in 1975, reflected on the state of his own oppressed people. 'Slowly but surely, we are losing the sense of time. We begin to forget what happened when, what came earlier, and what later, and the feeling that it really doesn't matter overwhelms us.' Twelve years later he commented more optimistically: 'Time is beginning to become evident again, as if we were rejoining history' (quoted in T. Butler 1989: 23). Indeed, the history of colonialism can be read in part as a story of one group of people attempting to expropriate the history, or social memory, of another group of people, and in so doing to dominate them. Conversely, the history of a people's struggle against its own oppression can also be understood as an insistence upon remembering its own history, and thus retaining a sense of identity.

To understand the workings of the social memory it may be worth investigating the social organization of forgetting, the rules of exclusion, suppression or repression, and the question of who wants whom to forget what, and why. Amnesia is related to 'amnesty,' to what used to be called 'acts of oblivion,' official erasure of memories of conflict in the interests of social cohesion (Burke 1989: 108).

Without memory, there is no history, and history, for its part, is the stuff of memory: Cicero's *vita memoriae* (history is the life of memory). And yet 'Both history and memory are coming to appear increasingly problematic...no longer...the innocent activities they were once taken to be. Neither memories nor histories seem objective any longer' (T. Butler 1989: 98). Again we are led to reconsider traditional concepts of objectivity.

In summary, claims that life history method is based on retrospective and introspective data are true, although whether such data are to be considered invalid depends upon the purpose for which they are used. If the object of the enquiry is strictly chronological biography, then the factual accuracy of accounts is paramount. Similarly, if the aim of the study is to investigate individuals' recall over time, then it is important for the researcher to know where a respondent's version of an event differs from what actually happened. However, as discussed earlier, even the perception of 'what actually happened' is itself something which can and often does vary with different observers.

Throughout this chapter, issues relating in one way or another to the concept of objectivity have come under question. I began by inviting the reader to join me in an exploration of the reasons why I conducted my study in the way in which I did. Implicit in the decisions I made were certain underlying assumptions regarding how we come to acquire knowledge about others and their social worlds – surely the realm of focus of the social sciences. I argued that qualitative and quantitative methods need not be set in competition with one another, but can be more constructively conceived of as the two parts of a bifocal lens, each yielding information of a different nature. I presented a brief historical background to these debates, in the hope that we might learn from the discussions of others before us. Notably, in the early part of this century, when case-study and survey methods were vying for the crown of respectability in the social sciences, many researchers advocated a complementary coexistence of the two. I hope this is a position to which researchers shall return. In my discussion of current methodological debates, I used examples from my own data to illustrate various points. The final discussion in the chapter focused on questions of truth and validity of retrospective data, the complementary processes of remembering and forgetting, and the relationship between individual and social memory.

Let us now turn from these methodological considerations, and meet the characters of the study, and glimpse at one version of the environment of their formative years. I use the words 'characters' and 'versions' to remind the reader and myself that what passes in these pages is an intersubjective reconstruction of the lives of the respondents and the times in which they have lived.

4   Personal Stories

> It's not oneself. It's my version of oneself.
>
> Mark Harris, biographer of Saul Bellow, in answer to the latter's protestations that he did not see himself in the way he had been portrayed (quoted in McCord 1986: 219).

Who are the respondents? This question is not as straightforward as it might appear. At one level, one can identify them by name, place and date of birth, together with a skeletal outline of their lives' activities. That is the level of response offered in this chapter. But one might also interpret this question at a much deeper level: who are the respondents really? What makes them who they are? Not only what do they do, but why do they do it? Reflections on these questions are woven throughout this book, and most particularly in Chapters 6, 7 and 8.

Here we shall consider the question in its most simple form. Nevertheless, writing these sketches has not been a thoroughly easy task, for several reasons. Obviously in our long hours spent together, I have learned far more about the people in this study than I could ever include in a few paragraphs on each of them. Thus, the choice of which biographical facts to include and which to omit was a leap of interpretation. I was guided in my decisions by a consideration of which events respondents themselves seemed to accord the greatest importance during our conversations. The most difficult aspect of the task was the overall mission of accurately summarizing a life, particularly ones which have been so long and so rich. My intention for these pages, then, is more modest: to relate a feeling for the kind of lives the respondents have led.

My work has been made easier by the great help of the respondents, who have patiently read and reread various accounts I have presented to them of their own lives. I have invited them to contribute to this process as much as they have desired, and the extent of their input has varied among them. The most common editorial suggestions which they offered to me concerned minimizing the number of pronouns which referred to them, either directly or indirectly; the quite striking modesty of many of the respondents perhaps does not come through in these descriptions. It has been difficult to relate the many and varied accomplishments of these individuals, while still conveying a sense of what they are like as people. The construction of these biographies was not altogether different from the process of assisted autobiography, described by DeWaele and Harre (1979), although, of course, my approach was less structured. Thus, what follows in these pages represents in many cases a joint effort by the respondents and myself. Finally, I might add that some of the respondents are relatively well known, and have been the subject of biographies and autobiographies. I have felt free to draw upon that material. Obviously if readers wish to read a more thorough account of the lives of particular respondents, they should consult the appropriate books. The sketches are divided into two groups, the ten core respondents and the five additional respondents. Within each section names are listed alphabetically.

The ten core respondents

Edward Charles

Edward was born in 1909 at Harrow, the youngest of five children. His parents were middle-class Anglican evangelicals, with a personal commitment to London's East End. Edward attended Harrow School, 'which I hated'. After leaving Harrow, Edward spent six months in Canada with a Canadian schoolfriend. Edward read Classics at Trinity College, Cambridge, which, in the late 1920s, was brimming with left-wing activity. However, Edward describes himself at that time as 'more interested in church things than political things'. After leaving Cambridge, Edward spent two years teaching English in the Middle East. When he returned to England, he began his religious training at Wescott House, Cambridge. Edward then broke his ties with the Oxford Group, an individualist Christian organization with which he and his parents had been involved. Edward took part in a group establishing camps for the unemployed, with the League of Nations Union, and it was then that he had his first political awakening.

At the age of twenty-six Edward was ordained as an Anglican minister. The parishes in which he has worked have been in poorer or mixed areas, which he preferred to more middle-class surroundings. During his first job, he met Ruth, his wife-to-be. Edward joined the Left Book Club (LBC), often spoke on street corners for the National Unemployed Worker's Movement (NUWM) and for the Aid to Spain Movement. On one occasion he spoke on a stand against Oswald Mosley. 'I remember saying cheerio to Ruth and wondering whether I was going to see her again.' He and Ruth housed a returned International Brigader and entertained Spanish refugee children. They have two daughters. They have been long-standing, active members of the Labour Party, except for a few years in which they renounced their membership because of the Party's anti-Soviet policies. After the war, Edward and Ruth went on most of the early Aldermaston marches of the Campaign for Nuclear Disarmament (CND). Also at this time, Edward got polio, and was very seriously ill for six months. He supported the struggle of the people of Vietnam against invasion and in particular the British hospital in North Vietnam.

During the war, the family lived in a blitzed area of the West Midlands. Edward spoke for the Russian Today Society in Birmingham, and managed a religious socialist newspaper, *Religion and the People*. Edward has always regarded the church as having a great potential to unite people from Eastern and Western Europe: '[It's] the biggest organisation that exists on both sides of the divide.' Edward has travelled extensively in the Soviet Bloc: the USSR, East Germany (five times), Bulgaria, Romania and Czechoslovakia. Edward was Chair of the Christian Socialist Movement for eight years. He is currently a Vice-President of this group, as well as the British–Soviet Friendship Society, and the British section of the International Christian Peace Conference.

Christopher Cornford

Christopher was born in 1917 in Cambridge, 'the middle child out of five. I had a brother either side of me...and sister at either end.' His father was Professor of Ancient Philosophy and Fellow at Trinity College, Cambridge, and his mother, the granddaughter of Charles Darwin, was a poet. He had a large and close family, and they lived in considerable comfort. From the age of nine, Christopher attended a preparatory boarding school in Surrey. The school was the same one that both W. H. Auden and Christopher Isherwood had attended about a decade earlier. Christopher recalls that the latter was regarded as 'a clever boy, but rather gone to bad at Oxford' because he was a socialist. Christopher's older brother, the poet John Cornford, who was very active in the Cambridge University Socialist Society, had a particularly strong influence upon him. While still a schoolboy, but no longer at boarding school, Christopher delivered the *Daily Worker* on Sundays, and, for his brother, monitored the *Manchester Guardian* for anything about war and military preparations. For a brief period in 1932, Christopher went to try his vocation as a mason's apprentice with Eric Gill. In 1934, he moved to London as an art student, where he joined the local branch of the Communist Party of Great Britain (CPGB). He was one of the anti-fascist demonstrators at Mosley's appearance at Olympia Stadium, and there he was beaten up by Blackshirts.

John went to fight for the republican cause in Spain, where he died on his twenty-first birthday. Meanwhile, Christopher continued his political activity. Eventually he returned to Cambridge, where in 1941 he became Secretary of the city's Communist Party. In the following year he was conscripted to the army, where he was in an artillery regiment. From that time forward, he no longer retained his Party membership. During the decade following his return from the army, he was not as politically active as he had been before that time. He was by this time married, and he and his wife were raising the first of their two sons.

From 1962 until 1979, Christopher was head of the Department of General Studies (i.e. Humanities) at the Royal College of Art in London. He describes his work: 'I could combine my convictions and my activism with my academic life, a very satisfactory combination.' In due course he was very sympathetic with the student revolts, which 'got me into trouble with my colleagues and the boss...I was regarded as a subversive element.' He also spent a brief time teaching at the University of California at Santa Cruz, which was 'absolutely bubbling with anti-war and generally left-wing [activity]'. In 1970, he became involved with the ecological movement, and was a signatory of Blueprint for Survival, the first major environmentalist manifesto produced in Britain. He sought to embody its ideas into the academic programme for which he was responsible by running an ecological study group. Christopher was Chair of the Cambridge branch of CND for two years, and he continues to combine his political commitment with his artistic ability. 'I do cartoons and lettering and posters and that kind of thing for the peace and green movements, because that after all is what I can do better than other people.' He is working on a study of the use of geometry in art, architecture and design, and has written articles and reviews for art and design journals.

Eileen Daffern

Eileen was born in 1914 in a conservative Yorkshire mill village on the edge of a strong, desolate landscape of moorland and dark stone walls. 'All that you know about *Wuthering Heights*, that's where I walked in my childhood. Laid upon the hills...I think that has bitten very deep into me.' She had one younger brother. Her upbringing was strict and religious but reasonably well-to-do: social life revolved around the Baptist Church and Sunday School. Eileen attended the local girls' grammar school, and, later, university, where she studied French language and literature. Eileen's first important contact with radical politics was on a boat going to Australia, where she met someone who was a member of the LBC. The voyage was spent discussing politics. After three years of living in Australia, New Zealand and South Africa (where her political awareness was quickened), she returned to England immediately before the outbreak of war.

The period of the 'phoney' war, pro-German elements in the British government, the fall of France, the German invasion of the USSR – all were politicizing events. She was swept into political action through union activity in Manchester, where she was working for a large chemical company and had become very friendly with militant scientists. It was then that Eileen joined the Communist Party, of which she has remained a member ever since. After a personnel management training course, Eileen worked in a Royal Ordinance Factory in the North West. In between shifts, she taught courses on elementary Marxism to dockers, organized meetings for women factory workers and campaigned for opening up the Second Front, 'chalking' slogans on Salford streets.

Her consciousness as a feminist grew as she moved to London to be part of a team of women creating and implementing progressive personnel policies for a large manufacturing company. When the war ended, the men returned to reclaim their positions; the identity of interest between workers and management, so remarkable during the war, was replaced by the old confrontation. Eileen lost her job for being a communist. She married, and travelled with her husband across the United States, studying industrial relations. They then settled in Canada for ten years, during which time Eileen had three children. She and her husband became very active in the Canadian peace movement, and organized a citizens' discussion group, Citizen's Forum, in conjunction with the Canadian Broadcasting Company.

The return to England was shadowed by the long illness and death of her husband. Eileen had to be the economic provider: she taught, first at secondary then at university level. She wrote several publications and through writing and teaching, she felt she was able to express and promote her political ideas. Eileen was active in the peace movement, and went on some of the early Aldermaston marches. At this time, lasting contacts with France, both literary and political, were developed. Eileen and her family spent summers in a small village in southern France which had a communist mayor; she still retains close links with a commune there. At the time of our first interview, Eileen had been retired for three years. Apart from her children and five grandchildren, she dedicates most of her time to working for peace and disarmament at regional, national and international levels, with a broad alliance of groups, but mainly with the United Nations Association and CND.

Jack Dash

When asked when he was born, Jack responds with some pride: 'on our national day, St George's Day, and the anniversary of the birth of Shakespeare', 23 April 1907. The family lived in South London. Jack was the youngest of four boys, and grew up in an environment of severe financial need. One image he often evokes, which was related to him by his older brothers, is that of his mother walking the streets singing, trying to sell bootlaces, with Jack as an infant in her arms. In order to feed the family, the father stole food, and once purposely broke his leg to collect insurance money. The family was evicted from their home on many occasions. Jack's mother died when he was seven, and from that time he was virtually an orphan as his father, once a teetotaller, had become an alcoholic. He was regarded as the neighbourhood orphan, and fed by other families. When Jack was fifteen, his father died, and Jack went to live with his older brother.

Jack left school at fourteen, and his first job was working as a hod-carrier. He laboured for an old socialist, who had been imprisoned for refusing to fight in the 1914 war, and the two of them had many political discussions. Jack listened to street-corner speakers, became involved with the NUWM, and became a member of the LBC. It was as a builder that he took part in his first strike. Jack married in 1931, and he and his wife had one daughter. They moved to London's East End, where they were to stay for nearly sixty years. In the building industry, Jack became increasingly politically active. Shortly after he volunteered to fight with the International Brigade, Britain enacted the Nonintervention Pact, and thus he was prevented from going. At this time, Jack joined the Communist Party, of which he remained an active member for the rest of his life.

During the Second World War, Jack volunteered for the Auxiliary Fire Service. The fire brigade formed a union, and Jack became the delegate for his station. Jack and some of the other firemen were politically like-minded, and together they formed a communist cell to discuss politics, and to go chalking. After the war, Jack began working on the docks in London's East End, where he was to stay for nearly twenty-five years. Immediately he joined the dockers' trade union, and eventually he became one of its leading spokespersons. During the time that he was a trade-union leader, dockers' pay rates increased by two-thirds. Although Jack had supposedly retired nearly twenty-five years before the time of our interviews, he remained very active politically, travelling throughout Britain, speaking on behalf of pensioners' groups and the unemployed. Jack died in June 1989.

Dorothy Greenald

Dorothy was born the second of six children to a working-class family in Yorkshire in 1903. As the first daughter, she was expected from an early age to share her mother's burden of work. Her father was a Labour supporter, her mother apolitical. The family observed religious practices, attending church every Sunday. At the age of twelve, Dorothy started work in the mill, attending school half-time. She left school altogether at thirteen, and although she had wanted to go to night-school, her mother insisted that there was enough to keep her busy at home. Years later, after her mother had died, Dorothy began taking history classes through the Workers' Educational Association (WEA). Dorothy's responsibilities at home included the financial management of the household, as she was the main provider for the family.

Dorothy was an active member of the LBC, where she met her husband Joe. Following her work at the mill, she was employed for a brief period at a bakery, and then began a job in a dentist's where she stayed for 'fifty five years and three months'. Particularly for the past thirty-five years, Dorothy's life has been completely absorbed by her community service and the peace movement, and the vast array of organizations with which she has been involved is the living expression of her commitment to socialism.

In 1951, before the existence of CND, she helped to found a peace group to protest against the nuclear bomb. The Labour Party, in which she had been very active, perceived her activities to be pro-Soviet, and upon her return from a trip to the Soviet Union, she was expelled from the Labour Party. Some years later, she joined the Communist Party, which she left after only a few months because of the Soviet invasion of Hungary. She was active in helping to establish the political journal, *The New Reasoner*. She later rejoined the Labour Party, of which she has remained an active member ever since.

In 1952, Dorothy began three years of service as a county councillor. She helped to start a family planning clinic, with which she has remained involved for nearly twenty-five years. For more than twenty years, Dorothy served as a court magistrate. For about a decade and a half, she was Chair of the juvenile court, and concurrently, for much of the time, Chair of the domestic court. She was very active on the local probation committee, and she later served on the Central Council of Probation in London, where she was Chair of Recruitment Training of probation officers.

For twenty years, Dorothy was involved with a weekend home for teenage boys with difficulties, a place which she helped to found. She also helped to form a group to help discharged prisoners, which joined with a similar organization nearby, and for nearly two decades Dorothy served as Chair of the consolidated group. (Later the group became part of the National Association for the Care and Resettlement of Offenders, NACRO.) This group collaborated with a priest to open the first detoxification centre in England. They also opened several hostels for homeless ex-prisoners, as well as establishing a furniture aid scheme, which organizes distribution of furniture to newly released prisoners and/or their families. This operation is still very active, and at the time of our interviews, it occupied most of Dorothy's time. Dorothy also remains a very active member of CND.

Walter Gregory

Walter was born in 1912 in Lincoln, the second of four children. The family was working class, his father a woodworker, a strong trade unionist, and a Labour Party supporter. Walter's first political activity was as a ten-year-old child, when he pushed Labour Party pamphlets through neighbourhood letter-boxes. The family experienced chronic economic hardship. His father's strong trade unionism resulted in his being blacklisted and subsequently suffering long-term unemployment. 'Some people occasionally are out of work, but poor old dad reversed the situation; he was occasionally in work. It was as bad as that.' Walter left full-time education at the age of fourteen to help with the family finances, taking evening courses in subjects such as book-keeping and shorthand. His first job was as a clerk, which he held for four years, before being laid off.

It was then that his political education began. He took classes in political subjects through the WEA. He joined the NUWM, an organization with which he became increasingly involved. From 1930 to 1935, Walter was often unemployed, although he occasionally had casual, short-term jobs. In 1934, he was arrested for chalking[1] and later that year participated in the NUWM hunger march, walking from Lincoln to London. He became very influenced by the leaders of that movement, and during this time he joined the Communist Party. Walter became involved in the anti-fascist movement, and was a member of the No More War Movement. However, his views on pacifism shifted when he no longer saw it as an effective response to 'the expansionist and vicious ideology' of fascism. Walter protested against the British Union of Fascists (BUF) when they came to the Victoria Baths in Nottingham, and he was slightly injured at this violent gathering.

During his years of unemployment, Walter had spent six months training with the British armed forces, where he learned how to handle a rifle. He put this knowledge to use when, in December 1936, he went as a volunteer to Spain as a member of the British Battalion of the International Brigade. Walter became a member of the Partido Comunista Espanol. He was made a lieutenant, and was wounded three times. He was taken prisoner during the Battle of Ebro in September 1938, and was condemned to death but then reprieved. He was forced to partake in what was called a 'pistol walk', in which about twenty captives were selected, ten were killed before the group, and the other ten were then interrogated. 'I was one of those that was lucky enough to be interrogated.' He was released in February 1939.

Upon Walter's return to England, he met and married his wife. He then joined the royal navy, with which he served for five years. By the time the war ended, they had one son, and were expecting another child. Walter got a job with the Co-operative Movement as a clerk. He became very active in his trade union, the Union of Shop Distributors and Allied Workers (USDAW), for the remainder of his working years. He has held the positions of Branch Secretary, Chair, Shop Steward, Joint Industrial Council delegate, and Union conference delegate. When he retired, he was made a life member of the union, 'which is the highest honour that a trade union can give me, for services rendered. I'm proud of that.' Since his retirement, Walter has travelled extensively throughout the country, speaking on behalf of the International Brigade Association. In 1986 Walter published *The Shallow Grave : A Memoir of the Spanish Civil War*, which met with much acclaim.

Rose Kerrigan

Born in 1903 to working-class, Jewish, socialist, Glaswegian parents, Rose was the second of four surviving children (her mother gave birth to six), and the only daughter. For the first three years of her life, her family lived in Ireland, where they had moved for her father's employment. After he was fired from that job for being too outspoken, the family lived from hand to mouth. They moved back to Glasgow, and lived in a one-room-and-kitchen flat.

As the only daughter, much of the domestic responsibility fell to Rose, and at eight, she was doing most of the family shopping. In her later years, she supported both of her parents and one brother with her modest wages. When she was eleven, her father, a tailor, went bankrupt; the family was forced to move again and all their furniture was impounded. At twelve, Rose played an active role in the Glasgow Rent Strike, convincing her neighbours to take part. The strike resulted in the Rent Restriction Act, which lasted until 1957. Rose left school at fourteen so that she could contribute to the family wages. Her first full-time job was in a department store, where she was eventually fired for defending a conscientious objector, the brother of one of her co-workers. She was accused of being pro-German. 'I said "I'm nothing of the sort. I'm not pro-anything. I'm anti-war."'

Immediately following the war, there was an epidemic of the Spanish flu, which killed many civilians. Rose caught the flu but 'came through. That's why I'm a survivor.' Her younger brother was not so fortunate; after catching the flu from Rose, he died of it. Rose attended a socialist Sunday School, and she joined the Communist Party when it was first formed. She has remained a member ever since. She met her husband, Peter, through a socialist group to which she belonged, whose members would go rambling together. He was to become one of the leaders of the Communist Party. They married when Rose was twenty-three. Following Rose's brother's death, her father went into deep depression. In the last five years of his life, he became so ill that his wife's full-time occupation was to look after him. When he died, she followed only nine days later. It was in this same week that Rose gave birth to her first of three children. Rose went to Russia in 1935, accompanying Peter, who was a representative at the Comintern.

Rose was Chair of her tenants' association, and sold the *Daily Worker*, a communist newspaper on Sundays. Peter spent much time in Spain, and Rose was very involved in gathering support for the Spanish republican cause in Britain. During the Second World War, the two lived in London, while their children were evacuated to Scotland. Rose worked for an insurance company as a collector, and there she organized the first women's branch of the staff union. She was also the only woman to attend the union's conference. While they were living in London during the war, their home was bombed. Although they lost most of their belongings, they were fortunate enough to escape unharmed. Eventually they settled in London permanently. Rose had various jobs (including demonstrating vacuum cleaners and washing machines, and conducting market research on dried eggs) to supplement her husband's small wages from the Party. For seven years she worked in a clothing factory, where she organized one hundred and fifty women into their first union. At the time of our interviews, she was dedicating most of her time to her local pensioners' rights group, of which she is Chair, and to CND.

Frida Knight

Frida was born in 1910, the fourth of five children, into a secure and cultured Cambridge home. Her father – a Stewart, who traced his ancestry back six hundred years to the liberator of Scotland, Robert the Bruce – was Chaplain of Trinity College, Cambridge, and the President of the Cambridge Musical Society. Her mother, a classical scholar, received the first first-class degree from Newnham College, Cambridge. Between the ages of fourteen and sixteen, Frida had a heart condition, and was in bed for almost a year, missing nearly all of her formal education during that period.

On recovering, she spent a month in Italy, where she was shocked into 'juvenile political awareness' by Mussolini's Blackshirts. In 1928 Frida travelled with her sister, a pianist, to Germany, to study violin. While there, she saw widespread unemployment and growing political unrest (clashes between Nazis and communists) and met many young Marxists. In 1929 she returned to England and entered the Royal College of Music. After completing her studies, Frida moved to the North of England, then an area in deep depression. She took the job of music and drama organizer at Manchester University Settlement in a deprived area; there she produced plays and opera with the unemployed, often with a strong political message. In 1935 she went with the British Drama League party to the Moscow Theatre Festival, which she found very stimulating and inspiring.

Frida then became a member of the LBC; she began work in adult education in Hull, where she started a Spanish relief committee and joined the Communist Party, of which she remains a member. In May 1937 she drove an ambulance for the National Joint Committee for Spanish Relief from London to Murcia, Spain, where she helped with relief work and in the local hospitals. Eventually she went to Madrid, where she wrote and translated articles for the Prensa (press office). She stayed there for two months, visiting the Front, speaking on national radio, and attending the International Writers' Congress.

Eventually Frida returned to England and worked as a full-time fund-raiser for the Basque Refugee Children's Committee, organizing meetings and concerts for them all over the country. Later, after Franco's victory, her work for the National Joint Committee for Spanish Relief involved supplying aid to the fleeing republicans. In 1940 Frida was in France, doing refugee work; she was caught during the Nazi invasion and interned in a prison camp in Besançon (then in Vittel) for more than one year. She managed to escape, and returned to England – with a message for De Gaulle hidden in a cigarette lining – to work with Free French Forces, for two years. In 1944 she married a socialist scientist, and by 1951 they had four children.

Frida continued her political work, going on all the early Aldermaston marches. When family life allowed, she attended peace congresses as a translator of Spanish and French, travelling to Hungary, Finland, the USSR and Ceylon. Frida has written about ten books (including translations), on subjects ranging from the French Resistance, to a biography of Beethoven, to the history of music in Cambridge. She continues to campaign indefatigably for CND, the United Nations Association, the African National Congress and the Campaign Against the Arms Trade.

Mary Waters

Mary was born in London in 1913, the middle of five children. Her father, a liberal, owned a wholesale toy and fancy-goods business, and the family lived very comfortably. As a child, Mary helped to collect donations for deprived children in Wales. Religion was 'a very, very big influence' in the home, and Mary kept her religious faith until entering college. For five years, Mary attended a boarding school in the country. Following this, she trained as a teacher at a college in London.

Mary's first teaching job was in the preparatory department of Bradford Girls' Grammar School in Yorkshire. The year was 1934, and Bradford at that time was plagued with 'colossal unemployment'. Through a friendship with a politically minded teacher, Mary joined the LBC. There were young Jewish refugees in the school, and thus she became aware of the international situation. Mary went as an exchange teacher to the United States between 1937 and 1938. Upon her return, she again taught, and, at the school where she worked, gas masks were fitted to the children. She also joined the International Voluntary Service for Peace, although she was not a pacifist. Through this organization she met her husband, Eric. He had been a pacifist, but as the war progressed he decided to join the Communist Party. Eric joined the army and was killed in service. Mary, too, had decided to join the Party, and she remained a member until late 1957. Mary spoke from soap boxes and on street corners on behalf of the Party.

After the war, Mary and her two small children moved to Cambridge, where she joined the local branch of the Party. She got a job teaching in a state school, and joined the teachers' union. When her sons had grown up, she became very active in the union, at one time serving as a national delegate on the Primary Schools' Committee. For eighteen years, Mary was Deputy Headmistress of the school. The eleven-plus examination[2] was the target of much of her political activity in the union. She explains the connection between her politics and this exam: 'Children of eleven are not, you can't test them at eleven and tell what they're going to be like at twenty-one. It's absolutely ludicrous... As a socialist I want everybody to have the maximum opportunity that it is possible, within the funds, to give them.' Mary was active in the early days of the anti-nuclear movement, going on many of the early Aldermaston marches and motorcades around East Anglia. She was also very active within the Labour Party. Mary demonstrated against Suez and Vietnam. More recently, she has been involved in the Nicaraguan Solidarity Campaign, and is an active member of Amnesty International and CND.

Elizabeth Wilson

Elizabeth was born in Surrey in 1909. Her father was a school teacher, and her mother headmistress of a church school. Elizabeth was their only child. The family was lower middle class, 'not particularly wealthy...but not particularly poor'. Until the age of ten, she was a pupil at her mother's school, but then she switched to the local secondary school. Elizabeth remembers it being 'quite a release to be away from somebody who was the headmistress at school and still the headmistress at home'. Although the family was not very religious, they attended church because of the mother's position. Elizabeth went to Homerton College, Cambridge, to train as a teacher. There, she became involved with the Unitarian Church. After college, Elizabeth joined a socialist society in London. In 1936, Elizabeth married and moved to Huddersfield in the North, where she was 'horrified by the poverty ...and unemployment'. Two mornings a week she cooked for an unemployed men's club. Elizabeth organized the selling of *Peace News*, became a member of the Peace Pledge Union, and was active in the local Aid to Spain efforts. She also joined the Society of Friends.

When the Second World War broke out, Elizabeth and her husband registered as conscientious objectors. They were instrumental in forming the Huddersfield Famine Relief Committee, which, like the Oxford Committee for Famine Relief (later known as Oxfam), was one of the small organizations that were created throughout the country during the war to put pressure on the government to allow food for children and nursing mothers into occupied countries. Elizabeth and her husband had four children, and during the war they housed a number of refugees. After the war, only the Oxford and Huddersfield famine relief committees continued to operate. Elizabeth was invited onto the Oxfam Executive Committee and their Asia Grants Committee, as well as continuing her work with the organization in Huddersfield. She was involved in the early Aldermaston and Weathersfield marches, and on two occasions she was arrested. Refusing to pay the two fines, she spent two weeks in a maximum-security prison in Scotland.

Elizabeth went on the first of what was to be a number of visits to India and the Far East. As a representative of Oxfam, she visited their projects and took slides which were useful when writing articles for local newspapers in Britain and, upon her return, speaking at meetings. She became the Deputy Chair of the International Co-operation Year, which led to the creation of the Huddersfield Community Relations Council. Elizabeth taught Asian children, set up an international women's society for English-speaking women, and established a home tutor scheme to help Asian women to become acquainted with their host environment and to learn basic English. This work led her to organize interfaith services and international dance performances at the Town Hall.

In the late 1960s, Elizabeth was very active in the anti-Vietnam protests. She joined a peace group going to Cambodia. She and one other person splintered off, and went directly to the 'rest and relaxation camps' for American soldiers in Hong Kong, where they passed out leaflets to soldiers, containing information on how to contact peace groups if they wished to get out of the war. Presently, Elizabeth teaches a class in Ikebana, Japanese flower-arrangement, at the University of the Third Age. She is Vice-Chair of the Huddersfield Famine Relief Committee, as well as being increasingly concerned with environmental issues. She is the Yorkshire area organizer for the Quaker Green Concern.

The five additional respondents

The five non-core respondents were each selected to complement or contrast perspectives of the ten core respondents. Thus, Trevor Huddleston was selected because of his international focus, and because of the amount of time he has spent living outside of Britain. In addition, he is the only religious respondent apart from Edward. Louie Davies and Ed[3] Frow were selected because I felt their perspectives as working-class, Northern, virtually life-time Communist Party members would enrich the sample. Janet Vaughan was selected because, as an active member of the Social Democratic Party (SDP), she is the only respondent who calls herself a socialist and yet does not support the Labour Party.[4] Finally, Jack Lindsay, who has lived in England for more than sixty years, was selected as the only respondent not born in Britain (although he became a citizen of both Britain and Australia). The biographies of these respondents are very brief, as the central purpose of their participation in this study was to illuminate aspects of the interview data of the ten core respondents.

Edmund Frow

Ed was born in 1906 in Lincolnshire to an agricultural working-class family. He attended a trade school, and in 1930 he moved to Manchester, and he has stayed in that area ever since. He joined the Communist Party in 1924 and continued to be a member up until one year before our interview. In the early 1930s, Ed was involved with the NUWM, and later was Chair of the local branch of the Communist Party. He was very active in his trade union as a Shop Steward. Together, he and his wife Ruth founded the Working Class Movement Library, which contains more than 15,000 books and 20,000 pamphlets relating to such subjects as the history of trade unionism, the Co-operative Movement, early Radicalism, Chartism, and the women's movement. The Frows are also joint authors of many books and pamphlets on the history of working-class struggles in Britain.

Louie Davies

Louie was born in Lancashire in 1909. Her mother was a working-class Tory, her father a Liberal. She left school at fourteen, and by the time she was seventeen, both her parents had died, leaving her and her older sister to raise three younger children. She joined the Communist Party when she was sixteen, and has remained a member ever since. Her husband was a foundation member of the CPGB. In 1937, the CPGB awarded Louie two Tolpuddle Martyrs awards for her effective work as a Party member. In every factory in which she has worked, she has succeeded in achieving 100 per cent trade-union membership amongst the workers.

Trevor Huddleston

Trevor was born in 1913 to a wealthy family. His father was a director of the Royal Indian Marines. His mother accompanied his father to India, and Trevor was raised by an aunt in England. He was educated at Lancing College, Christ Church, Oxford (where he read history), and Wells Theological College. In 1941, he joined the Community of the Resurrection, and in 1943 he was appointed Priest-in-Charge of the order's missions in Sophiatown and Orlando in the black suburbs of Johannesburg, South Africa. There he became deeply involved with the anti-apartheid struggle, to which he has dedicated his life. Trevor bought and begged instruments for the Huddleston Jazz Band, and it was he who gave the jazz musician Hugh Masekela his first trumpet. He also knew Desmond Tutu as a young boy with tuberculosis, whom he visited every week in hospital and brought books. Trevor is the Godfather and namesake of Tutu's son. After twelve years of living in South Africa – where he had become known as Makhalipile, 'the dauntless one' – Trevor's church directed him to leave. His *Naught For*

Your Comfort (1956), one of the first books to expose the evils of apartheid to an international audience, became a best-seller. He has been Bishop of Masasi, of Stepney, and of Mauritius, as well as Archbishop of the Indian Ocean. He is Chair of the International Defence and Aid Fund for Southern Africa and President of the Anti-Apartheid Movement.

Jack Lindsay

Jack was born in 1900 in Melbourne, Australia, to Norman Lindsay, the famous writer and artist, and his wife Katie. Jack received an honours degree in Classics from the University of Queensland, and several years later he moved to England, never to return to his native Australia. There, as a young writer, he started the Fanfrolico Press. One of the most memorable pieces of political poetry which came out of the inter-war years was Jack's 'On Guard For Spain' (1937). From 1941 to 1945 he served in the British army, first for the Royal Corps of Signals and then as a scriptwriter for the War Office. Jack has been an extraordinarily prolific writer of over one hundred and fifty books. *The Oxford Companion to Australian Literature* describes him as follows: 'Poet, dramatist, editor, historian, translator, classical scholar, biographer, novelist and critic, he has a formidable international reputation, especially in the last five fields' (Wilde *et al.* 1985: 419). The many people who knew Jack and who were influenced by his ideas include Bertolt Brecht, W. E. B. Dubois, Sigmund Freud, Robert Graves, Aldous Huxley, D. H. Lawrence, Jean-Paul Sartre, Edith Sitwell, Dylan Thomas and W. B. Yeats (Anderson 1984: 13). Among the various awards he has received are the Australian Literature Society Couch Gold Medal (1960) and the Soviet Badge of Honour (1968). He was made a Fellow of the Royal Society of Literature, the Ancient Monuments Society and the Australian Academy of Humanities. In 1981, Jack was made a Member of the Order of Australia. Jack died in March 1990.

Janet Vaughan

Janet, the oldest of the respondents, was born in 1899. Her parents were middle-class Liberals. At fifteen she was sent to North Forland Lodge 'for young ladies'. She studied medicine at Somerville College, Oxford; as President of the college debating society, she chaired the famous confrontation between Vera Brittain and Winifred Holtby. Janet later became one of the leaders in the Spanish Medical Aid Campaign. She was part of the Bloomsbury Group, and a cousin of Virginia Woolf. Sally Seaton in *Mrs Dalloway* is meant to be Margaret Symonds, Janet's mother. She joined the Communist Party, but left in the mid 1950s. Throughout Janet's professional life, she has been a pioneer in the field of medicine; she was one of the early proponents of social medicine, and had 'a small part in formulating the ideas enshrined in the Beveridge Report', which eventually led to the creation of the National Health Service. She set up the first blood-transfusion depots in 1939. Between 1945 and 1967, Janet was Principal of Somerville – Margaret Thatcher is one of her 'old girls'. In 1944 she was awarded the Order of the British Empire (OBE), in 1957 she was made a Dame of the British Empire (DBE), and in 1967 Oxford conferred on her the Degree of Doctor of Civil Laws Honoris. Although Janet had been very active in the local Labour Party, she eventually left it because of its position on two issues: (1) joining the EEC, and (2) nuclear energy.

It is not possible to provide one coherent summary of the biographies of these fifteen respondents. Rather, it is hoped that readers will have developed some sense of the diversity of both the background of the respondents, as well as the issues to which they have been committed. Now let us turn to consider the wider historical context in which respondents initially became radicalized, looking in somewhat greater detail at the major left-wing issues which have been merely mentioned in these biographical sketches.

5   A nation in turmoil: Britain between the wars

The road ran downhill into Spain,
    The wind blew fresh on bamboo grasses,
The white plane-trees were bone naked
    And the issues plain:

Louis MacNeice, 'Autumn Journal'

The inter-war period was for Western Europe, as indeed for much of the world, a time of great ferment: social, political and economic. England was no exception. In this chapter, I shall review some of the major events and movements of this time which might have been of particular significance to the respondents of this study, for this was the time of their young adulthood. It seems obvious that 'Individuals do not become mobilized out of a political void' (Marsh 1977: 22): a cursory knowledge of the social and political environment which forms the context of action of an individual or group of individuals is crucial in understanding the evolution of such people's political consciousness and activism.

Our historical review begins just before the end of the First World War, in 1917, the year of the Bolshevik Revolution. Vladimir Ilyich Ulyanov (Lenin), who had been living in exile for nearly two decades, successively in Brussels, Paris, London and Geneva, from where he wrote and distributed revolutionary materials, was able to return permanently to the Soviet Union on 23 October. Promising 'Peace, Land, Bread', Lenin successfully lead the seizure of government offices on the 6–8 November, an action which became known as the October Revolution (the month misnomer due to the change in the Russian calendar). In March 1918, the Bolsheviks shed the name 'Social Democrats' and became the Russian Communist Party.

The Third International, or the Comintern, was formally established on 2 March, 1919, to promote revolutionary Marxism as opposed to the reformist socialism of the Second International. (The concept of international solidarity of the proletariat can be traced to Marx and

Engels' *Communist Manifesto*, written in 1848.) Lichtheim comments that:

Without the Russian Revolution – to be exact, without the Bolshevik seizure of power in November, 1917, eight months after the fall of Tsarism and proclamation of a democratic Republic – there would have been no communist movement (1970: 269).

Lichtheim's statement, while calling attention to the importance of the Bolshevik Revolution, fails to account adequately for the breadth of communist support outside of Russia. There were communist seeds sprouting throughout Europe, and many would argue that if the revolution hadn't happened in that country at that time, it would have happened later, if not there, then elsewhere. Marx himself had predicted that the first proletarian revolution would occur in one of the more highly industrialized nations, and indeed, though the Bolshevik government did create the first fully Communist Party, Russia was by no means the exclusive bed of Marxist sympathizers.

The long-term impact that this revolution would have, not only on the Soviet Union but on the rest of the world, was not immediately perceptible. There are two significant reasons for this: first, Russia had been through a series of upheavals. The revolution led by the liberal intelligentsia in February 1917 had seized power from the Tsar, and had successfully aborted the first attempted Bolshevik revolt in July. There was little reason to assume that when the Bolsheviks did come into power the following November, they were ushering in a new era. Second, the attention of the world community, particularly of Western Europe and the United States, was focused elsewhere, namely on the events of the First World War.

It is, of course, not a coincidence that the Russian Revolution occurred when it did, within the context of the global war.

the immediate cause of the revolt was the inability of the existing order to manage a world war. Shortage of ammunition and food, a chaotic transport system, the burden of $5\frac{1}{2}$ million casualties all contributed to demoralization. The Tsar's government was so divided by petty feuds and intrigue that in twelve months there were four different Prime Ministers, three different War Ministers and three different Foreign Ministers (Palmer 1983: 332).

One of the first acts of the Bolshevik government was to end Russian participation in the First World War. On 3 March 1918, the Bolsheviks signed the Treaty of Brest-Litovsk, in order that the Germans might end their eastward advance. In turn, Russia agreed to surrender the Ukraine, Finland, the Baltic provinces, the Caucasus, White Russia and Poland. Although this treaty was invalidated by the German Armistice eight months later, the Russians paid the price of establishing grounds for a future stereotype of themselves as betrayers.

The First World War ended for the rest of Europe on 11 November 1918 with the German Armistice. The Allies then formed themselves into the Paris Peace Conference, which lasted from 18 January 1919 until 28 June 1919. The purpose of the congress was to determine a settlement with the Axis powers. At this time, the League of Nations was formed, as a peace-keeping body that would serve as arbitrator in any future international dispute so that further global conflicts could be avoided. However well-intended the founding of this organization may have been, in fact it became a rather ineffective body which was much-ignored in times of international crisis. Indeed, the United States never even became a member, as a result of the US Congress refusing to ratify the Treaty of Versailles, and Germany was only a member from 1926 to 1933. The final straw was that the League of Nations had no armed forces, and thus had to rely on non—military coercion to force compliance with international law. In the end, this proved to be ineffective.

Interestingly, though it was on the basis of President Wilson's 'Fourteen Points' that Germany and Austria–Hungary sought armistices in 1918, the Paris Peace Conference did not deliver what Wilson's programme had promised. Indeed, it could be argued that as the Paris Peace Conference saw the conclusion of one war, it set the table for the beginning of the next. 'The defeated states resented the fact that the terms were dictated to them rather than settled by agreed compromises between victors and vanquished' (Palmer 1983: 304). Retributive spirit ran high among the Allies: reparations for Germany alone were fixed at £6,600 million plus interest. In fact, this severe financial arrangement backfired, for effectively it prevented Germany from rebuilding itself. In addition, this arrangement instilled within the German people a bitter resentment towards those who had imposed upon them the shackles of such enormous debt, which exacerbated the harshness of the conditions under which they were already living. Arguably, this general national feeling of having been dealt with unfairly was one of the elements that made the German people receptive to the angry, proud and unvanquished spirit embodied in Adolf Hitler.

The losses Britain had suffered during the war were severe: eight hundred thousand dead, and another two million wounded. Indeed, 'roughly 12 per cent of all men mobilized in Britain during the First World War were killed' (Winter 1985: 92). The mortality rate of men who served and who were under the age of twenty-five in 1914 was one in four (p. 98), with the well-educated middle and upper classes suffering disproportionately heavy losses (p. 92). In the following years, Britain was to experience 'a more pronounced post-war boom and slump than the rest of the international economy' (Buxton & Aldcroft 1979: 9); while the 1920s saw a long-term decline in the basic industries of coal, textiles and heavy engineering (Branson 1975: 91), there was a great boom in such areas as private housing (Buxton & Aldcroft 1979). Woodrow Wilson, speaking one month after the end of the First World War, expressed a belief in the general progress of humankind, and a hope for what the post-war period might bring.

I believe that... men are beginning to see, not perhaps the golden age, but an age which at any rate is brightening from decade to decade, and will lead us some time to an elevation from which we can see the things for which the heart of mankind is longing (Mowat 1955: 1).

This optimism proved to be unfounded; sadly, 'The history of the twenty years between the two world wars is the history of the disappointment of these hopes' (*ibid.*). The hardships of the previous few years, though different in cause and nature from what was to follow, did not disappear with the end of the war.

The conclusion of the First World War saw changes on many fronts of British life. During the war, women moved from traditional women's occupations into munitions manufacturing; between July 1914 and July 1918, the number of women employed in Britain rose by 1,345,000 (M. Pugh 1980: 30). The implications of this, however, were not unproblematic; indeed, in many places women workers were greatly resented, for they 'showed that with little, or sometimes no, training they could perform industrial jobs hitherto designated as skilled work by men' (p. 31). Much of the official wartime propaganda emphasized that a woman's most important contribution to the national effort was 'to dispatch their menfolk to the front and not tie them to her apron strings ... a woman's most important function was to rear fighting men of the future' (*ibid.*).

The First World War had a regressive effect on the British women's movement. Prior to that time, there had been quite a widespread and growing feminist consciousness. 'Implicit within the feminist movement before 1914 was a much wider challenge – a challenge to masculine control over women and a vision of transforming relations between the sexes' (Rowbotham 1973: 168). However, 1914 saw 'the wrenching apart of the socialist and feminist movements' (*ibid.*), epitomized by the split between Sylvia Pankhurst on the one side, and her mother Emmeline and sister Christabel on the other.[1]

Christabel and her mother were fervently patriotic. They changed the name of the Women's Social and Political Union (WSPU) journal from

The Suffragette to *Britannia* and 'supported military conscription for men and industrial conscription for women. The WSPU suffragettes were among the first women to give men in civilian clothes white feathers of cowardice' (p. 116). Ironically, they found themselves on the same side as former enemies, such as Lloyd George and Winston Churchill, and denouncing 'conscientious objectors, passive resisters, and shirkers', including some of their old allies. So supportive of the war effort did the government see these women to be, that it even paid suffragette expenses for marches (*ibid.*). Sylvia, for her part, 'never ceased to attack "this capitalist war"'... The Russian Revolution and the triumph of the Bolsheviks made this separation impossible to overcome. Sylvia's future was with revolutionary socialism; her mother's with the Conservative Party' (pp. 116–117). *The Worker's Dreadnought*, a socialist feminist paper, proclaimed it was unable 'to assent to the old fashioned suffragist standpoint that the political activities of women must begin and end with two subjects, Votes for Women and venereal diseases' (quoted in Rowbotham 1973: 160): the women's movement must include, but not be limited to, the campaign for women's suffrage.

In 1918 the Representation of the People Act, which, among other things, granted the vote to women over the age of thirty, was passed. Many women who had worked for women's suffrage were quite cynical about the way in which this had come about. Spender (1984: 30) summarizes the feelings of Millicent Garrett Fawcett, one of the movement's leading campaigners for almost fifty years:

the vote was not granted to women as recognition of their war contribution or even because their case was strong enough to warrant legislation, but because there had to be a new franchise bill to include the returning service men who had lost their residence qualification for voting; and some women were included in this bill – designed for men – almost as an after thought.

Dora Russell, another leader of the movement, cynically reflected in 1925:

In 1918 they bestowed the vote, just as they dropped about a few Dames and MBEs as a reward for our services in helping the destruction of our offspring...They gave the vote to the older women who were deemed less rebellious (pp. 3–4).

Older women were generally regarded as more stable, more conservative, and more likely to follow their husbands' political preference. Indeed, in 1916 at the Speakers Conference on Franchisement, the government had made specific calculations ensuring that enfranchised women would constitute a minority of the electorate. Thus, even though granting women the vote was to be portrayed as a reward for their significant contribution to the war effort, this was patently not the case as most of those very women were under thirty. Despite having partial franchisement, women did not mobilize as a political pressure group, as many had feared (and others had hoped) they would do. This perhaps facilitated the passage of the Equal Franchise Bill of 1928, which granted the vote to all women, and effectively added five-and-a-half million women to the voter register. In 1929, women comprised 52·7 per cent of total eligible voters (M. Pugh 1980: 37).

1918 was a significant year for British women not only because of enfranchisement, but also because it was the year in which Marie Stopes published *Wise Parenthood*, a practical guide to methods of contraception. In 1920 Stopes opened the Mothers Clinic for Constructive Birth Control in Holloway, North London. During and immediately following the war there was strong pressure exerted on women to bear children. Indeed, during the Great War, the birth rate had fallen from 24 births per 1,000 (in 1910–1913) to 17·8 per 1,000 births (in 1917). 'In aggregate terms this meant a decline in number of registered births from around 880,000 per year before the war to a low of 660,000 in 1918' (Winter 1985: 253). In 1919, a popular magazine offered special tea trays to every 'proud mother of ten children'! (M. Pugh 1980: 36). Various voices of authority – press, church, science and politics – joined in a chorus promoting national fecundity, but to no avail. Whereas women born between 1841 and 1845 had an average of 5·71 live births, women married between 1925 and 1929 produced only 2·19 (*ibid.*). Moreover, divorce rates in 1918 were higher than ever before. The Matrimonial Causes Act of 1923 'meant that adultery was grounds for divorce for the wife as well as husband – an important equalisation in moral standards' (Rowbotham 1973: 112).

Still, even with these changes in women's lives, the women's movement was not able to recover the unity of purpose and quality of consciousness which had characterized it in the pre-war years. Strachey in 1936 observed that 'Modern young women know amazingly little of what life was like before the war, and show a strong hostility to the word "feminism" and all which they imagine it to connote' (quoted in Rowbotham 1973: 163). One effect of the split between socialist and conservative feminists was to blur the political analysis offered by the former, connecting questions of production with those of reproduction. Thus, politically minded young people saw feminism as irrelevant to their own lives and to the multitude of crises with which society was confronted.

In the context of the hunger marches, Spain, and anti-fascist young women who inclined toward radicalism had more pressing political choices. They were likely to be dismissive of feminism, because they only knew it as a limited movement and because they felt they no longer needed to be feminists. The women in left political organisations, including the Labour Party, could feel that they worked as individuals and that a specific consciousness as women was a kind of indulgence (Rowbotham 1973: 164).

This view echoes some of the debates presented in Chapter 2 regarding the relationship between class and gender consciousness, just as it foreshadows some of the data to be presented in Chapter 7. Enfranchisement had appeased those suffragettes who regarded their movement as being oriented toward a single issue. All who remained in the women's movement were socialist feminists who were not able to communicate effectively to potential supporters the broad base of their political agenda.[2]

The inter-war years are a particularly interesting period for any Labour Party historian. Though formed in 1900 as the Labour Representation Committee which combined all the socialist groups in Britain – notably the Independent Labour Party, the Fabian Society, and the Social Democratic Federation – it emerged from the First World War with a new vitality and strength. In 1918 the constitution of the Labour Party expressed a socialist vision, calling for 'the gradual building up of a new social order based...on deliberately planned cooperation in production and distribution' (Palmer 1983; 228). The Labour Party, however, distanced itself from the Communist Party of Great Britain, and indeed would not allow it to join, as Lenin had urged them to do. In 1922 Labour became the official Opposition Party, and in 1924 the first Labour government was formed, lasting for only ten months.

In 1929 a second Labour government was formed, led again by Ramsay MacDonald. MacDonald later became a controversial figure when, in 1931, he, with a minority of his Labour cabinet ministers, created a coalition government with the Conservatives, known as the National Government. As a result of this, many regarded him as a betrayer, both to his class and to the party which he had helped to create. One important effect of the formation of the coalition government was that it caused many Labour supporters to be cynical about their leadership, perceiving MacDonald as having been easily and willingly coopted into the system. For many, this paved the way for the consideration and sometimes acceptance of a more radical alternative.

Although Britain was plagued by domestic problems between the wars, let us first briefly examine its role as an imperialist power during this time. The spirit of 'Rule Britannia' had long presided over Britain's policies towards its occupied territories. During the inter-war years, however, this confident posture was challenged. While Britain continued to exercise firm control over many of its colonies – Kenya becoming a new colony in 1920 – there were significant exceptions to this, the two most salient being Ireland and India.

The importance for the Empire of keeping Ireland as an occupied territory was acknowledged both by its supporters and its opponents. Lenin, writing about the Irish rebellion of 1916, the Easter Uprising, stated:

A blow against the power of the English imperialist bourgeoisie by a rebellion in Ireland is a hundred times more significant politically than a blow of equal force delivered in Asia or Africa (1960: 357).

The British, for their part, also recognized the significance of their position in Ireland. In May 1921, shortly before his assassination by the newly formed Irish Republican Army (IRA), Field Marshall Sir Henry Wilson, former Chief of the Imperial General Staff, urged:

If we don't reinforce Ireland by every available man, horse, gun [and] aeroplane, that we have got in the world we would lose Ireland at the end of this summer, and with Ireland the Empire (Blake 1986: 29).

In fact what ensued in Ireland was neither what Lenin had hoped for, nor what Wilson had warned against. The British manipulated the situation in such a way that essentially the Irish were left to fight one another, taking different stances on the partition that was imposed upon them.

In 1919 there were still 43,000 regular British troops occupying Ireland. In addition to this, the Royal Irish Constabulary, a semi-military police force, numbered 10,000 (Branson 1975: 57). In 1919, the IRA was formed to fight against the occupying British and to work for a unified republic. The tensions and violence escalated until 1922, when there was a split in Sinn Fein between those who accepted the newly established Irish Free State, and those who did not. In question was the Partition Bill, which was to divide Ireland into two parts, one consisting of six of the nine counties of Ulster with a predominantly Protestant population, and the other of the remaining twenty-six counties of Ireland which had a majority of Catholics (Branson 1975: 56–66). In Ireland, the minority Protestant population, whose ancestors had come from Scotland at the time of James I, still felt a primary allegiance to the British crown, whereas the Catholic majority viewed the British as foreign interlopers who had appropriated jobs, houses and spheres of influences in their land. The proposed partition was destined for disaster. Nonetheless, the bill was passed, and at the end of 1921 a treaty was signed which provided for an Irish Free State for the twenty-six counties; this, however, still fell short of total independence. When Michael Collins, the original organizer of the IRA, accepted the Irish Free State, the IRA regarded him as a traitor. The country was divided between those who accepted the partition and those who did not, and civil war was waged until early 1923.

The situation in Ireland was arguably qualitatively different from that of other occupied territories, if only because of its geographic location in relation to the country of its oppressors. Ireland was at Britain's back door, and had lived with the fact of the Empire for centuries. This proximity meant that not only was the cost to the British of maintaining their imperialist status in Ireland small in comparison with the significant financial burden they incurred by their presence in more distant lands, but also that Ireland, for the British, lacked the exoticism of the other colonies (Maley 1987). It took on, rather, the character of a problem that simply would not go away.

India, on the other hand, was the prized possession of the Empire, the 'jewel of the [British] crown'. The rise of Britain's domestic problems, coupled with the complications of the international crisis, helped to create a situation in which relations with the colonies became problematic. R. A. Florey summarizes the causes of unrest in the following way:

The growth of large-scale production, the formation of trusts and monopolies, the predominance assumed by banking and finance, the action and reaction of overseas investment, had all affected the British Empire and had begun to disturb the relations of the various classes and races within it (1980: 49).

Nowhere could these problems be more clearly identified than in India. 'It was with India', writes Mowat,

that Britain experienced the greatest difficulties as an imperial power... throughout the interwar years. The war had stirred Indian nationalism, and had brought together, for the time being, the predominantly Hindu Congress party and the Moslems (1955: 110).

The radicalization of the nationalist movement in India was of great importance to the Third International, and the Communist Party of India (CPI) was founded in 1920. Because of the imperialist relationship between Britain and India,

India was the chief responsibility of British Communists, and while they were entrusted with promoting revolutionary movements throughout their country's colonial possessions, India absorbed most of their energies (Macintyre 1975: 290).

Two leading members of the CPGB were Indian, Shapurji Saklatvala, the Communist MP, and Clemens Dutt, elder brother of Rajani Palme Dutt.

R. P. Dutt provided the political analysis that formed much of the backbone for left-wing discussions relating to the British–India question. Macintyre, in his study 'Marxism in Britain 1917–1933', summarizes the arguments advanced by Dutt in his seminal *Modern India*, printed in Bombay in 1926 and in London the following year:

[*Modern India*] drew attention to the recent consequences of the growth of Indian industry. British imperialism had taken the Indian bourgeoisie into 'junior partnership' in a 'counter-revolutionary front.' Because they received a share in the spoils of imperialism the colonial bourgeoisie were coming to play an increasingly 'treacherous role' and the future movement must be based on the peasantry and working class (1975: 292).

That India, with the growing momentum of its nationalist movement, would become independent from Britain after two hundred years of being a colonized nation, seemed quite likely. The main question, however, was what form this new society would take. Unlike the Congress Party, led by Mahatma Gandhi, the aspirations of the CPI went beyond Indian independence: they wanted not to replicate but to revolutionize the existing structures of society, and it was to this political end that they worked. It is not surprising then that the struggle in India commanded so much attention from the CPGB.

The domestic situation in Britain, following a short-lived boom in 1920, was financially quite unstable. As R. H. Tawney wrote, 'In April 1920 all was right with the world. In April 1921 all was wrong' (quoted in Mowat 1955: 26). The reasons for this were basically overspeculation and inflation: the postwar economy could not sustain the production rates of the war years; markets were changing and industries were forced to accommodate themselves to the unstable demands of the new economy. The most devastating result was a steep rise in unemployment: in March 1921, 1,355,000 or 11 per cent of insured workers were unemployed. By December of the same year, that figure had reached over two million, or nearly 18 per cent (Branson 1975: 69).

Massive unemployment and the rise of fascism were the two main issues around which the left, led primarily led by the Communist Party, became mobilized; hard times made fertile soil for the promulgation of radical politics. The CPGB had been formed in 1920, and it was later to attract a great number of sympathizers, if not actual members; it was the impetus behind many of the major left-wing movements of the inter-war years (particularly in the Popular Front of the later 30s). In 1943, at the

height of its popularity, the CPGB had 55,138 members (Newton 1969:
160). However, the circulation of its newspaper, *The Daily Worker*, was
slightly higher, at 70,000 (sometimes reaching as high as 100,000 for
special issues).

Ralph Miliband summarizes the attraction to the Communist Party
during this period of history:

Unemployment and the Depression; the blandly reactionary face of Con-
servatism and the tarnished reality of British imperialism, the blatant
inadequacies of Labourism; the rise of Fascism; Spain appeasement; the
attractive certitudes of 'Marxist-Leninism'; the promise of a new world to be
gained by striving and strife; the immensely strong will to believe that the new
world was already being built in the Soviet Union and that it must be defended
from the permanent threat of the old world...What is remarkable is not that
many young men and women felt the pull to the left, but that there were not
more of them (1979: 16–17).

Finally, John Saville, himself of this generation, calls attention to the
leadership role of the CPGB in the politics of the 1930s:

without the Communist Party, the history of the 1930s, from about 1933–4
onwards, would have been very different. They provided the dynamic behind
the organisation of the hunger marches, much of the opposition on the streets to
Mosley, and a great deal of the extraordinary efforts that went to support
Republican Spain in the Civil War, including the recruitment of a high
proportion of the British section of the International Brigade from among Party
members. The Party was also central to the radicalisation of the student
movement, and its influence over intellectuals was not inconsiderable (1977:
248).

The CPGB offered an analysis of the situation which many found
plausible, meeting the urgent crises with a call for massive political
organization and action.

In the early postwar years, up until the mid 1920s, the trade union
movement had been gaining strength. However, it suffered a tremendous
setback in 1926 with the disappointing outcome of the General Strike.
The strike was organized by the Trade Union Congress (TUC) in
response to the Samuel Report, issued on 10 March 1926 by a Royal
Commission on the mining industry. The Commission had been created
by the Prime Minister, Stanley Baldwin, to mediate in a dispute between
mineowners and mineworkers. In an attempt to reduce the price of coal,
the mineowners wanted their employees to accept a severe cut in wages,
coupled with a longer working day. A. J. Cook, the miners' leader,
responded to these demands with the pledge 'Not a penny off the pay,
not a minute on the day' (Palmer 1983: 161). The Royal Commission

supported the claim of the mineowners for a cut in wages. Initially the role of the TUC was ambiguous, since it was trying

to persuade the miners to move from their position of 'no reduction in wages' to another which suggested 'no reduction in wages, unless...' [They were] trying to persuade the miners to accept the Report, and trying to persuade the government that the miners could be got to accept the report (Branson 1975: 175).

In the middle of negotiations, the mineowners posted notices ending the miner's contracts on 30 April. The following day the decision was made to call a general strike. The TUC leadership was anything but militant in its approach, and thus was 'anxious to stress that the strike had a limited and purely industrial object' (Branson 1975: 177).

The government, however, viewed the strike not only in terms of the particular claims being disputed, but also in regard to its more threatening potential to function as a revolutionary catalyst. Its concerns were somewhat justified, as undoubtedly some individuals must have viewed the situation as an opportunity to realize fundamental societal change. From the point of view of the government, much was at stake, for 'if the trade unions were victorious in this trial of strength, the existing power structure could be shaken to its foundations' (Branson 1975: 179). Much of the media reporting at this time expressed a heightened fear of revolution, and it made widespread appeal for the support of the general public by evoking patriotic sympathies. An example of this was a letter printed in the *Morning Post* by the Duke of Northumberland. Headed 'COAL WAR PLOT – MINERS UNDER THE THUMB OF MOSCOW. THE VANGUARD OF REVOLUTION', it read:

In this great crisis the issues are not between Capital and Labour, Employer and Employed; they are between those who love their country and those who are in league with its enemies (Florey 1980: 130).

Transport workers, printers, builders, heavy-industrial workers and, later, engineers all went out on strike. The plan was not for a universal and simultaneous stoppage of work, but stoppages by selected industries at varying intervals. 'The "first line"...included transport, printing and press, iron and steel, electricity, gas and building' (Branson 1975: 180). This was followed by other industries; in total, just under three million workers were called out. The government declared a state of emergency, and recruited special constables, volunteers to run essential services, and employed troops to maintain food supplies. After only nine days the TUC called off the strike, and accepted a compromise which the miners themselves rejected. Although the miners fought on for an additional six months without the support and cooperation of other trade unions, the effectiveness of their protest was severely limited.

Once the strike had been called off, and the government had been reassured of its firm control over the 'subversive elements of society', the outcome was used as a prime tool for political propaganda. Although the strike had only lasted nine days, the images that it evoked were stirring for many: the British people had displayed a strong spirit of unity as many contributed what services they could, responding patriotically to their country's call of need. Good had triumphed over evil; it was as if Britain had won a war, but it was a war against its own working-class citizens.

The Times ran an article on 22 May 1926, reporting the previous day's Empire Celebrations:

The Lord Mayor unfurled the Union Jack and the children saluted the flag and gave three cheers for the King... the Lord Mayor reminded the children of the extent and influence of the British Empire, of which they were the future citizens, and exhorted them to remain loyal and patriotic members of the Empire. It was a delight at any time, he said, to take part in a demonstration of that kind, but after the stirring and anxious days of the past fortnight, they were intensely proud of the patriotism and discipline and the regard for law and order exhibited throughout the country during that unfortunate period. He impressed on the children the value of education and urged them to make themselves fully acquainted with what the words 'British Empire' meant (Florey 1980: 56).

The immediate aftermath of the General Strike was the enactment of the Trades Union and Trade Dispute Act of 1927, not repealed until 1946, which made any form of general strike illegal. But even more importantly than that,

The General Strike ended a major epoch in the history of the labour movement. It destroyed the myth that a nationwide work stoppage could lead to a fairly bloodless revolution in which the system simply 'collapsed' (Jupp 1982: 3).

Cliff and Gluckstein echo this opinion, stating unequivocally that

The General Strike was a decisive turning point in British history... The sell-out brought to an end a long, although not uninterrupted, period of working-class militancy (1986: 282).

But while the outcome of the strike dealt a crushing blow to the trade union movement, the fact that three million people came out on strike, was, nonetheless, evidence of a strong solidarity and trade union consciousness among the industrialized working class.

The belief that you should be deferential to those in the class above you was being replaced by a belief that if you joined with others you could stand up and feel proud of your working class status. For years such sentiments had been expressed at trade union conferences and meetings. Now at last they were being put into practice (Branson 1975: 191).

Despite the disappointing results of the strike, this feeling, once created, did not vanish at the end of the strike. No longer would the rank and file trade unionists unquestioningly trust their leaders to represent their interests: some now regarded union organizers themselves as having been coopted into an essentially unjust system. Others interpreted the outcome as evidence of the overwhelming strength of the government, and hence did not perceive their leaders as having been empowered with the choice to 'sell out' or not.

Few at that time could have predicted that the years to follow would be even leaner than any they had recently experienced. The crash of the New York Stock Exchange on 29 October 1929 strongly affected the entire world economy. Britain, itself already in severe financial difficulty and one of the closer trading partners of the United States, was in a particularly vulnerable position. The major consequence of the crash was massive unemployment; by 1932 there were 2·8 million unemployed workers in Britain. National and Conservative governments preferred policies which, in hindsight, can be seen to have exacerbated the problem, rather than relieving it. The Labour Party, too, whether in power or in opposition, at no point in the inter-war years had had an effective policy for tackling mass unemployment (Pelling 1975; Pimlott 1977).

It was in this climate that the National Unemployed Workers' Movement (NUWM) gained its greatest momentum. Headed by such well-known public figures of the left as Wal Hannington and Harry McShane, the NUWM encouraged unemployed workers to regard the organization as a 'trade union of the unemployed' (Jupp 1982: 25). As previously stated, many of these people looked on the TUC (as well as the leaders of the Labour Party) with great suspicion, and saw betrayal by the organization's leadership as virtually responsible for their present plight. Although from 1923 to 1925 the TUC and NUWM had a Joint Committee, after this the TUC regarded the NUWM as 'Communist-dominated' and ceased all cooperative efforts.

This allegation was not unfounded, though not everyone regarded such a label as pejorative. Tom Bell, in *The British Communist Party* (1937), writes of the NUWM that

its leader comrades were Party members and worked in the closest collaboration with the Party Central Comittee. The Party indeed was the main inspirer of the whole of this movement (quoted in Jupp 1982: 25).

Pelling (1975) suggests, however, that part of the NUWM's effectiveness and appeal lay in its leaders' willingness, on occasion, to put the interests of the unemployed ahead of those of the Party Central Committee. Thus, the relations of the NUWM's leaders (themselves Party members) with the Central Committee, were by no means unproblematic. Overall, it can be stated that the major attraction of the NUWM was that it provided an organization for those who had been displaced and in many ways discarded by the economic system. Moreover, it provided a political explanation for their difficult situation. The NUWM offered an alternative response to the general ethos of poverty, discouragement and despair. Employing a strategy of speaking on street corners to elicit support, the leaders of the NUWM spoke in a language that was accessible to many, and the problems to which they addressed themselves were those of the everyday man and woman.

Hence, the poverty and hard times of the early thirties created an environment which caused many to re-evaluate the capitalist system which had rendered them unemployed. As Jupp writes, 'Marx was seen as essentially an economist with a theory of capitalism which explained the Depression' (1982: 132). The severity of conditions witnessed if not experienced by everyone, invited a left-wing critique of society, particularly from intellectuals and those less well-off. Thus in the face of this despair, there was for many a feeling of great hope, a belief that revolution was around the corner, as they interpreted the decay about them as evidence of the decline of the capitalist system.

One of the most effective forms of protest organized by the NUWM was that of the hunger marches. While these had begun in the 1920s, as the economic situation worsened, the movement grew in the 1930s, both in terms of actual participants and of national recognition. This was an effective form of protest because of its success in attracting national support; as the unemployed marched through the various cities, where they presented their case to the townspeople, they were often met with warm meals and a place to sleep. Equally important, they provided the workers themselves with a sense of unity which better enabled them to sustain a fighting spirit. The hunger march of 1934 was received with much more public support than was that of 1932, and again the march in 1936 was the most successful of all.

The Jarrow March, or Crusade, as it has often been called, which also took place in November 1936, was separate from the one organized by the NUWM. Kingsford, in his *The Hunger Marchers in Britain 1920–1940*, makes the point that while both marches had as their object the same immediate goal (i.e. to protest against unemployment, which had reached 73 per cent of insured workers in Jarrow), the Jarrow

March was essentially far less radical than any organized by the NUWM. The Jarrow March was to be represented as non-political, with no association with the wider left-wing movement, much less with the communists. Consequently, Kingsford argues, the Jarrow March attracted much more support, earning for Jarrow 'the image and name of hunger marching which belonged properly to the NUWM' (1982: 221). Thus, he refers to 'the myth that it [the Jarrow March] was representative of the British protest against unemployment' (*ibid*).

In November 1936, the NUWM hunger marchers presented a petition to the House of Commons which referred to the

grievous hardship which is being endured by great numbers of unemployed men and women by reason of their loss of physical well-being, the breaking up of many of their homes, the wretched condition of the villages and towns, and the harsh incidence of the family means test (Kingsford 1982: 216).

As one conservative paper, *The Hertfordshire Mercury*, summed up the effect of seeing the marchers: 'What the eye does not see the heart does not grieve at' (Kingsford 1982: 200). Kingsford states that by 1936

It was common knowledge that half the nation was not getting enough food and that the army could not get the physically fit men it wanted... Hearts had been moved by the appearance of the [emaciated] men who, however misguided, had chosen the rigours of a long march in order to raise their voices on behalf of the victims of a great social evil (1982: 200).

The climate of opinion had changed, and what had hitherto been seen as a left-wing, even communist-inspired activity, was now viewed as a legitimate response to a dire situation.

In 1934, however, there was a shift in the focus of the left from national to international problems. Although the issues which had initially occupied the left such as massive unemployment (and its corollary effects) still persisted, the political events that were happening elsewhere, particularly in Germany, were increasingly alarming, and were seen by many on the left to have potentially strong international implications. In March 1933, the German Nazi Party, with Hitler as its leader, had come to power in Germany.[3] Within weeks of the election victory, reports of Hitler's crackdown on Jews and socialists, and his creation of concentration camps, had appeared in British newspapers, and it was not long before the first Jewish refugees from Germany began to trickle into Britain.

However, in 1933, the British general public did not take much notice of events in Germany. Rather, it was Italy, in the character of its ebullient leader, Benito Mussolini, that had captured the imagination of many. Mussolini had started out as a socialist, an activist and a journalist, but he had left the Socialist Party in 1915 over the First World War. In October 1922 Mussolini, heading a coalition of fascists and nationalists, was appointed Prime Minister, on the strength of his anti-communist credentials. It was not until 1928–1929 that he established a fully fascist government. This coincided precisely with the economic crash of 1929, which caused many to question the viability of capitalism and of democracy, and to regard the case of Mussolini with interest and admiration.

Italy presented, to many, the picture of a country that had turned from chaos to order, from widespread poverty to comparative affluence... To the inhabitants of countries which appeared to be losing their pride and their imperial past, this regeneration of 'Italian self-respect' seemed one of the most important features of the regime (Griffiths 1983: 13–14).

Praise for Mussolini was widespread in Britain, even coming from relatively unlikely sources such as George Bernard Shaw, who wrote to a friend in 1927 that Mussolini had gone 'further in the direction of Socialism than the English Labour Party could yet venture if they were in power' (quoted in Griffiths 1983: 20). One of the popular slogans at the time was 'In Italy, the trains run on time' – things were seen to work. The greatest support, however, came from those Tories who were most worried about Britain's economic situation and who had come to question the future of capitalism (Griffiths 1983). The economic depression of the late twenties and early thirties had caused many to critically examine democracy's capacity for dealing with the complexity of problems in the modern world. While such severe circumstances caused some to adopt a socialist critique, others were attracted by the models of dictatorship offered by Mussolini and Hitler.

Perhaps the best-known, though by no means the only, expression of British support for fascism was the British Union of Fascists (BUF), started by Sir Oswald Mosley. Up until February 1931, Mosley had been a member of the Labour Party. He was a 'brilliant and ambitious man, considered by many to be a potential Prime Minister' (Griffiths 1983: 31). In his book *The Greater Britain* (1932), Mosley wrote, 'Fascism today has become a world-wide movement, invading every country in the hour of crisis as the only alternative to destructive Communism' (p. 154). Much of the appeal of fascism was its pronounced anti-communism, just as on the left anti-fascism was often confused with communism. Mosley called on those who wished to join the BUF to 're-write the greatest pages of British history by finding for the spirit of their age its hightest mission in these islands'. In return, he offered them 'the deep belief that they are fighting that a great land may live' (pp. 159–160). Within a year and a half, the membership of Mosley's organization had reached twenty thousand, while that of the CPGB was at that time hovering at just above five thousand (Newton 1969: 159). Members were fitted out with black shirts, an identification from which they drew their name. Mosley, with his slogan 'Britain First', initially stood in complete opposition to any concept of international fraternity and struggle, although after 1934 this changed. Originally regarded as a challenge to the growing sympathy for the radical left, the BUF entertained a wide range of support, 'including romantically-minded white collar workers and semi-literate toughs in search of excitement' (Branson & Heinemann 1971: 282). Indeed, much of his support came from very 'respectable' elements of society.

The BUF orchestrated many rallies throughout the country. One which gained particular notoriety was that held at Olympia Stadium on 7 June 1934. At this meeting, in which the Blackshirts violently evicted anti-fascist protesters from the hall, many 'eminent and respectable eyewitnesses were outraged at what they had seen' (p. 284) and withdrew their support. W. J. Anstruther-Gray, Conservative MP, commented, 'I had not been at the meeting for more than a few minutes before all my sympathies were with the men who were being handled with such brutality' (*ibid.*). Similar views were echoed by others; Mosley's base of appeal began to weaken, not because of intellectual disagreement or disapproval, but rather because of the vulgarity and 'foreignness' of its tactics. Thus, while

> Mosley undoubtedly had admirers in important social positions...and had access to a wide range of the politically influential...the violent character of the BUF and its unashamed adoption of foreign symbols made it unattractive to many who might otherwise have agreed with some of its policies (Jupp 1982: 57).

What is important here is not the rise and fall in popularity of Mosley the individual, but rather the fact of the significant appeal of his policies within British society. There were other pockets of fascist sympathy. For instance, the *Anglo-German Review*, established in November 1936 and targeted at a pro-German readership, was so popular in its first six months that it could afford to cut its price from a shilling to sixpence. The readership settled at about twelve thousand, where it remained until 1939. Many eminent figures used this forum to express their faith in Hitler. In 1937, Lady Londonderry wrote of her impressions of Hitler, whom she and her husband had visited twice in the previous year. He was, she felt, 'symbolic of the new Germany', 'a born leader... an arresting personality'. He 'stood for peace and for friendship with the English. He had saved Germany from Communism, and "may well be called upon to save Europe"' (Griffiths 1983: 275). Again, one sees the sympathy for fascism growing out of an anti-communist sentiment.

At the same time, there was in Britain a growing popularity of left-wing ideas, not only in the industrialized working class, who had shown their support for supposedly radical organized political action in the General Strike, but also among the intelligentsia. The Fabian Society, originally founded in 1884, came to have an increasingly high profile because of such members as George Bernard Shaw, and Beatrice and Sidney Webb. For many on the left, the Soviet Union represented hope and possibility – a new frontier. Many, like the Webbs, went to the USSR and returned with glowing reports of what they had seen. The popular appeal of the left grew, and though not all expressed their political sympathies through joining the Communist Party, many were fellow travellers, or as Lenin called them 'me-too communists' (Curare 1973: 3).[4]

One example of the popular appeal of left-wing politics can be seen in the Left Book Club (LBC), which was founded by Victor Gollancz in May 1936. The LBC published many notable authors: Woolf, Malraux, Spender, Orwell, Snow and Attlee, among others. The significance of the Club was that it 'showed how widespread was the desire to understand the crisis from a socialist viewpoint' (Branson & Heinemann 1971: 276). But the LBC was more than a mere publishing venture. Small groups organized themselves throughout the country to meet and discuss the monthly selection. 'The aim of the club' as described in one of its introductory leaflets,

is a simple one; it is to help in the terrible urgent struggle for World Peace and a better social and economic order against Fascism, by giving (to all who are determined to play their part in this struggle) such knowledge as will greatly increase their efficiency (Reid 1979: 194).

Although the Club had a lifespan of more than a decade – it died in 1948 – its peak in influence and membership was in its first few years. At its third anniversary rally in 1939, 'it was announced that the membership had grown to 58,000 and the groups to 1,200. Fifteen million leaflets had been distributed, two million bound books and half-a-million each of two pamphlets sold' (Reid 1979: 195). In short, 'for a whole generation, it had meant a unique and irreversible process of socialist education' (Branson & Heinemann 1971: 277–278).

Clearly, the LBC had emerged as a response to the political and social environment. The Club, though not technically a communist organization, had many Party members, was closely affiliated with the Party, and generally published books which were pro-Soviet and supportive of British communism. Of course there were exceptions to this, particularly when rifts developed within the left, over such issues as the German–Soviet Pact and the Stalinist trials in the Soviet Union of many Bolshevik leaders in the late 1930s. Even Gollancz, who has admitted that the LBC did sometimes 'compromise with intellectual integrity' (Hoggart 1986) in order to advance most effectively its political message, edited a collection of essays called *The Betrayal of the Left*. These difficulties, however, which did not surface until much later, were not particular to the LBC, but were mirrored in the wider left movement.

Meanwhile, in 1935–1936, the Abyssinian War provided unequivocal evidence of the inefficacy of the League of Nations. Mussolini had decided that he would create an East African Italian Empire, and despite attempts by the League of Nations to intervene, Italian troops invaded Ethiopia in October 1935. The significance of this was that not only did it give further evidence of the international spread of fascism and reveal the depths of fascism's imperialist nature, but it shattered all illusion that the League of Nations could function as an effective arbitrator in international disputes. Hitherto, many had hoped, unrealistically, that confrontation could be averted by negotiations through this international body. Moreover, the international ostracism which Italy incurred because of the invasion helped to create a bond between Hitler and Mussolini, and in 1936 the Axis was formed between the two powers.

As noted earlier, by far the most organized and outspoken voice of anti-fascism was the Communist Party, and the Party gained many sympathizers, who, if not positively communist, were strongly anti-fascist. Thus, when the Spanish Civil War broke out in July 1936, in Britain it was the Communist Party which answered the call for international help from the Spanish republicans. In the summer of 1935, the Communist International at its Seventh World Congress had called for a united anti-fascist struggle in every country. In the Spanish elections of February 1936, the 'Frente Popular' defeated the nationalists, and formed a coalition government, initially primarily comprised of liberals, but later including socialists, anarchic-syndicalists and communists as well.

It was against this republican government that Francisco Franco led his revolt. On 1 October 1936, Franco was named generalissimo of nationalist Spain, and one month later his government received recognition from Hitler and Mussolini. The Spanish Civil War has often been referred to as the dress rehearsal for the Second World War. With both Hitler and Mussolini supplying Franco with not only weapons but considerable troops, it was clear from the beginning that the significance of the war extended well beyond the Spanish borders.[5] With the military strength of the Germans and Italians added to the nationalist cause, the republicans, if they were to remain unassisted, stood little chance.

The International Brigade, organized by the communists, was thus formed to coordinate international efforts in aid of the republican cause. Philip Bolsover, writing in 1939, describes the international flavour of the Brigade:

They came from all the corners of Europe. They rode under trains across half a dozen international boundaries. From Greece and Bulgaria and Jugoslavia and Hungary where liberty had always been difficult to hold, they made their way to Spain (quoted in Been 1984: 174).

The Soviet Union was the only country which supported the Spanish government outright. Other countries, such as Britain and France, had adopted a policy of 'non-intervention', ostensibly in the hopes that this would cause Germany and Italy to withdraw their support from the nationalists. In fact this policy had no such effect. Germany and Italy had no intention whatsoever of withdrawing, and the fact that that course of action was preferred for them by other nations was of little import. Within this context, then, the non-intervention policy could not be regarded as a neutral stance: it was a policy which effectively aided the fascists, by denying the republicans the possibility of buying arms and other supplies that would help them to sustain their struggle.

What was the response of the British people to Spain? Although there were surely some who supported the government's policy of non-intervention, as the war progressed and as this policy came to be understood as intervention-by-ommission, public opinion began to shift. Particularly on the left, there were many whose passions were ignited by the Spanish Civil War.

For them the conflict seemed to sum up all the great issues of the day, the defence of a freely elected government against overthrow by an armed reactionary clique, the cause of civil liberty and human rights, the universal cause of poor people against their rich oppressors. 'It is better to stand and die than to live on your knees' La Pasionaria had said, evoking a response not just in Spain, but half the world over (Branson & Heinemann 1971: 312).

The republican cause had an increasingly wider base of support in the British public. That it captured the heart and imagination of many of the great writers of the day is well documented (Cunningham 1986). In a poll taken by the *Left Review* in 1937, five writers supported Franco, sixteen had no preference, and one hundred were pro-republican.

Domestically, such support found its expression in such organizations as the National Joint Committee for Spanish Relief, which coordinated efforts between other groups. However, the cornerstone of the movement was the local Aid to Spain committees which existed in almost every town, and were responsible for such things as the collection of food – twenty-nine foodships in all were sent – raising money for medical supplies and aid, as well as functioning as an educational organization, pamphleting and holding meetings to gain wider recognition and support for the republican cause. A total of more than £2 million worth of cash and goods was contributed to help the Spanish people (Green 1970: 317).

Finally, the most significant expression of British support for the republicans was the British Battalion of the International Brigade. Because it was not an 'official war' no exact figures are available, but according to rough estimates, about 2,000 British men volunteered to fight, of whom 1,200 were wounded and 500 were killed.[6] Due to the official policy of non-intervention, this direct involvement was considered unconstitutional, and in January 1937, it became illegal to volunteer, to recruit volunteers, or to aid volunteers for the republicans. The Battalion was organized by the communists, and half of the volunteers were members of the CPGB.

Judith Cook's *Apprentices of Freedom* is about the British Battalion – who they were, why they went, and what they encounted once they got there. In her introduction she comments that the collective public memory of the Battalion is that which was seen through the eyes of its 'distinguished participants'. Yet, she writes,

95 % of the Britons who fought in Spain came from working-class backgrounds, from the ship yards, mines and hunger marches. Few had ever been abroad before and most of them had to leave their families behind them in great hardship. On their return, they did not sit down and write of their experiences, yet they were the British Battalion of the XVth International Brigade (Cook 1979: ix).

For many the Spanish Civil War represented a challenge to put political principles into action, and the participation of the British working class in the republican cause was an extension of the same struggle they had been forging at home. Spain represented the international fight against fascism and oppression.

The outcome of the war is history. By July 1938 the nationalists held three-quarters of the country, and on 15 November the International Brigades paraded in Spain for the last time, where they were bidden farewell by Dolores Ibarruri, 'La Pasionaria':

Comrades of the International Brigades! Reasons of State, political reasons, the welfare of that same cause for which you offered your blood with boundless generosity, are sending you back, some of you to your own countries and others forced to exile. You can go proudly. You are history. You are the heroic example of democracy's solidarity and universality. We shall not forget you, and when the olive tree of peace puts forth its leaves again, mingles with the laurels of the Spanish Republic's victory – come back! (quoted in Green 1970: 324).

The fighting continued for another five months: in January, Barcelona fell, and on 28 March, Valencia and Madrid. Three days later, all fighting ceased.

With the nationalist victory in Spain, the scene had been set for the beginning of the Second World War, and the continuation of the struggle against fascism.

6 Radicalization: coming to commitment

> there is always a honeymoon period in life, when you fall in love ... with
> the job that is really worth your life. Nothing can take the place of that
> period. That is *the* moment, and ought to be, and is.
>
> Trevor Huddleston (Caradon *et al*. 1967: 59)

It is hoped that the previous pages have instilled in the reader an
awareness of the political urgency which characterized the inter-war
years. Haunted by the aftermath of the Great War, reeling from the
consequences of an economic crisis of unprecedented dimensions,
Britain appeared ripe for political change. The more desperately wrong
things seemed to be, the more people believed in the possibility of a
fundamental restructuring of society. As documented in the previous
chapter, both the left and right saw in this time a great, perhaps unique,
potential for the realization of their respective visions of society. The
result was mass political education and participation. But how did this
grand scenario translate into the daily lives of ordinary people? In this
chapter we shall explore how and why the respondents of this study
came to their political convictions.

In Chapter 3, I argued that retrospective data was most useful in
indicating to the researcher what, over time, has remained or become
important to the respondent regarding the way in which he or she has
come to understand his or her life story. Thus, what I am presenting
here is not, of course, a reconstruction of what actually happened in the
lives of the respondents, but rather how respondents remember and
ultimately have made sense of what happened. We do not begin at the
beginning of the story as such; rather we begin at the end – that is the
present day – and look back at the beginning, trying to reconstruct what
has happened from that time forward.

Our task, then, is not to predict but to explain. One recalls here the
words of Freud, reflecting on the construction of causal explanations:

Even supposing that we have a complete knowledge of the aetiological factors
that decide a given result ... we never know beforehand which of the determining
factors will prove the weaker or the stronger. We only say at the end that those

which succeeded must have been the stronger. Hence the chain of causation can always be recognized with certainty if we follow the line of analysis, whereas to predict it along the line of synthesis is impossible... The synthesis is thus not so satisfactory as the analysis; in other words, from a knowledge of the premises we could not have foretold the nature of the result (1920/1979: 395–396).

Thus, this chapter does not address why these individuals, and not others, became politically active; rather our focus is on why these particular people understood and subsequently responded to their environments in the way in which they did. The only thing which can be stated with certainty is that the respondents of this study experienced their environments in such a way that they became politicized. It is our task, then, to identify those factors which must have been the stronger, because it was they in the end which prevailed.

Respondents' stories of radicalization identify three important influences in the awakening of their political consciousnesses: identifiable individuals, including those who were personally known to them and those who were not; intellectual stimulants (such as books, movies, formal and informal education); and the role of highly visible organizations (such as the CPGB and the NUWM). These three influences, to varying degrees in different lives, combined to transform the way in which respondents understood their lived experience.

Before proceeding to our discussion of the accounts of radicalization, it is worth noting that these three influences might, and indeed most probably do, have a catalytic function in the lives of many individuals, helping to transform actual lived experience into a particular understanding of that experience. One is reminded here of Aldous Huxley's comment, 'Experience is not what happens to you, it's what you do with what happens to you' (quoted in Kegan 1982: 11). But, to state that certain categories of influences exist is merely a first step in an analysis of the content and attraction of those particular influences. A deeper understanding of how and why an individual became radicalized in the way in which she did demands an appreciation of the intersection between historical context and personal circumstance. It is precisely this intersection which we shall explore in the following pages.

'Gut socialism' and working-class activism

It's the gut communist or the gut socialist is the most reliable... Come from shortage of food, you know, evicted from their home, unemployed. That's what we call a gut reaction... gut reaction through gut experience (Jack Dash).

One of Jack's earliest memories is of coming home from school, and seeing his mother sitting on a bucket on the pavement, crying, the family having been evicted from the home and all the furniture taken. He remembers his family seeking refuge in the theatre (his mother had been an actress before her marriage), and sleeping in the stalls after the audience had gone home. His mother died of tuberculosis when he was seven, and at fifteen he was orphaned. He explains the effect that these and other, similar experiences had upon him. 'I'm a gut communist. I've been hungry...I mean these things are unforgettable.' Jack was the youngest of four boys, and the only one who later became a socialist. Indeed, one of his brothers became a sergeant in the army, in which he served for twenty-six years. Some might argue that because of their difference in age, these brothers had not in fact encountered the same experiences at the same formative age. While this is true, it would be insufficient to explain the radical difference between their outlooks as a mere function of the age differential, particularly since the family had never been well-off, even when the parents were living. The fundamental difference between Jack and his army sergeant brother was not so much their lived experience, as the way they made sense of that experience.

Jack's first political teacher was a socialist pacifist whom he met while working as a hod-carrier in London's East End. The man told Jack to read certain books, and then to come back and discuss them. 'That was laying, not overnight, but it laid the foundations that made me enquire more and read more...The soil was being fertilized.' Reading the books suggested by the old socialist and discussing them with him had a deep effect on Jack:

It laid the foundations, helped me to understand it, you see by reading it fiction-wise, it's much easier to understand. Where the characters are working-class people, you know, and their struggles, and you identify yourself...you know the problems that are facing them because you're facing it or been through it.

Jack identified himself with the working-class characters in the books he read; the problems which faced them were problems which he had faced in his life. He was receptive to the political message of the books because of its direct applicability to his own situation. Identifying himself with the characters, being simultaneously outside the situation (as a reader) and inside (through familiarity), helped to bring about a change in him.

I was aware something was happening with me; you know, that I wanted to be a political person...I aligned myself with what was being written in the books. Jack London, he had the greatest impact on me of all...It fitted into my brain, and then it was clear, and I knew something; I've got to become a political person, I've got to take part in the struggle. In other words, I really became class conscious.

For Jack, political consciousness was predicted upon class consciousness. He came to identify himself, in the words of Marx, not only as being of his class, but also for his class. He wanted to be a political person, and to take part in the struggle. Through the experience of speaking with others, and reading strongly political fiction, Jack came to see himself as a member of a whole oppressed group of people who experienced similar harsh living conditions for similar reasons.

The third influence which raised Jack's political consciousness was the high visibility of the left-wing groups, and in particular the street-corner speakers to whom he often listened.

The CP and the left of the Labour Party and the socialist groups would hold their street-corner meetings, and they would spell it out night after night wherever the corner, their corner, they were speaking...And if you had a political grounding what I had, then it only reinforced it more and more...You was listening to a fella talking in your own working class way of talking. So you could relate what they was saying to your own experience. They wasn't talking the guff. They wasn't trying to talk in an education manner. They was just saying it in working class, and you related it.

Jack's description of the language used by the street-corner speakers, 'your own working class way of talking', highlights the importance to him of being able to identify himself personally with what was being said. Clearly the success of street-corner speakers in communicating their message was not only due to the content of their speech, but also to its form, and the combination of the two served to facilitate a connection between the orator and the audience. In later years, Jack would himself become a famous orator, attracting crowds of people who identified with what he said and how he said it.[1] In Jack's description there was a perceivable shift in the way he saw the world before and after he became politically conscious. Without his political understanding, he led his life 'looking for better times, hoping for better times'. With it, however, he viewed life with a new clarity, which included in it a pronounced role for himself. 'It fitted into my brain and I knew something. I've got to become a political person. I've got to take part in the struggle.' His political analysis gave him an understanding of why he was unemployed and this understanding gave him the power to do something about it.

Had Jack not become politicized, he explains, he 'would have just been lumpen, and carried on in the same way, accepting things explained by the newspapers, not making no critique of it and just looking for better times, hoping for better times'. His new political consciousness allowed him to understand past experiences from a new perspective.

I began to relate these things back in time when...my mind was being developed politically. I was able to look back and make the analysis of things. But until then, I just accepted things, you know, just accepted life without questioning life.

Jack is conscious of revisiting past experiences and examining them from his subsequently acquired political perspective. Becoming political, however, meant he wanted to take part in the struggle. Whereas previously he had felt he was just looking for better times, he now felt himself newly empowered to help create those better times. Jack's awareness of his class identity was heightened by the political lessons he had learned from the old socialist, from Jack London, and from the street-corner speakers. 'Understanding why you're poor is not to leave your class. It's to want to move everybody along with you.' Jack's expression of class consciousness highlights the inadequacies of Tajfel's social mobility/social change continuum, discussed earlier. For even while Jack, as an individual, could have probably 'improved' his class status (the option taken by his army sergeant brother), this was not something he chose to do. He recognized that his own position was part of a larger social structure, and it was that structure, and not just his position within it, which became the target of his efforts for change.

Walter's political education really began when he was laid off from his job as an office worker, and developed with his subsequent involvement with the NUWM. Walter recalls that at the time he was laid off, he began taking classes in political subjects through the Workers' Educational Association (WEA). His teacher, though a 'very middle-class little sort of lady' was quite left wing, and his intellectual pursuits helped him to understand why he was unemployed. Walter felt that he had been denied his rightful place in society.

I'd got a right, I'd got a duty to have a job to play a part in society, and society was saying 'we don't want you just yet. Do you mind going into cold storage?' I resented it, bitterly resented it. It was a terrific shock to a youngster.

It was this very anger that made Walter receptive to the political analysis he heard in the WEA classroom and preached on the street corners. 'Because my bitterness and annoyance made them all very very acceptable to me, I felt here was somebody that was on my side and that I could identify myself with.' Recognizing that there were others who were in a similar situation to his own, and who were fighting for their rights, instilled in Walter a sense of belonging to a wider group, and through this belonging, a sense of empowerment. As with Jack, Walter's political awakening was the result of becoming class conscious. In both cases, the two processes were not altogether distinguishable, as one naturally fed into and reinforced the other.

Walking to London in the NUWM hunger march in 1934 was 'the really big turning point after which there was no going back...Here I was actually doing something.' Walter joined the Communist Party because he perceived it to be taking action.

You do something. You street chalk, you go on a demonstration, don't wait for the member of Parliament to get up and make a pretty speech. You do something about it ... The Communist Party was a party of action.

Walter's politicization was not a mere appreciation of abstract concepts; it was, rather, inextricably tied to the attraction of being able to take action in a situation which had hitherto rendered him immobile. In becoming politically active, Walter felt that his energies were no longer being wasted; he was not being asked to sit in storage, but rather was taking an active role in affecting his environment. He was a member of a group which was fighting back. Walter describes the comradeship he experienced on the walk:

[We were a] close knit, close knit group. We slept down on the floor together and if there was soap and water available, we got washed together and we ate together and it was wonderful.

The leaders on the march had a particularly strong effect on young Walter. 'Without a doubt my political views were formed by contact with ... Wilf Jobling and Bobby Elliot, the hunger march leaders.' Before joining the march, Walter was 'a nice quiet little lad, brought up in a traditional way', while those he met on the march were 'full-time professional revolutionaries'. By the end of the march, Walter was a committed political activist.

The cases of the two women working-class activists, Rose and Dorothy, differ slightly from those of Jack and Walter, simply by the fact of their gender. While their politicization was also a result of understanding their actual personal circumstances, they experienced double oppression; they suffered in material terms not only because they were working class, but also because they were women. The differential treatment allocated to male and female children in both women's homes was marked.

Rose recalls the effect that seeing wealthy people, whose circumstances contrasted so sharply with her own, had upon her as a young child.

I remember as early as seven or eight years of age, and thinking that it was very odd that there were so many people who could afford to be dressed up. We lived around the corner from the Royal Theatre ... we used to go down and watch them go into the theatre from the taxis and wonder ... here we could hardly buy our own shoes. That made me feel that there was something wrong, somewhere. Why did these people not share their money with us? ... I never felt anger and I never felt envy. I just felt it was wrong somehow.

Perhaps if her family had not lived within viewing distance of the Royal Theatre and she had not had the opportunity to compare her family's situation with that of others, she would not have fully realized that not everyone experienced the same poverty as her family.

Rose's early exposure to politics, combined with the severe living conditions (a hand-to-mouth existence), helped her to confront certain aspects of her environment. Her political understanding of her situation came not only from comparing her situation with that of others, but also through speaking with her socialist father, whom she describes as 'the supporter of all lame dogs', attending socialist Sunday School, and listening to street-corner speakers. The family home was very near to Glasgow Green, which, Rose explains,

was like Hyde Part corner in London. Everybody spoke at little meetings. We used to go there every Sunday morning, one of my brothers and I. So I was up to here in politics from a child.

She describes her mother as 'the one who dealt out the punishments, and also exploited me to a great extent. I always had all the work to do, being the only girl with three brothers.' Her early attitudes towards men grew out of her experiences at home. For while her father was 'a real radical' and supported the suffragettes, 'it never really equated him with doing anything in the house or anything like that'. She explains that she 'couldn't be bothered with men really... I thought men got too much of a good time, I was more or less a drudge in my family... But I felt rebellious that the boys weren't asked to do the things that I was asked to do.' (Interestingly, however, she blames this inequality of workload on her mother.)

In and out of the home, she learned to defend herself and, if necessary, to fight for what she perceived to be rightfully hers. Rose's responsibilities to her family increased with the years; eventually she supported her parents and one of her brothers with money she earned through a sewing business she had started. From a young age, Rose had a fighting spirit, and was determined that she would influence her environment. She explains her politicization by saying, 'when I was very young, I understood it instinctively'. But that instinct was itself a result of an exposure to politics which provided an adequate explanation for the oppression she experienced.

Dorothy's family situation was similar in many ways to that of Rose, with the exception that Dorothy's parents were not politically minded. She was the oldest daughter, and the second oldest child of six. Her elder brother had had meningitis as a child.

He always got a bit softer treatment. Myself, I got the hard treatment. My mother used to give us good hidings... she used to beat us... I always fought against it, I never gave in... I used to say to myself. I don't care if she kills me... Because inside I was sort of fighting back anyway.

Dorothy would sooner have had no life than a life of submission and being beaten down. She recalls that she was 'brought up to believe that everybody else was always better than us, and that you felt there was something wrong with you. You weren't the equal of the other people.' The family was very poor, and the three children shared a three-quarter-size bed. Dorothy started work half time when she was twelve, getting up at 5:30 a.m., walking two-and-a-half miles, and working ten hours a day, for not more than 15p a week (working and going to school on alternate days). In Dorothy's home, too, responsibility for the household fell to her, and she, like Rose, eventually became the main provider for the whole family. She lived at home until she was forty 'because I had to look after my father until he died'.[2]

But Dorothy was determined that she would not be defeated by the oppressive environment in which she lived. By the time she was exposed to left-wing politics, she had been fighting back for a long time. Politics gave her yet more strength, as from it she gained a wider perspective on her own situation. As she grew older, she came to understand the social reasons behind the harsh circumstances of her family and those about her. In a letter to me she explains:

So due to lack of Education and any inspiration in the home later comes the desire for enjoyment in Knowledge and Education hence first joining the Ethical Society, then the WEA and Left Book Club – creates a strong enough desire for practical socialism and drives you on to want to change the lives of your Poverty stricken neighbours – I would say this is why I am me.

The history class she took at the WEA had a strong effect upon her.

Then one became acutely politically aware and was able to sort of look at issues and think more about it. And probably think more intelligently about it... history made you look at things in a different way... It made you think deeper about things really.

From that time forward, Dorothy became increasingly interested in politics and socialism. It was while attending meetings of the Left Book Club that she met her husband. 'He was 100% socialist... I was conscious of the fact that I wanted to know more about it, and that I could find out more about it from [him].' In Dorothy's case, the politics matched her own experience, and the poverty of her early life would continue to motivate her to help others. 'I feel at one with people that are at the bottom. And with all the hardships they have. I can feel, not only sympathy, but understand their position and understand what they feel and want to get them out.' Here Dorothy expresses a strong sense of class consciousness and solidarity, and it has been this which has functioned as the primary motivator behind her political activism.

The four people described in this section experienced a relatively similar process of politicization. Although they were exposed to politics under different circumstances and at different ages, in each case the politics made sense to them because of their direct experience of oppression. Jack expresses the role of experience in his education:

The greatest teacher of all...has been unemployment, poverty. Poverty's the greatest teacher, provided you want to understand why you're poor...The greatest university in the world is life. Life is the university and industry has been my college.

For each of these four, the role of conventional education was negligible; all of them had finished full-time schooling by the age of fourteen (though both Walter and Dorothy later attended classes at the WEA, which had considerable impact upon them).

Of the working-class respondents, only Rose came from an overtly political family; her father was a socialist, and she attended socialist Sunday School from a young age. While Walter's father was a strong trade unionist, his political activity seemed to be of a limited sort. However, like Rose, Walter's political activity, in the form of pamphleting for the Labour Party, pre-dated the genuine awakening of his political consciousness, which did not come until many years later when he was laid off his first job. The situation was just the reverse for Dorothy and Jack, both of whom came from apolitical families. Their first political activism was a direct expression of their political beliefs. Because Rose was 'up to here in politics from a child', she did not share the experience of the other three, in which becoming politically conscious brought with it the perception of greater control over one's life. For Jack, Walter and Dorothy, their political awakening was a powerful and empowering experience, for even while it did not alter the material conditions which they suffered, it did offer them the possibility of being able to change those conditions, not only for themselves, but for others as well. They were, in Walter's words, 'actually doing something'.

Class consciousness was an integral part of the working-class respondents' political consciousness; their radicalization was a process of understanding why they were poor. In this way, direct experience in early life played a central role in the nature of the way in which their political consciousness was raised. However, the mere fact of being unemployed, or living hand to mouth, was not in itself a sufficient catalyst for radicalization. Without an analysis of the situation, individuals might have experienced themselves as simply unfortunate, victims of circumstances beyond their control, or possibly even blameworthy for their situations.

Such analysis was stimulated by encounters with the three sources of influence identified earlier: various people; books and schooling; and the high visibility of left-wing organizations. Through such influences, working-class respondents came to understand their own experiences of oppression in a wider political context. This enhanced their class consciousness, as they no longer perceived themselves as isolated individuals, but rather as members of a larger, oppressed group.

'Identifying with the underdogs' and middle-class activism

The world of these three quarters of an acre of land became very complete, because you didn't have to go outside it for anything. Everything was provided for, and the environment was lovely to play in...one went into the fields and occasionally one went into the town, but one lived in a very sort of protected, insulated, cosseted environment. And later on, of course, when I became politicized and a communist, I felt a deep sense of inferiority because I felt, well, working-class kids don't have this same fantastic amount of privilege and protection and ease and security (Christopher).

Christopher's description both of the physical environment in which he grew up, as well as his later reaction to it, encapsulates the tension experienced by most of the middle-class activists. Christopher came to question his cosseted environment as a result of his politicization. To understand this process, it is, again, most instructive to examine the intersection of the historical context and his personal circumstances. Again, the catalysts which forged the bridge between these two trajectories are the same three general influences which were operative in the radicalization accounts of the working-class activists.

In the case of Christopher, the importance of one individual to his radicalization is more pronounced than in the accounts offered by any of the other respondents. Christopher describes his relationship with his brother John:

We were in school together and we were inseparable. I've never understood how it was that John tolerated me. I think perhaps because I so adored him and so admired him, I just wanted to be with him all the time, and listen to everything he had to say about any subject.

The subject which stirred John most was that of politics; by the age of sixteen he was a committed Marxist. Not surprisingly, then, he was the source of Christopher's earliest political tutelage.

It never occurred to me that he could be wrong about anything, so I felt sure he was right. On the other hand, I didn't feel that it applied to me...until one day...he said 'You could be a communist too', and it was rather like St. Paul on the road to Damascus, bang, flash, wollop...I began reading the Third International pamphlets he had with him.

John exposed Christopher to left-wing literature, and the latter responded by making a concerted effort to educate himself about the issues. After about a year, he joined the Communist Party.

However, the seeds of Christopher's political awakening had been germinating for several years. He had grown up in the wake of the First World War, and had been very influenced by the many anti-war books which were published during that time. He explains the strong effect this literature had upon him:

I read...*All Quiet On The Western Front* which absolutely knocked me over with horror and compassion and outrage...and I also read Graves' *Goodbye To All That*...from all of these sources, one got a notion of life in the trenches in '14–'18, and I was so upset about this. In fact I think it's almost true to say that nothing that I experienced during World War Two, in which I was a soldier, horrified me as much as reading those books did.

Christopher also recalls the effect which several movies had upon him. One Russian film in particular, *Road to Life*, in which the protagonist reminded him of John, 'bit into my soul. I went to see it two or three times in one week.' As a result of these impressions, Christopher developed strong anti-war feelings, calling an anti-war meeting in his school, and refusing to join the Officer's Training Corps, which was required of every student.

It is neither possible nor necessary to draw absolute distinctions between the three sources of influence. For instance, it was through John that Christopher came into contact with the Communist Party. Nonetheless, the Party itself came to exercise a considerable influence on the development of his political thinking. Similarly, the Russian movie affected him deeply not only, and perhaps not even primarily, because of its message, but also because the protagonist reminded him of his brother. A comparison between the accounts of Christopher and Rose is interesting here. Christopher's affiliation with political people and groups preceded his own political awakening; in this sense he was similar to Rose. Yet he also experienced an almost cathartic moment, in which he realized that these political writings and events had, or could have, personal significance for him and the way he led his life; Rose reports no similar moment.

Christopher explains that the environment was ripe for left-wing analysis: 'it was difficult for any intelligent person not to begin to wonder about the political state of affairs and whether the society we were in was the kind that ought to exist'. He elaborates upon this:

You can see it, can't you, how unemployment, fascism, war preparations, political reaction...one knew that all the right-wing conservatives were really anti-semitic and pro-Hitler in their heart of hearts, and they really wanted Hitler to attack Russia...one saw in Russia this wonderful, creative, just, egalitarian society with infinite potential, and everything seemed to add up, and everything seemed to cut the same way.

Christopher's focus was clearly on the international situation. His attraction to left-wing politics was primarily a result of attempting to make sense of the mounting world crises. He describes his political awakening as

a real conversion...you suddenly see the world in a different perspective, the world becomes much more luminous and exciting and comprehensible and involving and significant and you feel that you have a sort of function in the world, as distinct from being a little dry leaf that is blown around by the wind.

Christopher's description is a very powerful one. In becoming politicized, his concept of the world and of himself was altered. Through applying his political ideas to his own lived experience, he came to re-evaluate the previously unquestioned, unproblematic material conditions of his life, his cosseted environment.

The awakening of Christopher's political consciousness was followed almost immediately by a flurry of political activity. As with many of the respondents, the more resistance he encountered, the stronger his left-wing self-identification became. Declaring oneself to be a socialist is to define oneself in a positive, as well as in an oppositional way, as group membership derives its meaning in contrast to other groups. A strong feature of socialism, particularly pronounced in the 1930s with the rise of global fascism, was that it was anti-fascist. Christopher describes his involvement at the Mosley rally at Olympia Stadium:

I got up and started yelling anti-fascist slogans and a bunch of these Blackshirts converged on me and yanked me out of my seat and dragged me along the corridor...I was thrown down some concrete steps and some of my teeth were loosened by a well-aimed punch from a Blackshirt...I managed to...make my getaway, crowned with heroism that I'd actually done what the party said and made a disturbance and got beaten up.

In this situation, the opposition he encountered was not only ideological, but physical as well. Christopher was proud to have taken part in the anti-fascist demonstration. Far from being a little dry leaf, he was making a public stance for his principles. Being beaten up for doing so left him, in his eyes, crowned with heroism. Once having encountered resistance and having risked his personal safety for his political beliefs, the beliefs became more internalized, part of his immediate, personal experience. Through his political discussions with his elder brother, his reading, and joining the Communist Party, his radicalization was complete.

Frida was raised in an environment very similar to that of Christopher. Indeed, they are the only two respondents who knew one another growing up; their families were part of the same Cambridge community. Having lived in a relatively self-contained and protected environment, Frida began to ask political questions with the rise of fascism. 'I really woke up in '33, when the Jewish persecution began.' Her parents had a big home, and were able to offer their hospitality to a number of refugees, 'but they didn't look on it as a political thing, they probably looked on it as humanitarian'. Frida was one of five children, and though none of them have been as politically active as she, all but one have been considerably engaged in left-wing politics over a long period of time. From this information, one might surmise that the home environment was relatively conducive to an endorsement of left-wing causes, even while, as Frida notes, her parents would not have regarded their many involvements as political.

Interestingly, however, Frida remembers feeling that she didn't fit into that environment, which was very academically oriented. Because of her long illness, her regular schooling was suspended at an early age. During this time, she grew estranged from the community that under other circumstances would have been hers. 'I think I was always the stupid one in the family, the unacademic, uneducated one, and my sympathies were strongly with people who were underprivileged.'

During her convalescence in Italy, Frida recalls seeing the Mussolini Blackshirts, and the strong impression that made on her. 'That was very upsetting... One saw that there were these things happening. First them, and then the Jewish question, [and] all the terrible unemployment in Germany at that time.' In the early thirties, Frida became increasingly politicized, through exposure to Communist Party members, street theatre, and the unemployed in the North, and through travelling to the Moscow Theatre Festival in 1935. However, it was the Spanish Civil War which was the turning point for Frida. 'The Spanish war brought me right over to the left.' Frida was given the opportunity to drive an ambulance to Spain. 'One feels "I must make this decision and do it"... you just have to take that decision.' The decision to go to Spain was the culmination of a process which had been ongoing for some years. The decision itself involved much more than whether or not to go to

Spain. It was, as well, her declaration to herself that she would play as active a role as possible in addressing what she perceived to be the social ills surrounding her.

In Frida's description of her radicalization, there is no one individual who stands out as having been particularly influential. Nor does she refer to books which changed her thinking, and she actively dismisses the role that formal schooling played in her development (although one might argue that its absence was itself a formative influence, particularly as it set her apart from those around her). However, the importance of family sympathies should not be underestimated. Her parents were very involved in the Aid to Spain movement, a cause in which many of her siblings were also engaged in varying capacities. In addition, her theatrical and musical involvements led her first to the North of England, where she encountered poverty on a scale which she had not previously witnessed, and then later to Germany and the Soviet Union. Finally, she had much exposure to left-wing analysis of the political situation, both through her travels and through personal acquaintances, including Christopher's brother John. The combination of these factors proved to be very forceful, and while she had been politically sympathetic with left-wing causes for some time, it was not until she made the decision to go to Spain that she felt herself to be fully politically committed.

Eileen was the only daughter of a mother whose own expectations had been thwarted early in life.[3] The effect of this on Eileen was twofold: her mother was determined that Eileen should be able to continue her education, yet at the same time her mother beat her regularly. 'She was so frustrated, I think, that it took that form.' Thus in the opening minutes of our first interview, she explained, 'my mother had a great influence on my radical thinking, negatively and positively'. Eileen did not experience the double oppression that Rose and Dorothy did, because the material needs of her family were generally met. Nonetheless, the intersection of group membership is quite interesting in her case: being middle class, she and her family enjoyed relative prosperity, particularly in comparison with the other neighbourhood families. Yet, being female, she was beaten on a regular basis in her home, and thus knew oppression, not because of her class but because of her gender. However, the connection between 'the feminist thing', the socio-economic disparity in the neighbourhood, and politics in general did not come for some time.

Throughout Eileen's life, there have been particular individuals who have exercised a strong influence in the development of her political thinking. In her early years, these people, both known (such as women in the neighbourhood) and unknown to her personally (Edith Sitwell, Virginia Woolf, and Winifred Holtby, all of whom had spoken at her university), tended to be women, or 'heroines'. 'I had my models of women ... I had plenty of heroines when I was a girl, and I think latterly, it's been heroes.' Eileen explains her understanding of the role of heroes and heroines in her life:

They'd sustain you because they are on the same wave length as you. I think that's it ... Who are your heroes and heroines? They're people who you think believe as you do, but are much better than you. And so you can admire them. I have a great capacity for admiration, but not for many people.

At college, Eileen 'would have liked to be friends with sociology students and people who were doing politics ... I just never had that courage because I felt out of my depth'. There, she got lost in music and religion. 'I used to go and play for six hours on the piano and get rid of my loneliness ... And then I turned to religion.' Throughout this time, her 'rebellion was seething underneath', until finally 'when I did rebel, I rebelled bitterly'.

There was a variety of experiences which contributed to this rebellion. However, the 'cataclysmic period', the time of Eileen's 'political bath', was when she was working as a secretary for a marketing manager in Manchester.

I suddenly discovered that he wasn't thinking about the war at all, but all that they were doing in this division was having ideas about the markets after the war ... I read funny reports that said we shouldn't build great blocks of flats because these can become places where workers get together ... into subversion, revolution and all the rest.

Her awareness had already been awakened by reading books of the Left Book Club, and discussing ideas with various people. But this experience made it all real; it connected the abstract ideas to her own life. Eileen's rejection of God and religion was part of the process of becoming political.

Right and wrong and the evangelical influence ... is very easily transposed into political thinking ... You can see how I kept my moral certitude ... The religious thing ... had been going slowly, but that was the end of that. You didn't rely on a God who would put things right.

Having become politicized, Eileen was no longer timid, because she felt she understood what needed to be done. She describes her radicalization as having been

a very sudden illumination, that you saw a pattern to life, and you understood how life operated. But it wasn't chaotic as you kept thinking. And it didn't depend on God ... It was the scientific approach to life ... and understanding, and illumination so that you could cope with life and you had something that showed you how it worked and that you could take part in that, that you were a part.

Having a conception of how life operated was central to Eileen's self-perception of being able to take a part (to be active), and of being a part (to belong).

Edward, Mary and Elizabeth's politicization was related to, if not a direct result of, their understanding of religious teachings. The perceived connection between socialism and Christianity is most pronounced in the case of Edward, who is an Anglican minister. Edward's conception of Christianity made him receptive to socialism.

Socialism ... is sharing, and in particular sharing with people who are least advantaged, and capitalism is grasping ... It was self-evident that sharing was more in line with the issues of the New Testament than grasping ... socialism was a Christian way of living.

The intersection between the two he describes as 'dialectical ... each playing into the other'. Central to the connection between them is the belief that to work for socialism is to work for the realization of God's will on earth.

When we pray 'Thy Kingdom Come on Earth as it is in Heaven', this is a very serious prayer, and one that will in the course of human development be made actual ... That means fighting against all the obstacles which are preventing it happening now.

Edward speaks of a 'dynamic God working in history'. (Not surprisingly, the sentiments expressed by Edward here are shared completely by Trevor, for whom Christianity and socialism are also inextricably linked.)

Edward's parents were deeply religious, particularly his mother, and were members of a Christian fundamentalist organization. Thus, he was raised in an environment in which the expression of deep commitment – of a totally non-political nature – was a part of daily life. When Edward broke with this fundamentalist group 'it was the final cutting of the umbilical cord ... The sort of religious upbringing that I had didn't make sense to me' because it was concerned with abstract issues of morality but ignored the plight of the underprivileged on earth. Edward had, in a sense, expanded the parameters of his parents' commitment, dedicating himself not only to religious principles, but to their practical application.

At Harrow, Edward did not identify with his peers.

I was always one of the underdogs. I was never much good at games and that's what you needed to be ... I used to feel more sympathy with people like the house butler ... than I did for my colleagues. They were the underdogs like I was.

One can hear in Edward's words the tension between his own class background and his early sympathies with those outside his class. These feelings did not find their expression in political analysis until many years later. 'Two things obviously had to worry everybody; one was the threat of war, and the other was the terrible suffering of the unemployed.' Edward's interpretation of the Bible had brought him to work with the unemployed and underprivileged, but still this was not complemented by a political perspective until he became a member of the Left Book Club and was intellectually influenced by what he read. He had been a strong believer in the League of Nations, but Mussolini's invasion of Abyssinia shattered this belief.

It could have been prevented, but we didn't operate it [the League of Nations] properly. Why didn't we...? John Strachey [*The Theory and Practice of Socialism*] told me why: it was because of capitalism. I read this and I was convinced, and I've been convinced ever since.

His worldview was thus both political and religious, and his understanding of the world altered him. 'I had much more confidence then than I had had at school ... the clearer you could see an issue, the more confident you are in supporting it. And I was very sort of clear about it at that time.' Edward joined the Left Book Club, and spoke on street corners for the NUWM and later for the Aid to Spain movement.

Certain individuals did play an important role in Edward's politicization, particularly in making clear the connection between Christianity and socialism. He says, 'I can think of so many people I owe a lot to in showing me what I think is the way.' Among these people was his Godfather, Dick Sheppard, who was a well-known priest and a founder of the Peace Pledge Union. He was, Edward remembers, 'absolutely fearless. He would speak out on what he thought, and to hell with anybody.' Edward recalls presenting to him his plans for what he would do in London's impoverished East End. 'I said to him "do you think that's too wild?" He said "Too wild? Too wild? My dear chap, be as wild as you possibly can, don't let anybody tame you."' Edward also describes Stanley Evans, a politically active left-wing priest who had an 'enormous impact' on him, and who was an inspiration for him. Together they organized the pro-Soviet, pro-socialist newsletter *Religion and the People*. Edward's politicization can thus be understood as a result of his growing understanding, and as a deepening, of his religious faith.

Mary's early religious upbringing played an important part in laying the foundations for her later political beliefs.

You haven't...got to suffer yourself necessarily to mind about other people ...perhaps even more when you're comfortable, you after all do read, don't you...one saw...the tragedies on the streets, because there were the maimed soldiers from the war and...groups of Welsh miners singing, because there was tremendous unemployment, tremendous, terrible unemployment...One didn't not know that other conditions were there.

Again, the comparison of one's relatively comfortable situation with that of others less fortunate was an important initial step to becoming politically aware. However, the awareness of such difference was a necessary but insufficient condition for interpreting the cause of social inequality; although Mary was aware of these other conditions, her consciousness was not a political one. This shift occurred when she began teaching in Yorkshire. There she met another teacher who had studied at Oxford, and had been very political there. Through her, Mary began reading books of the Left Book Club and became more politically informed. This coincided with her exposure to an environment in which the devastation of unemployment was far more visible than it had been in Surrey.

Mary explained the attraction to the left-wing politics of her friend: 'It was because I'd taken the New Testament seriously as a little girl.' Further, it was 'being with somebody who was used to the feeling that we could do something about the wrong things.' Although Mary had lost her religious faith before she became political, the social tenets of that faith still influenced her perception of right and wrong. Her political understanding, however, provided her with a practical course of action which she could take in order to fight for those principles.

Elizabeth's politicization was perhaps the most gradual of all the participants of the study. She recalls a dream she had in early adulthood, about coming to 'some kind of attitude towards life which on the whole suits you and belongs to you, doesn't belong to anybody else'.

I was in a little boat, just a little lugsail, it was a tiny little boat and it had only got one sail...I was setting sail across the sea on my own. On my right...there was a huge steamer...and everybody on board, they were dancing and laughing...it was setting off, it knew exactly where it was going, they were all going together and they were having a merry time. I didn't want to go on that steamer, it didn't belong to my type of thinking at all, but I was really quite terrified of setting out in this little lugsail. I realised that that's what I was doing and what sort of person I was, and you couldn't be other than that.

In this description, Elizabeth differentiates herself and her life plan from what she perceives to be the happy-go-lucky, pre-planned paths of other people. It is evident throughout the passage that she values her independence and the exploration of the unknown (even while the prospect of setting out alone might have been frightening). Moreover, she does not see herself as a passenger on a ship steered by someone else, but rather as the person in control – inasmuch as one can be on a sailboat, allowing for fluctuations in the environment. While this dream expresses certain aspects of her life plan, it is not overtly political, although it does communicate that she would not be happy dancing and being merry all her life. Not only the image, but also the language she employs is striking. This life plan is uniquely hers, as she affirms, 'it doesn't belong to anyone else'. Her self-image is very pronounced, as is her general construction of the environment (broadly interpreted as the world), and her place within it.

While she was a socialist even before college, she has become more politically active and radical every subsequent decade of her life. The process of her politicization can be best understood as an unfolding of her religious beliefs. As a child, religion did not play a very important role in her life, although she had attended church regularly. At sixteen, she began reading about Buddhism, Confucianism and Hinduism, 'which opened up my mind considerably... From that time I was a Unitarian, although I didn't know that such things... existed.' However, while at college she encountered the Unitarians. 'It was such a joy to find something that you had been looking for that opened a tremendously wide vista to you.' In Unitarianism she found 'greater spiritual understanding, of respect for spirituality in anybody, the whole world over... It wasn't just a Christian thing, and all the rest were heathen.' This last sentence reveals the potentially political element of religion as she understood it. It opened doors to the rest of the world, rather than closing them.

Huddersfield, to which Elizabeth and her husband moved several years later, offered a stark contrast to the relatively comfortable living conditions she had seen in the South of England. 'When I came to Huddersfield, there was tremendous unemployment and poverty here. In fact I was horrified. Huddersfield after Cambridge seemed a dreadful place.' Elizabeth's work in the soup kitchen brought her into direct contact with the impoverished. Although she and her family lived very comfortably, Elizabeth decided to take an active role to improve the plight of others. Because the shortage of food seemed to be the most immediately pressing demand, her political activity focused on famine relief, not in the Huddersfield area alone, but across the globe. Unlike other famine relief committees set up in England whose 'only concern [was] for the nursing mothers and children in Europe... [the Huddersfield committee focused on] the different standards of living in the world'. In this work with world famine relief, her religious and political beliefs found their meeting point.

The class interface

The particulars of the stories vary, as lives do, and yet, with all of them there is a sense in which politicization was experienced as a recognition of the familiar, something which made sense, which perhaps had even been intuited but had not found formal expression. Through their politics, respondents felt they had found their way. Jack Lindsay recalls the effect that reading Marx had on him: 'From almost the first moment I felt that at long last I had come home; I had found the missing links ... ' (1982: 761). But the stories are not identical; there are some interesting contrasts and comparisons to be made between the working-class and middle-class respondents' accounts of becoming radicalized. These fall roughly into five broad categories: (1) the role of class consciousness in radicalization; (2) the importance of religious beliefs to political understanding; (3) the question of national versus international focus of initial political orientation; (4) the process of radicalization and the question of unique moments; and (5) the perceived shift in locus of control as a result of radicalization.

In all of the working-class respondents' accounts, becoming class conscious and becoming politically conscious were two closely inter- twined, and perhaps at times even indistinguishable, processes. One recalls here the regularity with which respondents made reference to seeing that there were others like themselves. Everyone around them experienced the same economic hardship as themselves; becoming political meant, amongst other things, recognition of the existence as well as of the importance of this group membership. Proclaiming solidarity with their class was thus an integral part of their politicization.

As discussed earlier, social identity theory posits that the concept of group membership is only meaningful when there are multiple groups. Part of saying who one is, is saying who one is not, and moreover, who is not in one's group. This has interesting implications for our present discussion. Jack describes himself as 'deeply class conscious. I knew what the battle was. It was us and them.' He describes his 'deep hatred for capitalism. Monopoly and international cartels, I have a deep hatred for them. I hate them, you know really hate them, and despise them as well.' Again he emphasizes that these feelings have come 'through my life's experience and my politics.' For Jack, lines of group membership are determined by individuals' relationships to the means of production.

He declares emphatically: 'It's never changed from the given line, us and them, never changed, not with me it hasn't. And I won't let it change.' But is 'us' only to include other working-class people? Jack's response to this is qualified. 'It's the gut communist or the gut socialist is the most reliable.' About non-working class activists, he says:

Well, you welcomed them, but you were always prepared for a sell-out. Like the intellectuals who joined the movement and joined the CP...But after all, Lenin was an intellectual. When the intellectuals join the Party, all you've got to do is to be on your guard. But you must accept them.

Jack acknowledges the importance of the intellectuals to the movement, but at the same time he is quite sceptical of activists whose politics do not come from their lived experience, as they did with him.

Because Walter's politics were so intricately linked to his own experience – most of the people with whom he was in association shared the harsh experience of unemployment that he had endured – he regards more privileged socialists with a bit of caution.

Class identity, I suppose, is important. For an upper class person to adopt a socialist outlook on life, is if anything unusual, I would say. They've got to be very convicted, very honest with themselves to do it.

In saying that socialists who are upper class must be very honest with themselves, Walter implicitly introduces the question of motivation: why would people of privilege renounce a system which so obviously benefits them? How is this renunciation expressed? In words alone? Can the appreciation of the abstract concept of social equality really function as a catalyst for the awakening of a socialist consciousness?

Walter says that his feelings about his own social class have been 'all-important' to his political work. 'I was with my own people on the hunger marches, I was with my own people on the lower deck of the Royal Navy.' Elsewhere, however, his feelings appear to be more ambiguous. Speaking about a middle-class man who was killed on the Ebro Front in Spain, he says, 'He should never have gone to Spain, an educated person like that...he was much too important to the British working class back home to be just used as a, cannon fodder is hardly the word, but...' The implications of this statement are not altogether clear: should only working-class men have risked their lives for the republican cause?[4]

While working-class respondents became politicized by 'understanding why they were poor', for the middle-class participants radicalization meant applying intellectual, abstract concepts to situations which did not directly impinge upon their own circumstances. Thus they spoke not only of their class, but of the importance of class, with much less frequency; they did not, by and large, perceive it as being central to their political radicalization. The most pronounced expression of this is in Mary's response to a question regarding her family class background:

I don't think it's important. But I suppose if someone was doing research on it they would have shoved me down as lower middle class. (In other words, in your own mind that wasn't important?) No, I mean I was just a person.

Mary's comment that she was 'just a person' implicitly rejects the significance of her class membership. When I tried to probe further on the question of the importance of class, she responded, 'Obviously what I should like most would be a classless society, and certainly I come myself from what obviously was and still is a middle-class, but I'm not really sure what you're getting at.' And yet the meaning of this question was very clear to working-class respondents. Elsewhere, however, Mary does speak of the importance of knowing of the harsh living conditions of others, as cited earlier. The recognition of severe social contrast appears to be a necessary but insufficient condition for the awakening of a socialist consciousness. Locating one's position on the social hierarchy does not in itself lead to the identification of oneself as a socialist. It is, rather, the way in which one explains the existence and maintenance of social difference which contributes more significantly to the process of radicalization. Moreover, one might push the observation still further, to argue that the appreciation of one's relative privilege is not, in itself, as forceful a politicizing catalyst as appreciation of one's relative deprivation.

Christopher describes the importance of class to his political outlook. He says that in the environment in which he was raised, there was

an ethos whereby being rich and ostentatious and having big cars and things like that was vulgar and stupid and uninteresting and that working people had a kind of dignity and worth which people who just made their money in the city didn't have.

This produced in him almost a sense of inferiority because of his own class status, which remained with him until he joined the army in 1942.

I was still a member of the Communist Party, and had a standard outfit of beliefs...particularly about the working class being the revolutionary class...I found in the army that my mates...were not in every respect superior to me, not even physically...I certainly could no longer regard [them] as the sort of mythic heroes that working-class people had been built up as.

The way in which Christopher describes his earlier attitudes towards the working class implicitly acknowledges his own naivety; to him, they were unknown mythic heroes. Again, one can appreciate the subtlety of the 'us and them' dynamics of self- and other-identification. Christopher, as a communist, sought to distance himself from the interests of his class. Still, however, his lack of familiarity with those outside his class produced in him an unrealistic image of the working class – one which many would characterize not as the product of class consciousness, but rather of romanticism.

Again, social identity theory is potentially useful in the discussion of the relationship of class consciousness to the process of radicalization. For working-class respondents, radicalization meant that involuntary group membership (class background), and voluntary group membership (becoming a socialist, and affirming one's solidarity with one's class), were in fact complementary and mutually reinforcing processes. In a sense, one could say that their social identity was enhanced. The same was not true for middle-class respondents, however. For them, while membership of the involuntary group of family class background was constant, feelings about that membership shifted significantly. In this way, the very basis of their social identity was radically altered.

The 'us and them' dichotomy poses a particular dilemma for middle-class socialists. Because of the inevitable split between their voluntary and involuntary group membership, they will never fully belong to one side or the other. Even in their fight for socialism, they will be with the working class, but never of them. Freire, in *Pedagogy of the Oppressed*, discusses the transformation of consciousness which radicalization of middle-class individuals must entail:

Discovering himself to be an oppressor may cause considerable anguish, but it does not necessarily lead to solidarity with the oppressed. Rationalizing his guilt through paternalistic treatment of the oppressed, all the while holding them fast in a position of dependence, will not do. Solidarity requires that one enter into the situation of those with whom one is solidary; it is a radical posture...true solidarity with the oppressed means fighting at their side to transform the objective reality (1972: 34–35).

It is significant that 'true solidarity' does not mean pretending to be a member of the oppressed group, but rather fighting at their side. A middle-class socialist need not deny or feel guilty about her class background. She should, rather, acknowledge, accept, and even use it to further the cause she believes in. Ultimately this is not only the most honest, but the most constructive approach. The involuntary and voluntary group memberships are no longer set in direct opposition to each other, but the resources derived from the former are used to benefit the latter.

Frida was not unaware of her fortunate position regarding finances. 'I was lucky because...most of the things I did, I got paid my subsistence,

I was never properly paid for any of these things I did. I suppose my parents had a good income and I was never bothered.' Her statement that she was never bothered does not mean that she did not care about her own middle-class background, but rather that she would use this fact to the best advantage of the cause she believed in. Because she was less dependent upon a steady wage, she had a freedom of choice which many others lacked. 'This feeling that one comes from a middle class origin is quite a strong one... I think what one does is use whatever contacts and position or money one's got to work for the movement.' Frida's attitude is a very practical one: she will use money, position, and all other amenities that come with being middle class to further the cause of the movement. She aligns herself with the disadvantaged, while not pretending to be one of them.

Thus one can see that the role of class consciousness in the process of radicalization was very different for working-class and middle-class respondents. The reasons for this might be several: (1) Working-class respondents had direct experience of oppression. Understanding socialist principles was thus not a purely abstract exercise, as it had direct application to their lives and the lives of those around them. That class was an important and divisive social influence was made clear to them by the material conditions of their daily existence. (2) The experience of relative deprivation might be more forceful than that of relative privilege in encouraging people to perceive social issues in terms of class. (3) There was a tension between involuntary and voluntary group membership for middle-class socialists. Being middle class might appear to undermine or even threaten the way they identify themselves as socialists. For working-class respondents, these two categories reinforced each other.

The importance of religious influences on the formation of political beliefs seems to vary significantly between respondents, and slightly between classes. In one form or another, it was present in the early lives of all the middle-class respondents, whereas this was not the case for the working-class respondents. In three of the middle-class cases (Edward, Mary and Elizabeth) religious beliefs appear to function as the basis of political ideas. But even in the lives of the other three middle-class respondents, religion had been a strong early influence. Although Eileen had been very religious as an adolescent, part of her political awakening was a full rejection of her religious beliefs: 'it didn't depend on God'. Frida never speaks of herself as being particularly religious, even as a child. Still, her father was a minister, and one can assume that religion must have had a central role in family life. Christopher's father, though not himself a believer, was the son of a clergyman. Christopher recalls that his father would read to his children the twenty-three tales of Tolstoy. 'He loved those tales and so did I and we all did. They are profoundly Christian stories...' Throughout these accounts, religion appears to have been at least a formative influence.

This is true in only two cases of the working-class respondents: Rose and Dorothy. Rose's family were observant Jews, and stories of preparation for the Sabbath or for Passover run throughout the accounts of her childhood. She remembers, 'I believed in my religion right up till I was sixteen. I used to go to the synagogue on my own because of course I like to listen to the choir... and another reason was that it took me away from the chores.' She recalls someone saying to her '"people say God knows, it means nobody knows". That's stuck in my mind all my life – it's absolutely true.' Rose became an atheist at sixteen, rejecting her religion 'though not [her] people'. She explains that her socialism had replaced her religion: 'When I learned about socialism and I realised that everybody was equal... I didn't have the same attitude to life as just a religious person who thought the Jews were the chosen people.' When she married a non-Jew, her parents would not attend her wedding. Dorothy's family went to church regularly. At one point in our interview, she says 'I don't think I've ever enjoyed my life. It's always been a life of duty really...' Her husband, sitting nearby, then interjects 'Methodism, that's what's responsible...', to which she quickly responds 'I don't think the Church of England is anything to do with me. Nothing whatever.' Despite the fact that both Rose and Dorothy rejected any form of religion once they grew older, it was, nonetheless, an important part of their growing experience.

Jack describes the role of religion in his early life. He explains why he was a choir boy in the church: 'you ought to get something to eat, with the charities you know, they used to bring round food to church and meals was given out, that was the reason...it was a materialistic approach, what gains I could get from it in terms of the charity organizations'. As a child, he won awards for his knowledge of religion, but still he did not accept those beliefs as his own:

'cause it didn't make any intelligence to me...I used to go to Hyde Park and listen to the discussion and meetings on religion for and against it and I related it to my own life, you know if there was a God why was we going hungry. And it gradually built up. From a physical living experience, and I couldn't accept it no more, with war how could you?

Summarizing the role of religion in respondents' radicalization, we can say that in three cases – all middle class – it was very important, and in an additional five – three middle class, two working class – it was present if not overly significant. For Jack, religion was only marginally important, and in Walter's entire account of his upbringing, there is not one mention of it. The only respondent who seemed actively antagonistic towards religion was Louie. She left the church when her mother died.

The parson said, 'Louie', he says, 'why don't you call me father?' I said 'I lost my father in the war and there's nobody else who'll take his place.' I says 'I'm not coming to church any more if I've got to call you father.' 'Can't you call me vicar?' I said 'I'll call you nothing. I'll not be in religion any more'.

She then tells the story of a religious teacher she had.

She used to do the sign of the cross, and I used to follow her deliberately ... I said 'You keep kneeling down' I says 'I shall fall over you every time.' And I fell over her oh at least six times ... Deliberately. It caused a stir every time. And I said 'I'm finishing with religion. I've had enough. I don't believe in it.'.

Clearly Louie did not feel that the religion she was taught had much relevance to her own life – a sentiment which, while expressed less dramatically, seems to be shared by several of the respondents. Overall, the present analysis indicates that the role of religion was slightly more important in the lives of middle-class respondents than in those of the working-class respondents. One might speculate that a possible reason for this was that middle-class respondents came to identify with those who were materially disadvantaged through their understanding of religious doctrine, and thus indirectly. Working-class respondents, in contrast, could identify directly with those in need; for them religion did not function as an introduction to the problem of social injustice.

A third contrast between the accounts of the two groups is again a tentative one. While to say that middle-class respondents were radicalized around international events and working-class respondents around more pressing, domestic ones would be an overstatement, there does seem to be some weak division along these lines. It is important to stress here that this observation is limited to accounts of radicalization only. Thus while many of the working-class respondents became thoroughly involved with international issues, this was not their initial introduction to politics. The example of Walter illustrates this point: he went and fought in Spain, but he had first become politicized on the NUWM hunger march, with which he became involved because of his own unemployment. This contrasts with comments made by several middle-class respondents regarding the importance of the international events in their own radicalization – this is most noticeable in the accounts of Christopher (the combination of unemployment, fascism and war preparations), Frida (the Spanish Civil War) and Edward (Abyssinia).

The final two points for discussion are not of contrast but of similarity between the two groups. Generally, the way in which respondents experienced their radicalization was as a process. The three possible exceptions to this are Christopher, Trevor and Eileen. Christopher describes the effect of his conversation with John, and the realization he had that he could be politically involved, as being 'rather like St. Paul on the road to Damascus, bang, flash, wollop'. Still, while the effect of this one conversation upon him was great indeed, in Jack's words, the soil had already been fertilized.

Trevor remembers a distinct 'moment of choice' in his own political development. He was invited to attend a meeting of the African National Congress (ANC) in Johannesburg. 'I can remember the actual moment, it was a Sunday morning...I had to throw in my lot with them or stay on the sidelines, achieving nothing.' He describes this occasion:

I remember it so clearly because it was then – and as a direct result, I suppose, of a build-up in myself of the necessity to act rather than just to observe, to act in a political way as well as being a pastor in a caring way as far as one could do this – it was from that moment that I identified with the ANC, and that led on in future years, after the Nationalist government came to power in 1948, to a different kind of battleground altogether (Huddleston 1990: 30).

Again, we hear in this account the crystallization of a long-term process. Although Trevor can identify a particular moment when he consciously chose to join the struggle, in fact this decision was itself based on a political awareness – a recognition of 'the necessity to act' – which had been developing in him since his arrival in South Africa.

Eileen's account of her radicalization, while different in its particulars, is somewhat similar to the two cited above, in that she experienced it as a 'sudden illumination'. She expands upon this later, however. 'Mind you, if it hadn't been there, it would have been somewhere else, and it would have happened in another way. There isn't just one way. So I'm not romantic.' Her concept of sudden illumination becomes clearer in the following passage, also a description of her radicalization:

ideas don't just appear, do they? It's an accumulation. It's the old Engels [saying] isn't it?...he's explaining...qualitative changes, and how the kettle is boiling and suddenly the water turns to steam. It becomes something else. Now it's taken that water a long time to boil.

Eileen's comment here highlights the importance of examining the process, rather than the moment, of radicalization. To overemphasize the unique contribution of one particular event to an individual's radicalization would be to adopt too narrow a perspective on the transformation.

Lastly, the accounts of radicalization reveal that respondents, in the process of becoming politically conscious, and thus altering their worldviews, came to regard their own lives in a significantly different way. In the first chapter, we discussed how the perception of personal control is influenced by one's worldview, and that people experience themselves as powerful not only when they are in powerful positions,[5] but when they develop a political understanding of the social structure and the dynamics within it. Perceiving themselves as understanding the operative political influences which function to create and sustain inherently unjust social structures, they achieve a certain clarity regarding their personal direction and purpose in life. Several respondents, notably Jack, Walter, Christopher and Eileen, specifically remark that becoming political gave them a new sense of control over their lives, as they no longer perceived themselves as isolated individuals but rather as members of a larger ongoing struggle. While the remaining six respondents do not explicitly address this issue, the general tone of their accounts is, at the very least, sympathetic with such a view. Thus, there is no evidence that the extent to which respondents experienced a shift in their perception of control over their lives and their environment as a result of the awakening of their political consciousness was affected by their class.

Throughout this chapter we have seen how respondents' political consciousnesses were awakened by a combination of influences. It was the way in which respondents understood their experience, rather than the content of the experience itself, which functioned as the catalyst in their radicalization, and which ultimately formed the foundation of their socialist consciousness. At the intersection of the personal (their lived experience), the political (their wider understanding of societal power dynamics), and the historical, was born their commitment to socialism.

Clearly, the fundamental difference between the politicization of working-class and middle-class activists was the role of direct experience of oppression. Working-class individuals had known poverty and unemployment. Their radicalization was not precipitated by these experiences themselves, but by their understanding of those experiences. Once they had identified themselves as members of an oppressed group, and had begun to examine the structural causes of their oppression, they were ripe for engagement in political analysis and ultimately for radicalization; direct experience was transformed into a basis for political understanding. For obvious reasons, left-wing political analysis did not speak to the lived experience of the middle-class activists in the same fashion. They had had comparatively comfortable lives, and were thus more likely to begin with an intellectual and experientially more detached analysis of the situation. Thus, for working-class activists, the various political influences illuminated the cause of their oppression, while for the middle-class activists, the process of politicization was slightly more indirect.

However, lived experience and historical circumstances are not in themselves sufficient to determine the development of a socialist understanding of the world. Rather, they merely provide the matter which will comprise the elements to be organized in the individual's meaning-making system. Eileen reflects upon this process. She begins by remarking that none of her ideas are her own, but that they come from her perception of the world, noting that that is the difference between materialism and idealism. She then adds:

We look at life...you're bombarded with perceptions. It's what you pick up...it's fascinating: why do some people pick up some things from the outside world? In a sense, it seems to me that that would be your individual contribution to how you are. It's how you make sense of the many, many things that you see in the world.

7   Political conviction and the social self

There is no such thing as cowardly temperament ... A coward is defined by the deed that he has done ... the coward makes himself cowardly, the hero makes himself heroic ... What counts is the total commitment, and it is not by a particular case or particular action that you are committed altogether.

Jean-Paul Sartre (1956: 301–302)

We have just seen how respondents became radicalized; through their words, we entered a period of time which was far different from our own. Indeed, in the political climate of the present day, it is difficult to imagine what it must have been like to walk down the street, listening to orators on the corner, people who were well versed in Marxist theory and who were explaining existing conditions in a highly political and accessible way. In the 1990s, it takes a leap of imagination to picture the existence of a group such as the Left Book Club, let alone the huge popularity it enjoyed. All of this and more makes that period seem a long time ago – and perhaps it was.

But some of the people who were active then are active now – their commitment has persisted across the years that divide that time from this. The story of political commitment which began at that time was to be, for some, a long story indeed, a story which would last the whole of a lifetime. For the respondents in this study, radicalization was but the beginning; political commitment has become the cornerstone of their lives. It is not only an expression of the way in which they see and understand the world around them, but also has strong implications for the way in which they perceive themselves and the purpose of their lives.

The meaning of commitment

Until now, I have been using the word commitment as if its meaning were unproblematic. In the opening lines of *Personal Commitments*, Margaret Farley remarks upon the difficulty of defining, and even adequately describing all that is packed into this one word. She writes:

Never...has one word seemed so powerless to carry the questions and the human experiences I want to probe. The problem may be that 'commitment,' in the face of the great variety of persons' lives, is too abstract a term. It becomes an umbrella word, in danger of making some of our most profound experiences superficial or obscuring the vast differences in our personal histories. My stake in using this particular term is not great. It is just that I cannot find a better one (1986: 1).

Farley's book sensitively documents the role of commitment in every-day human experience. Individuals commit themselves in a variety of ways, ranging from posting bail (thus committing oneself to returning for trial), to signing a lease for an apartment rental, to the less specific commitments made in a marriage ceremony. Yet all of these, along with many other examples which Farley provides, are commitments which are, at least superficially, immediately identifiable; they are marked by ceremony, signature, exchange of money, or some other observable, if symbolic, action. A commitment, Farley states, is an expression of intentions, 'by it, we attempt to influence the future, and by it we bind ourselves to someone or something' (p. 12). But intentions are not always met, and commitments are not always honoured. Some commitments pass with time (such as a rental lease), while others are meant to be forever binding (such as marriage). In these examples, the behaviour which marks the commitment also functions as a bridge between the present and the future; as the future is necessarily abstract, and the intention can only be realized through time, the individual is limited in her ability to give tangible evidence of her commitment in the present. Society provides a variety of symbolic gestures, public expressions of commitment, to accommodate this need.

But is commitment intention alone? Because, as Farley comments, commitment can be an umbrella term, important differences regarding intended meaning can be easily obscured. In this way, language imposes limitations on the ability to distinguish between those commitments, or intentions, which are met and those which are not. Can we only speak meaningfully of commitments after they have stood the test of time, thereby regarding marriage ceremonies, signing leases, etc. as statements of intended commitment, rather than as commitment itself? Might such public statements be understood more accurately as expressions of a current state rather than as predictors of a future one? At one level, these are semantic questions. It makes little difference to anyone how we choose to label something, as long as the parties involved share an understanding of what it is they are doing. But this linguistic ambiguity reflects a larger uncertainty: how do individuals know when they are committed? Is commitment an attitude, or an inner sense, which, once arrived at, is unalterable? Or do certain commitments contain within them a flexibility which allows individuals to accommodate to new and changing circumstances, while still retaining the core of the original intended commitment?

It is important to formulate these questions, for in so doing the complexity and depth of the concept become apparent. There are many variations contained within the concept of commitment. When speaking of it, one must consider the following questions: (1) Is it a statement of intention, or a description of an actual state of affairs? Is it socially identifiable, marked by ceremony, membership, signature or shaking of hands? (2) Is the commitment situation-specific and transitory, or is it long-term? (3) Is it expressed through professed belief only, or is there an action component as well? (4) Is it a low- or high-priority commitment?

This study deals with a very powerful and distinctive form of commitment which answers these questions in the following way: (1) It is a description of not merely an intention, but also a fact. It is not marked by ceremony, and although organization membership does feature prominently, it is not an expression of the commitment as such, but rather an extension of a political viewpoint. (2) It has endured for more than half a century. (3) It has strong belief and action components. (4) It is, and has been, a high priority in the lives of the respondents, sometimes functioning as a singularly motivating force behind major life decisions, and always as an integral part of their daily lives. I shall now discuss these four features – intention, duration, action, and priority – of commitment in more detail as they relate to the respondents of this study.

Respondents' political commitment cannot be fully understood as a statement of intention, although it is that as well. It is, rather, one of the most pronounced characteristics of the lives these people have led, and shows every sign that it will continue to be so. In the accounts of respondents' radicalization, there was no identifiable ceremony which marked the advent of their commitment. For them, becoming and being committed was, and is, a process. Griffin regards the term identity 'not as a noun but as a verb: to look at the *process* of identification rather than the formation of a static social identity' (1989: 189). So, too, the naming of oneself as a socialist is an ongoing process of identification. Elizabeth, after describing her dream of being in the little lugsail, comments 'I have never had a dream telling I've arrived, but frankly in this world you never arrive anywhere... It's being on the way, the actual doing [which]... is the important thing.' Political commitment is not something which is arrived at: it is not formally contractual, and is not usually ushered in by a public statement. Unlike marital commitment, for instance, which has a decisive moment of beginning, marked by the wedding ceremony, and which can have a clear end, divorce, or death, political commitment is more opaque in definition, though no less real in actuality. Whether or not commitment has a decisive and formal moment of inception might be more an indicator of the content of the particular commitment than of the strength of conviction behind it.

Some of the life-time Communist Party members interviewed in this study might claim that political commitment can be measured by membership of the Communist Party, and they mark the advent of their political commitment as the day they first joined. For instance, when Frida says that the Spanish Civil War 'brought [her] right over', what she means is that it was then that she decided to join the Party. However, this description would not be acceptable to others who are strongly committed to socialism, but who for one reason or another are not, or are no longer, Party members. Of the ten main respondents in the study, four have been in the Communist Party for approximately fifty years or longer (one for seventy years), another four joined in the inter-war years, but left either before the Second World War or in the late 1950s, and the remaining two never actually joined the Party, although they were generally sympathetic with it. Party membership, then, would not be an appropriate operational criterion of socialist commitment, as it has been understood in this study. It is, however, the one way in which the political commitment of some of the respondents may be perceived to have had an identifiable moment of beginning.

That the statement of commitment in respondents' lives is not only one of intention but of description relates directly to the fact of its longevity. Indeed, from the point of view of the respondents, the fact that commitment has survived the test of time is an affirmation of its very existence. For instance, rather than generally regarding fellow-travellers as persons who were once, but are no longer, committed, respondents would be more likely to question their initial, apparent commitment, stating that had it been genuine or well enough thought out, such persons would not have abandoned it, nor it them. Walter describes someone who had radically changed his commitment, saying 'You've almost got to say he couldn't have been committed.' The political commitment of the respondents, seasoned over half a century, has proven to be of a more fortified nature.

Perhaps one of the most outstanding features of the commitment of these respondents is the extent to which they have expressed their beliefs through corresponding actions. Indeed, it is this very action component which distinguishes them, activists, from others, non-activists. Of course all people everywhere have some beliefs, and invariably their lives are constituted by a series of actions. What is unusual in the case of these respondents is the extent to which there is a synchronicity between these two; their actions are purposefully informed by beliefs. Beliefs, in turn, are not strictly abstract, but exist in relation to, and are a product of, the individuals' perceptions of the world. As such, they reflect any alteration in this perception. Thus, in the lives of these activists, beliefs inform actions, as actions inform beliefs; the two are symbiotic.

The idea that belief must be expressed through action is one which is shared by all of the respondents; indeed this is central to their general view of life. For them, commitment is the meeting of belief and action on a regular and sustained basis; political commitment is the belief in a political and social agenda, combined with a willingness to work for the realization of the long- and short-term goals contained within such an agenda. Commitment then has both a psychological and physical aspect to it, demanding a total investment from the individual. Farley comments on the relationship between being and doing:

A willingness to do something seems, moreover, to follow upon our sense of being bound to whomever or whatever is the object of our commitment. Our very selves ... are tied up with this object, so that we do not just appreciate it or desire it, but we are in some way 'identified' with it. Our own integrity seems to demand, under certain circumstances, we do something. The object of our commitment has a kind of claim on us, not one that is forced upon us, but that is somehow addressed to our freedom (1986: 15).

I stated previously that the lives of the respondents are testaments to commitment as it is manifested in both belief and action. Not surprisingly, the respondents have a strongly pronounced consciousness of this fact, which is reflected in their descriptions of commitment. Typically, then, the idea that commitment must have both belief and action components is not merely an abstraction for them, but is something which they have realized through their way of living.

If you believe in something, you tie in your belief with action ... It's the hard work that's part of the commitment. It's the combination ... between action and a belief in action (Eileen).

I don't believe in abstract beliefs ... There are an awful lot of people just give lip service to a thing, but they don't do anything about it ... If you believe in a thing, you should try to do something about it (Rose).

I've always said 'if I was a Christian, I would sell bibles'. If I believe in something, I work for it (Jack).

We can say the creeds till we're black in the face, but the criterion is whether we act on them...if we don't act on them, we don't really believe them (Edward).

To sincerely believe in something you've just got to do something about it (Walter).

There is a kind of categorical imperative...to act in such a way that you give things a push, however small, towards what you believe to be the good destiny (Christopher).

I can't understand how people don't [act on their beliefs]...I think you must take some action...You can feel yourself committed, but unless you can do something about it, I don't think you feel the compulsion of a committed person (Frida).

Unless you act upon it, you're not doing anything, are you? It's so easy not to act on it. You can hold any belief as long as it doesn't disturb you (Dorothy).

I've always been frightened of words, and of course in trying to arouse the conscience of the world, you've got to use words. You've got to use language, you've got to be able to communicate. And yet there's a great danger in that because people can be only too satisfied with words and not action, and so I've always tried to combine what I've said with a form of action (Trevor).

These thoughts are reminiscent of the explanation which Albert Schweitzer offered for why he had turned to medical practice:

I wanted to be a doctor that I might be able to work without having to talk. For years I had been giving myself out in words...this new form of activity I could not represent to myself as talking about the religion of love, but only as an actual putting it into practice (1933: 114–15).

Janet, too, felt that through medicine, she was acting out her socialist principles. Indeed, she comments, 'How anyone could do medicine in those days and not become a socialist I find hard to understand! It was so obvious that so much illness and suffering was due to poverty' (Caldecott 1984: 111). Thus it was that she became dedicated to 'social medicine' – and in so doing, was able to practise her political beliefs.

Mary directs her attention to the relationship between belief and action, although she does so using slightly different terminology: '[Commitment] is your promised intention to follow a course that you believe in.' In her life, commitment is not intention alone, for she has acted upon her beliefs for a long time. However, what is interesting about employing the word intention is that it forms a bridge from the present into the future, as discussed earlier. In the case of the respondents, intention could be understood to mean an intention to continue to be as they have been and are being; thus a bridge between past, present and future.

The fourth and final feature of commitment which I shall discuss is that of its priority. This aspect is closely related to the belief-and-action feature examined above, for while individuals might be broadly sympathetic with a particular viewpoint, unless it is regarded as a high priority, it is not likely to be expressed through sustained action. The reason for this is apparent: because of various limitations, particularly those of time and finances, individuals experience competition between professed commitments, and choices regarding allocation of those resources must be made. There are, of course, circumstances which might militate against individuals being able to act on their beliefs, such as physical incapacity.[1] Moreover, acting on a belief might not be the most accurate indicator of that belief's high priority for the individual, if, for instance, to act on it is somehow more convenient than not to, or is done in the absence of competing claims. Still, while noting the existence of exceptional circumstances, one can assert that, generally, beliefs which are consistently expressed through action are of a higher priority to individual actors than those which are not.

As an individual's life circumstances change, so might the way she chooses to allocate her time. The organization and reorganization of priorities is not necessarily, or even usually, a conscious process. Nonetheless, it is through the process of prioritizing commitments that individuals make essential statements, to themselves and to the social world, of whom they perceive themselves to be. Again, Goffman's *Presentation of Self in Everyday Life* comes to mind; people act in a particular way so as to communicate to others, and to themselves, who they are. What is outstanding with the respondents of this study is that their commitment to work for socialism has remained a high priority throughout their adult lives. Again, this is reflected not only through their actions (most importantly), but also in their discussion of the meaning of commitment.

Commitment means that whatever you're committed to is the most important thing in your life (Edward).

Commitment means that whatever you undertake, you do it. That there's no half measures. That you put everything into doing it (Dorothy).

You accept a goal in life, and you commit yourself to it, and you have no abstractions away from it (Jack).

The word commitment means that if you believe in a thing, and you commit yourself to it, that you should do it absolutely 100 % within your capacity. Don't do anything lukewarm, half-heartedly. You have to have it here and here, in your head and in your heart (Rose).

For Christopher, the question of priority is precisely the one with which he was struggling at the time of our interviews. He seeks to establish a balance between two sides of himself: the artist and the political activist.

Given that there are only twenty-four hours in a day... how do I apportion limited time between those things?... That is a very acute problem in my life right now... I know that if I were to do more activism... it would have to be at a heavy cost to my work as an artist... That's the big tension and two-way pull: the studio and the street, if you like to put it in a journalistic manner.

While Christopher does try to combine these two sides of himself (by doing all the political artwork for various newsletters, demonstrations, etc.), the tension between priorities has not been fully resolved. He compares himself with his brother in this regard. 'I think I'm very different from John because I think for John activism was life itself... I don't have quite that feeling.' Throughout our interviews, the theme of the competition between these claims on his time and energy re-emerged.

Thus far, I have discussed the political commitment of the respondents in terms of its role as a statement of intention, its longevity, its belief-and-action component, and its high priority in their lives. Before examining how this commitment influences their social and self-perceptions, it is important to re-emphasize the role of experience in the formation of commitment. We have already seen that individuals' beliefs and actions are products of the way in which they have made sense of the material conditions which they have encountered in their lives. This sentiment is expressed time and again in their description of where commitment comes from.

[How do we form commitment?] By life's experience. My life's experience... When I see the youngsters today, I have a deep feeling for them, because I've lived it, I've lived it (Jack).

The seeds [of commitment] are there early on, but they do grow and flourish and spread out, so they're spreading out tentacles... It's only when you're older and you look back that you see what happened (Elizabeth).

You develop [commitment] through your experiences. It's this belief in something outside your own personal interests, isn't it? It's getting a perspective of our own life in the wider world... It comes from your childhood experiences. I think that's very, very strong. Plus, you look at your ancestors and you see there is a thread running through (Eileen).

Experiences help you later on, to be both committed and firm, and know what you're doing is right (Dorothy).

[How do we decide what to be committed to?] Ah well, that needs intelligence. That needs a bit of reading. You get that from experience, and from reading, you know, history and... economics... finding out what happened before and what conditions, how people came to certain conclusions (Rose).

In the passages cited here, there are three identifiable themes: (1) Commitment comes from the combination of lived experience and the way in which such experience is made sense of. (2) Commitment, like a seed, grows. It is a process, a gained perspective on one's life, and on life in general. (3) Commitment can function as a connector between the past (ancestral, and wider historical) and the future (dictating intended course of action). Thus it is evident that respondents do not perceive their commitment as something which is either temporally or experientially apart from themselves. Rather, it is a thread that exists throughout and across their existence, connecting their personal past, present and future to each other as well as to the greater passage of time. Additionally, it links not only their life course to the ongoing historical process, but also links them in a more immediate sense to the lives of others.

Social orientation of the self

Eileen describes her reaction upon reading the transcript of our first interview:

I found it rather shocking because I felt it was very self-indulgent. I think that's what hit me and I think after our discussion I had felt the same... my reactions were, 'Oh dear, we do try to get away from our egos – how do you break out of the circle of your ego – and here I am locked into it.'

Speaking in terms of the danger of getting locked into the circle of one's ego, Eileen is not comfortable dedicating prolonged periods of time to speaking about herself, not because she cannot do it, but because she perceives it as being self-indulgent. Moreover, the activists tend to be very materially oriented and a discussion on the abstract concept of self would have very little interest to them if it were not grounded in observable reality. Thus Mary comments: 'I don't really think of myself as having an identity.' Later she expands on this:

It's a funny word [identity] isn't it... I mean if I do something that I wished I hadn't, I think about it, [but I] certainly don't bother to think about an identity... I suppose I would only think of myself in terms of... what I like and... what I do... Perhaps you as the younger generation think more in that kind of way. I wouldn't think many people go on consciously thinking about themselves really.

Both women seem to be implicitly questioning the usefulness of thinking about the individualized self: to what end would one engage in such an activity? The function of reflection, they would argue, would be to transform reality; self-analysis for its own sake is not a satisfactory use of intellectual capabilities.

One example of a respondent identifying herself in relation – in this case in opposition – to others can be seen in Dorothy's response to the question of how she would describe herself. She says 'I don't know. I only know that I am the entire opposite to my sister.' She then proceeds to describe her sister. It is interesting that this is the closest that Dorothy comes to describing herself – through a thorough description of another person.

Elsewhere, in one of her letters to me, Dorothy reflects that 'It had never occurred to me to look at what I had been doing with my life, so the self-examination has made me evaluate.'[2] Dorothy does not mean that her actions were without purpose, but rather that she does not think about herself as an individual actor; she does not think about herself as a self, but as a social agent. In preparation for our interviews, Dorothy compiled an extensive list of her various involvements through the years. Through doing this, she came to a realization about herself:

It's only since I've looked back at things that I have sort of been involved with and I find that everything I've been involved with, and its been around twenty years, and it's been in a good healthy state where I could leave it... Really I was quite surprised.

When asked how this revelation made her feel about herself, she responds:

It's just a dead feeling really. It's gone and it's still going and it's successful and that's all that matters. Quite honestly I don't have any feelings about any of these things and if it hadn't been for the interview I wouldn't have looked back and made an assessment.

Later in the interview, she insists that all that she has done 'is no credit to me... It's no credit to me at all,' and again, 'I have no feelings about it other than it's something that's absolutely necessary. That's it... it doesn't reflect on me at all, personally.' Dorothy is not alone in her experience of being interviewed. Indeed, for all of the participants, it was unusual to devote an extended period of time to thinking about themselves, their life experiences, and the motivations behind many of their actions.

Thus the most revealing information which emerged from the direct questions on self-description was the lack of relevance and/or importance attributed to this category by the respondents. Taking the six hours with each individual as a composite whole, and thus reviewing the total self-presentation across interviews, two salient themes emerge: (1) Participants tend to see themselves and others as essentially social beings, attributing little importance to individualized elements. (2) Politics in general, and political activism in particular, is central to the way these individuals think of themselves.

The stories which respondents tell reflect a strong connection between themselves and the environments in which they live, as well as a consciousness of this connection. Earlier, we discussed the role of class membership and lived experience in the formation of respondents' political commitment. We saw that through radicalization, working-class activists became conscious of being members of an oppressed group, while for the middle-class participants, this process resulted in them identifying themselves with, but not of, those victims of social injustice. Clearly, respondents' personal histories influence the way in which they perceive their relationship with others who are in need. The result is that working-class activists appear to be motivated by a desire to help others whom they see as being very similar to themselves, whereas middle-class respondents speak of their work in the more abstract language of conscience, justice and social rights.

Broughton remarks upon the limitations of the liberal concept of role-taking, speaking of the 'reduction of mutual human communication, understanding and recognition to relations between roles' (1985: 375). Role-taking, he states, is 'anti-dialogue', unnecessary and insufficient

for knowing or understanding the other... We learn about the psychological and moral reality-for-the-other through direct communication with the other... In so doing, we relate as simple self to the other, rather than as self-in-the-role-of other (1985: 376–377).

While the point that Broughton makes is a compelling one, it is not without its own limitations. The possibility for one individual to understand another is greatly enhanced if the two share some form of life experience. Without this, a person's ability to make sense of what the other is trying to communicate is impaired, for, lacking relevant experience, she is restricted to the use of her imagination. For example, through political analysis, people who have never experienced un-employment might understand its causes; that does not mean, however, that they know what it's like to be unemployed. Whereas middle-class respondents might sympathize (as simple self to other) with those in need, working-class respondents have a capacity to empathize, relating to others' experience of impoverishment as if it were their own.

Dorothy remarks:

I think I can feel at one with people that are at the bottom. And with all the hardships that they have. I can feel, well not only sympathy, but understand their position and understand what they feel and want to get them out.

During her time as a magistrate, she remembers feeling 'at one with most of these people that came before the bench. I couldn't look at them and be anything different than myself'. Asked if she could ever conceive of herself losing her commitment, she responds, 'No, never. I can't, it's so, it's part of me.' She categorically states that she does not feel any different from any of the people whom she has helped.

Walter, when describing the plight of the young unemployed today, uses the same language as he did when he was speaking about his own early experiences of being unemployed. Today's youth, he feels, are receiving a similar message to the one which he heard in the early 1930s: 'society has told them "we haven't got a job for you" so youngsters have taken society's word and they've opted out. They've learned to live on the dole.' Walter can empathize with the youth, knowing from his own life what devastating effects long-term unemployment can have.

Jack often refers to the influence that his early experience has wielded on him throughout his life:

I've always, ever since I've grown up with it, to what we call the down and outs, I never shunned them, I always go up and talk to them, and identify myself with them... When I see the youngsters today, I have a deep feeling for them, because I've lived it, I've lived it... I've lived their experience.

Later he makes a similar statement:

You know I see a bloke unemployed, an old tramp, I've got a feeling for him, because I've been hungry, I've been bootless, and I can identify myself, and when he's there cold and shivering, I know what he's going through.

Jack sums up his feeling of connection with others, not only the oppressed, in saying, 'when I look at another human being, I'm looking at myself'.

Rose describes this connection in a slightly different way:

'Do as you would be done by.' That really sums up everything. There's nobody really wishes themselves ill... You can live your life like that, then you don't go far wrong... My religion is 'do as you would be done'.

While ostensibly this might be resonant of Broughton's self-in-the-role-of-other critique, in fact her application is ultimately a social one, and not one which reduces all form of human interaction to the individualized unit. That her intended meaning is pro-social and political is evidenced in the following statement:

If you believe that an injury to one is an injury to all, which is the first principle of trade unionism, it's [a] helpful attitude. We don't live alone, we condition each other... We live for ourselves and for each other. And if we get that attitude to life, then a helping hand is always there.

Dorothy, Walter, Jack and Rose all speak of the connections which exist between themselves and others, particularly those in need. Their memories are not short; having once experienced hardship and poverty themselves, they can readily identify with the difficult situations of others.

Middle-class participants tend to speak of their identification with a cause or movement, rather than with a particular individual or group of individuals in need. They are not 'at one with people that are at the bottom'; they have not 'lived their experience'. One exception to this is Trevor, whose description of commitment seems to bridge the gap between a primarily abstract perspective and one which is materially grounded:

I've always taken it for granted that it [commitment] meant identification, not just with a cause, but with the human element involved in that cause. That meant that you identify with the oppressed, if it's a society which oppresses.

Although Trevor himself had come from a well-to-do family, and he describes the Oxford of his day as 'an Oxford of immense privilege ... outrageous privilege really', when he went to South Africa, he insisted on living in the black township rather than in the area designated for whites. He writes:

It was Sophiatown and Soweto that matured me, because I *felt* apartheid, as it affected the people I was looking after (particularly the young and the old), when I saw every day of my life what apartheid did to them (1990: 20).

He speaks with disdain of the white liberals in South Africa who have 'never, actually never, set foot in a black township, let alone lived in one'. He feels 'They don't understand what they're talking about' because they speak of things about which they have no experience, nor have ever even observed. The way in which he has led his daily life expresses a joint commitment to abstract principles and to an identifiable group of people.

In this regard, Trevor is unique among the middle-class respondents in the study. Even while they may sympathize with the 'down and outs', they also do feel different from them, separated as they are by a world of experience. Thus, their descriptions of the motivation behind their activism tend to be abstract. Consider the following statement by Elizabeth:

I think once you begin to see the guiding you're deeply nourished by it, and you don't gad about and do things without thinking them over ... and weighing them in your heart first, as to whether it's the right ordering or not.

Establishing and living by a right ordering means dedicating oneself to something which is worthwhile, not, as Elizabeth says, 'silly and frivolous'. She also speaks in terms of 'enriching experiences' and 'a feeling of at-one-ment' when she is guided by right ordering. Other middle-class respondents speak of the importance of 'working for peace', 'deeper structures' and 'categorical imperative'. This kind of language contrasts with that of the working-class activists, whose sense of connectedness is less philosophical and more grounded in their direct experience.

The role of organizations

Another manifestation of this social orientation, important because of both its political and psychological implications, is the pivotal role played by organizations in sustaining the commitment of the respondents. They do not take very seriously reformist or revolutionary efforts which individuals may make as individuals, and in their own lives they have always orchestrated their political work with a wider movement or organization. In the case of the lifetime Communist Party members, one particular organization, the Party, pervades all aspects of political life. For the remaining six correspondents, while the role of the organization is equally important, there is no one organization which is accorded a similarly central position.

One is reminded here of Nelson Mandela's explanation of how he sustained his commitment to the anti-apartheid struggle during his twenty-seven years in prison. How was it that he did not become inward-looking, focusing on his own daily sacrifice? 'I don't think of myself. I think in terms of the organization to which I belong' (BBC transcript of 'Everyman', 18 March 1990). Quite simply, it was his membership of the ANC which kept him going, knowing that he was part of a larger movement, and that he was not alone.

All of the fifteen respondents direct their work organizationally because of their strong beliefs that only in such a way will they be politically efficacious. It is also true, however, that long-term affiliation with an organization or network of organizations yields certain psychological benefits which enhance the individual's experience of her political commitment. One of the most important benefits which individuals derive from their group membership is that of support (both emotional and intellectual), which contributes to the creation and maintenance of a sense of belonging.

Jack, when asked what has been the most important relationship in his life, responds, 'being a member of the Communist Party'. Later he reflects that in an organization, 'you are now with your kind...without that you sort of become an individual, a negative, you know, an individual. You're helpless.' Frida, also a lifetime Party member, refers to the poem 'Mon Parti' by Louis Aragon, in which the poet describes

the strength it's given him...to have a party with hundreds and thousands behind you...We're not only the English Party, we've got all the communists of the world. I mean this is something that is sustaining, you know, however small we are here, there is this great mass of a people who think exactly like us.

Eileen experiences the same exhilaration as Frida does from belonging to a world movement:

You belonged to something and you were part of an organization, that is very, very important indeed. And you felt if you went to France, you had friends there, you knew you had friends all over the world, it was an open Sesame...I went to America, I was in touch immediately with people who felt like I did...I felt strong and part of something that was a world movement.

When Mary moved to a new town after the war, she was still a member of the Communist Party. She describes the ready-made network of acquaintances which was made available to her through this membership:

You see, when you come new to a town, you need some way of getting to know people, and although I didn't stay with the Party for that purpose, the fact is that was my way of getting to know people and they were very nice people. So you see my friends would nearly all be communists.

Frida, Jack, Eileen and Mary are all expressing their loyalty to, and belief in, the Communist Party, as well as the strength which they derive from being members of it. These feelings are also shared by Rose, in whose life the Party has played an equally important role. But all of the respondents have similar feelings if not about the Communist Party, then about the emotional importance as well as the political efficacy of working with and through organizations. They identify themselves strongly as members of a group, and they derive much strength and sustenance from their affiliation with like-minded others.

Mary says she feels that 'one individual [who is] not a member of anything, is quite useless' and that 'one individual carries no weight...I don't really take individuals very seriously'. Walter feels that organizations are 'all important, the individualism far, far less important', and Edward says 'We'd be lost without them. You couldn't do anything.' He then elaborates upon his view of being part of an organization:

if you took any individual in the peace movement, any of the thousands who go on demos and so on, and said to them what difference have you made, none of us individually, separately could say 'I've made much of a difference.' Even though we have made a difference together.

Ed speaks emphatically of the importance of organizations:

There is nothing like an organisation. There is no substitute in any way. No individual could ever attempt in any way, shape or form, or even two or three individuals. You really need a collective, you really need to be with a group of people, an organization, and a collective to be successful... the limitations of one person's thinking, one person's activity is far too little to change things. You need to be able to have this close interchange of ideas, this discussion, this collective work as a team.

Christopher states that while organizations are politically important, one sacrifices a portion of oneself to be part of the larger whole. He refers to his Party membership in the 1930s as 'walking on one leg without using the other'. Speaking of the drawbacks of organization membership in general, he comments:

I think organization is a necessity in political and public life, but in some ways a rather regrettable one. Because the more you identify with an organization, the more aspects of yourself you probably have to suppress. There is a conflict there... between one's own unbridled impulses and that which the organization, however enlightened, says you should do. Organizations by their very nature militate against spontaneity and creativity.

In the discussion on the prioritizing of commitment, we saw that Christopher felt tension between pursuing his art work and dedicating himself fully to his political involvements. Whereas earlier Christopher's conflict was expressed in terms of its personal dimensions – how should he apportion the twenty-four hours of his day – here his reservations concern the very nature of organizations. It was as a member of the Communist Party that Christopher felt himself to be most suppressed. One reason for this might be that his social identity was profoundly influenced by one particular group, as compared with an alternative in which multiple group memberships created a more complex network of identity, thus allowing a greater potential for diversity of self-expression. Again comparing himself with his brother, he says, 'He could realize himself in that medium of action [political activism]. I can't.' Most of the respondents would be more similar to John than to Christopher, in this respect.

Still, even while Christopher acknowledges the constraints which organizations impose, he does nevertheless regard them as a political necessity. He has been an active member of various political organizations since his early radicalization, and he has made many close friends through these associations. That he does believe in the importance of working through them is evidenced by his long-term involvement with them. Elizabeth believes that it is unreasonable for one to expect to have all of one's needs met by any particular organization, explaining that they are

like people... there are things that you like in it, but you don't like everything. But you have... to accept a certain number of things that you're not in sympathy with, thinking of the overall.

All of the respondents would agree that, whether it is regrettable or not, organizations are indeed a necessity of political life. However, that is not all they are. A sense of belonging and strong friendships are often the result of the many years of involvement with an organization or cause. When Frida and Eileen speak of being part of a world movement, their enthusiasm extends beyond their belief that the greater the numbers, the greater the potential for success. Indeed, their membership in the Party gives them a feeling of being part of a larger whole. Eileen comments, 'We are all belongers. We all want to find a place for ourselves.' Both women refer to the positive feelings they had from being with people who share their views. In this way, they have not only made personal friends but they have also felt part of a larger whole. Frida says:

I don't want to be just the one person who thinks 'I'm the only person who believes in it, and it must be right because I believe in it'...One has to believe that there's a big movement, [and] that it's the right thing.

In Frida's statement here, there is evidence of both the personal and political significance to her of being a Party member. When she says that she doesn't want to be 'just the one person' she is expressing a very familiar human sentiment – a desire to know that there are others like herself. In the language of social identity, she wants to locate herself in a group. However, she connects this personal perspective to a political one, implicitly asserting that the existence of a big movement lends legitimacy to the cause; simultaneously, it augments one's perception that one's commitment is 'the right thing'.

Elizabeth speaks of the 'joy and pleasure' she gets from belonging to 'a community of like-minded people' and Rose reflects that 'if you're interested in politics and join a party, you make your friends around these people'. Christopher recalls that even as a child 'the people I liked tended to be socialist and the people I didn't like tended to be Tories'. When asked what benefits, if any, Elizabeth felt she had derived from her activism, she responded without hesitation, 'the people that I've met'.

Dorothy describes her experience:

If the people are sympathetic to what you're trying to do, well you can't help but make friends with them, can you? I mean you were all working to the same end, and it's a happy situation.

Dorothy also speaks of the 'loyalty' she feels 'to the other people that are in it'. Walter, in whose life the Spanish Civil War played such an important role, is involved in the International Brigade Association, which is still a very active organization. He tells of the support and lifelong friendships he has gained through his affiliation with the International Brigade. Elsewhere he explains, 'I made friends with people in the political movement... it just became my life.' Members of organizations come to depend on each other; they help to sustain each other's commitment, while at the same time reasserting their own. Thus, organizations play an integral role in the lives of the respondents, because of both their political and personal importance.

Throughout the interviews, it was evident that participants were remarkably strongly oriented toward their social environment; they experience themselves as members of a community to which they feel responsible. As Rose says: 'one does not live for oneself alone... we condition each other, we live for each other'. One manifestation of their overt social orientation was that they tended to speak of themselves in relation to other individuals (known and unknown), and groups of individuals (organizations). As the respondents are all very anti-individualistic in their political outlook, it is not surprising that they would not concentrate on themselves even, or perhaps most particularly, when speaking about the underlying meaning in their lives.

Respondents' self-perceptions are built upon their political beliefs, and through their political actions they confirm, time and again, that they are political activists. Let us turn, now, to consider another aspect of their identity – that of gender – examining the role it plays in respondents' conscious self- and other-perceptions.

'If I'd been a woman': difference, what difference?

In considering questions of gender identity, it is important to recall the history of the women's movement in the first quarter of this century, discussed in Chapter 5. The First World War caused a split amongst the suffragettes, or perhaps revealed a schism which was already there. Some were campaigning for the vote only, while others saw their efforts as being part of a more fundamental restructuring of a patriarchal, capitalist society. Many young socialist men and women during the inter-war years saw feminism as being irrelevant to the political struggles of the day, a bourgeois indulgence which diverted attention away from the 'real' issues of class politics.

As it was during these years that respondents were politicized, perhaps it should not be surprising that in this study issues relating to gender, and acknowledged as being so, are most striking by their absence. When I ask Mary – a single woman for most of her life, and a single working mother for much of it – about the 'feminist side of things', she responds, 'You see that wasn't nearly so much an issue. It had been, of course, as you know, with the vote, but no. You see it became a real issue long after it would bother me at all.'

Still, while there are historical reasons why the role of feminism may have been negligible in the lives of the respondents, there are other influences to be considered. It is somewhat curious that respondents address gender issues so infrequently, given that much current socialist discourse is informed by a feminist consciousness, with many arguing that 'the struggle against exploitation and the struggle against domination ought not to be counterposed' (Brenner 1989: 247). There is an acknowledgement of 'the importance of other dimensions of oppression' (*ibid.*). Moreover, respondents are aware of the influence that feminism exerts on the political agenda of the left. Yet it seems that 'feminist issues' are perceived as an abstraction, if not a distraction, by many, indeed most, of the respondents. Here we seem to hark back to the question of multiple group membership and the politics of recognizing multiple dimensions of difference, discussed in Chapter 2. Perhaps the most interesting aspects of respondents' perceptions of gender difference is the pointed discrepancy between their stated beliefs – which tend to minimize or deny any difference – and the way in which they speak of individuals personally known to them (e.g. spouses, parents, even themselves) – which reveals another story. This is equally true for most male and female respondents, although not for all of them.

This discrepancy is highlighted in the cases of both Jack and Walter, as they speak about women in general and then about their own wives. Jack proclaims with pride that

If I was a woman, if I'd been born female, and I'd lived the same circumstances as a female as I have as a male, yes I would have been a member of the Communist Party and I would be fighting and arguing amongst house-wives...fighting mentally, politically, discussing it with them. I mean if I worked as a housewife and they was talking about the price of bread going up...I'd give them the politics of it. Or if they were grumbling about 'Oh, they're on strike again' and that, then you'd have to explain why they're on strike.

At one level, Jack is saying that he'd have been the same as a woman, or at least have had the same politics as he has had as a man – that is, with a small qualifier 'if [he'd] lived the same circumstances'. While the realm of his political activity would have shifted from the docks to the kitchen, he imagines a continuity of political consciousness between the two situations. This is the only time when Jack describes a politicized woman: when he himself is transposed into a female body. Even here, he is out organizing the housewives who need to have explained to them why the men are out striking or why the price of bread is rising.

Usually, however, Jack's references to women and womanhood – and there are many – focus on images of self-sacrificing mothers and wives:

when I think of womanhood and I know from my own experience that no matter how poor they are, when the dinner's come on the table, mum's got the smallest [portion]. Still making that sacrifice like she did when she gave birth from the womb...Working class mothers, to me there's nobody like them.

Many times in our interviews, Jack comments, 'Apart from the sexual side, I've got a strong feeling for women... I always found you get much more help from a woman that you would from a male' (notice even the contructions – woman and male – are not parallel). He likes women, they've been good to him. They make sacrifices, and let the men folk get on with the job. When asked if his own wife shares his politics, he explains:

More or less acquiesces... when I come and say there's a struggle in the industry, I'd always explain to her, perhaps weeks and weeks before a strike was going to happen...and she used to say 'It's your industry, you know what you're doing. I suspect it'd bring more food for the table.' You know, proper good working-class healthy look ahead.

Jack does not see real women, i.e. women whom he knows, as being political. His own wife is 'not politically minded at all... she couldn't be interested in what I was talking about as a Marxist student, you know. Dialectics. There's millions of people that can't get on with dialectics.' There is a marked disparity between Jack's hypothetical, politicized woman and his description of women who are known to him.

In the following passage we can also see a noticeable shift between Walter's description of women in general and that of his wife, Gladys, in particular. To my question, 'Do you think that being a man has influenced your political activity, in other words the things you've done and how you've done them?', he responds:

No, I don't. I see no problem with this question. I would insist that's quite irrelevant. After all on the hunger marches there were women's sections. In Spain there was plenty for women to do...The first English person to be killed in the Spanish Civil War was Felicia Brown, a young girl...There again, like Gladys, women are inclined to get tied down by domestic duties, although I claimed I did my share during the difficult days, but I still got more freedom than perhaps Gladys had to get away from the home on trade union work. Plus the fact, of course, a man inevitably works full-time. Which of course Gladys never did. She always had a part-time job, so that she could do the two jobs – home and earn a few pounds. Er no, question of male or female, doesn't arise. Not at all.

This passage can be divided into three sections: in the first part, Walter makes a general statement on the lack of importance of gender

difference, for which he then offers supporting evidence. The words
'There again' herald a new message containing at least an implicit
acknowledgement of difference: men (like himself) inevitably work and
women (like his wife) are inclined to get tied down by domestic duties.
The last two sentences quite abruptly return to the original position, and
there is no attempt made to reconcile the apparent inconsistency, nor
even a recognition of it.

But Jack and Walter aren't alone in this regard. Elizabeth states, 'I
don't think I'm very conscious of being a woman... I'm just a human
being.' And yet, as our interview progresses, the toll that balancing her
responsibilities as a wife and mother has exacted from her becomes
increasingly clear. She hints at this difference when she says:

I think to be a good housewife you get a jolly good training really in keeping the
needs of your family, the needs of the house, the needs of the food, and all the
rest of it, and they're things you've got to keep on the boil, or simmering all the
time. Whereas a man can go into his study and shut out the outside world... A
woman has got to keep an eye on all these other things, and be responsible for
them.

These do not sound like the words of a woman who is not conscious of
her gender. Her earlier statement is even more surprising when one
considers her own experience. She describes a very difficult time she
went through:

I was relying too much on him [her husband] and his attitudes and trying to be
a good wife. I mean I think it's something to do with the kind of loyalty and
bringing up your children and all the rest of it... I just felt life wasn't worth
living. My roots were just in a hollow with no nourishment. I was cut off
completely.

In fact, it was immediately following this time that Elizabeth 'opened
out and started doing all these things'.

Dorothy describes herself as always having been 'a woman in my own
right'. Later she says, 'I can't identify with anybody else, only working
class, and I'd never pretend, whoever I was with, that I was anything
other than working class.' The tension between class and gender, or
class consciousness and sisterhood, reveals itself in the following story.
Dorothy recalls her relationship with a titled lady whom she met while
working on the Central Council of Probation in London.

She had a flat in Belgravia Square, and she invited me in for a drink. My
immediate reaction was to say to her 'If I come in, it won't be for a drink, it will
to see how you live'... But I had a super relationship with her, she always came
to sit next to me... she'd say 'Oh, I've just been with the kids'... or you know,
talk about her personal things really on a very warm and friendly basis... She
was a straight cousin of the Queen's.

Although Dorothy and the titled lady do have 'a super relationship', communicating on a warm, friendly basis, it is nonetheless clear that Dorothy cannot identify with her; the difference in their worlds cannot be bridged by their shared gender.

Other women address the question of gender difference from a more explicitly political angle. Rose and Frida, both lifetime Communist Party members, follow in the classical socialist tradition. Both feel that separate women's organizations are divisive of the movement. Rose – who describes herself as 'an early women's libber' who did not wear a wedding ring because 'I wasn't going to wear the band of slavery' – says categorically:

I never was [involved in any women's separatist organizations] because I always believed... that we should make our way through our own merit, not necessarily expect differentiation for women. We are human beings... it's the system that's wrong... once you alter the system... you don't need to have separate women's things... I don't need to be in a woman's group because I recognize that the real enemy [is] the ruling class... We [men and women] can't live without each other.

Frida expresses similar feelings:

I don't feel particularly drawn to the feminist movement, perhaps I ought not to say this, but I feel that the feminists are putting a great deal of energy, this is the rather way out ones, they put a tremendous amount of energy into being women first, you know, when we really need all our strength to get together and get social improvements throughout the movement.

Perhaps in an attempt to minimize the grounds for regarding men as the enemy, both women cast aspersions upon the image of women as victims of male violence. Rose tells a story about when she was nineteen and a man was following her.

I turned around and I looked at him... from top to toe, [I] never said a word. He turned round and left me and I walked across the street. That's absolutely true. You see, I've a theory that men don't like being taken down in any way... Women, if they do all the encouraging in most cases, mind you, I'm a woman's woman, but... I feel that our own sex are much to blame for an awful lot that happens to them, in my opinion.

Frida and I discussed the series of rapes which occurred at the live-in peace camp at the US Cruise missile base in Molesworth, Cambridge-shire. These incidents had attracted much controversy within the anti-nuclear movement; many, like Frida, felt that the peace camp had already had enough bad press without the women who reported the rapes adding to its troubles. 'They were made such a lot of... I don't know quite how far they were genuinely issues. It's very difficult because the women become very emotional'.

Only Eileen and Christopher explicitly address what they identify as feminist concerns. Particularly Eileen makes the connection between these broader issues and her own life. At nearly every phase of her biography, she charts the development of her feminism: her childhood (both home life and friendships with women in the village); attending a single-sex school; early politicization; her job during the war; her marriage; and having children. Her strong feminist consciousness is present in every story she tells. And yet she too is a lifetime member of the Communist Party, and she too became politicized when feminism was seen as something quite apart from, perhaps even in opposition to, socialism.

Christopher's views on feminism remain more philosophical and less concrete. He says, 'I see us all now as being in a vast psycho-drama, which we only dimly understand, but of which feminism is an enormously important, perhaps the most important and central, aspect.' In a testimonial of his beliefs which Christopher wrote for the purpose of this study, he elaborates on this idea. He speaks of feminism as being

a new emergence as important as any our species has so far experienced, comparable with the advents of speech, of writing, of philosophy, of science, to name some of the principal ones. For it is as though half of humankind, hitherto only sporadically heard from, is in [the] course of re-inventing itself, re-examining its own past and radically criticising the institutions and mental habits that have immemorially conditioned it, and creating new roles and possibilities. These I believe will be more intelligent, sensitive and humane – as well as innovative in directions we can't foresee – from the tired old patterns of masculine-conditioned existence: warfare, aggression, domination, repression, coercion, exploitation, competitiveness and all the rest of the historical horror-show.

Christopher accuses himself of being 'by temperament addicted to seeing human affairs in terms of grand evolutionary sweeps and transformations which I seem to detect as underlying normal everyday "reality"'. One of the daily manifestations of this colossal trans-formation which he identifies is that 'politics is no longer confined to the specialism of that name: it is everybody's business'. He refers to sexual politics, 'the politics of who does the washing up or fetches the children from school'. Indeed, as I visit Christopher in his home, it is clear that his grand ideas translate into his own kitchen.

Summarizing this section, we can say that for most of the respondents, gender is not a salient social categorization. Only two participants address the importance of feminism in their lives, Eileen from a practical perspective, Christopher from a philosophical one. Based on the interviews, it seems, then, that respondents are not generally conscious of gender being a central aspect of their self-perception. Gender consciousness is not part of their political consciousness; indeed for some the former might be perceived to undermine the latter.

Activism: a way of life

Eileen recalls a comment which another lifetime activist said to her: 'It's the way we live, Eileen. We'll never live any other way, till we die, will we? It's a way of life.' Activism is not merely something which the respondents do, nor even just a part of them. It is them. During their long, accumulated years of engagement, they have come to define themselves through their activism, thus Mary's comment that she could only think of herself in terms of what she likes and what she does. In our discussion of commitment, we stated that just as respondents' beliefs are expressed through their actions, so do their actions reaffirm their beliefs. A corollary of this is that the very doing of the political action enables respondents to perceive of themselves as politically engaged.

Earlier, we stated that the concepts which one uses to identify oneself are not only a measure of self-perception, but are themselves socially constructed (Griffin 1989; Reicher 1987). The naming of oneself as a socialist is itself an important step, as we have seen. However, through the years, this has come to be one of the most fundamental and enduring aspects of respondents' self-definition; it is at the centre of what they believe, what they do, and the basis upon which they share one of their most important group memberships. The identification of oneself as a socialist is an ongoing process – one which is restated and re-created in the very actions of daily life. Socialist identification is thus composed of being (indicating consciousness) and doing (performing actions consonant with one's beliefs).

Dorothy explains her approach to her work in the following way:

My immediate reaction is 'here's a problem, how can we solve it? What can I contribute? Probably there's some satisfaction from being able to do something, from knowing the sources to go to, where you can get other help.

She describes herself as one who is 'really 100% active'. Dorothy, as well as the other activists, has developed what I term a 'culture of responding'. By this I mean that individuals who have been involved in political activity over a long period of time are likely to continue to be active in the future. Political action, however, is not unreflective, but rather has built into it a history of past actions, and incorporates their underlying purpose as part of its own. In this way actions past, present and future are part of a larger, self-perpetuating continuum of purposeful, directed action. This culture of responding comprises two essential components, both in evidence in Dorothy's statement above: (1) the ability to perceive problems; and (2) the desire and capability to respond to such problems through action.

Social identity theory posits that the number of situations an individual perceives as being relevant to a particular group membership increases as awareness of that membership becomes more pronounced. Similarly, with growing politicization, individuals' perceptions of the parameters of the political domain expand, encapsulated by the cliché that the personal is political. Indeed, this has been the case with these participants, who, through the years, have developed a heightened sensitivity to their social and political environment. This is what is meant by the first component listed above, that of perception. The second component is related to the belief/action link: once participants perceive a particular problem and they feel that some sort of action must be taken to alleviate or, if possible, correct the situation, they are likely to identify a specific course of action which they themselves can undertake to effect such change.

Dorothy explains her approach to many of the problems she encountered while working as a magistrate: 'I knew what the problem was. I had some idea of how it should be put right ... I knew it was wrong and it shouldn't be allowed to go on.' She describes her community involvement in a similar way:

initially I've seen 'here's a problem that needs working on'... It's something that appeals to my inner self... I see... that somebody's life is so miserable and depressing... that this just isn't right... I then involve myself 100 % to get it put right.

For Dorothy, perception of a problem leads almost invariably to taking some sort of action. In a most genuine way, the problems Dorothy encounters become her own, and she involves herself totally.

The second component of the culture of responding, that of 'desire and capability to respond', indicates a proclivity on the part of the respondents to act on problems which they perceive; as Dorothy says, it appeals to her inner self. Respondents cannot merely identify a problem, discern a possible course of action for themselves, and do nothing about it. Perception brings with it a call for action – and the connector between these two processes is what Rose labels responsibility, 'something which is created between you and your environment'. Ultimately, she says, responsibility is 'the way you live'. For Rose, the concept of responsibility is a dialectical one – it is something which happens between an individual and her environment. Walter expresses a similar idea:

A sense of responsibility is brought on by observing the world outside, and feeling strongly about some of the issues and that something ought to be done about this, that or the other.

Responsibility then is not something which is imposed upon one person by another or by a situation or even by an environment. It is, rather, something which is created by the existence of a situation which ignites in an individual (or group) a need or call to respond. An individual's increased social awareness and sensitivity to the situations of others is more likely to produce in her some sort of response, for when no problem is perceived, the question of taking action does not arise. In this way, responsibility is as Rose describes it, a way of living, a quality of responding to the environment.

We have already seen how middle-class and working-class respondents differ in the way in which they relate to disadvantaged individuals or groups of individuals. Working-class participants, who have lived through similar situations, tend much more than their middle-class counterparts to identify personally with those in need. Middle-class respondents, in comparison, tend to speak more about the movement or the cause. This might be related to an earlier observation regarding respondents' national and international orientation in the initial stages of their radicalization. This difference is also reflected, although not in a very pronounced form, in the way in which respondents discuss the meaning of responsibility.

Walter protests that

People ought to see just how bad things are. But they don't... I think it's a middle class attitude, that they are doing very well, they're sorry for everybody that isn't, but anything that must be done to remedy it, must not interfere with their comfortable social standing. They're doing extremely well out of society and they can't understand why everybody else isn't. They've done, why can't you... They've got to see it, but they cannot understand it.

When Walter says that 'people ought to see how bad things are,' he means that they ought to be more affected by what they see. Crucial to being affected by the sight of poverty is understanding it; without some sort of political analysis, reactions are reduced to ineffectual sentimentality.

Jack states unequivocally that 'responsibility comes from life's experiences'. He believes that those who do not try to alter the poverty around them often may not do so because

They don't want the struggle. It's not deeply rooted in them... It's a selfish way out, you know... they're only concerned with themselves and getting away from it. They don't feel part of the brotherhood of humanity, 'Let's do it together, let's do it collectively.'... They sympathise, pull out a handkerchief, but when it's time to make a personal effort...they don't want to do it...They're only being emotionally disturbed in the sense of understanding of it. They don't look for cause, only see the effect.

Sentimentality, being emotionally but not mentally disturbed by the sight of poverty, is more likely to result in wet handkerchiefs than in effective political action. Political analysis, looking for causes rather than effects, yields an understanding of the situation which encourages individuals to take collective action. Thus, feeling responsible (being mentally and emotionally affected by the social environment) and responding (taking action) are intricately bound in the lives of the respondents.

The focus of Christopher's concept of responsibility is more universal than either Jack's or Walter's. He explains:

For example, if we take the notion of responsibility for the planet and the welfare of all its creatures, humans, animals, birds, fish, plants, and the environment that they depend on, it seems to me that any act which promotes that welfare, any act of good stewardship as they call it, is a good act. And any act which disregards that welfare, for example, promoting nuclear power or dumping of nuclear waste, or burying chemical waste at sea...seem to me to be absolutely wrong because they are contrary to the notion of a caring stewardship, for what is here, the creatures and the natural environment...

Rose's description of responsibility as a creation between an individual and the environment seems to be, particularly at a physical level, similar to Christopher's statement here. Christopher is nothing if not oriented toward his environment, which includes, but is not limited to, the plight of human beings. But even while Rose would support the work concerning the wider environmental issues which Christopher addresses here, her own focus, and that of the other working-class respondents, has been on the disadvantaged human element in that environment. Edward speaks about the responsibility people have

to all other of God's children...because of the technical advances of the age...we know when there are people starving in Africa, etc...whereas in the past we never would have known it. And so we're responsible to them and we're responsible to the people next door and everybody in between.

His concept of responsibility is directed toward people everywhere, 'all other of God's children'. Edward focuses on the human element, but not exclusively on the plight of the oppressed.

While the particular focus of responsibility might vary slightly between middle-class and working-class respondents, all of the participants embody the culture of responding; all of them perceive problems in the environment, and they feel a compunction to act accordingly.

This pattern of behaviour has existed over a protracted period of time, and it has become characteristic of these individuals. Thus it is that they are lifetime activists.

In some situations, however, the culture of responding becomes so accelerated that it deprives individuals of essential moments for pause in their lives. Eileen refers to this as getting 'caught up in...over-response'. She speaks of an 'over-developed' sense of responsibility. 'That's what people are always saying to me, that I have two right shoulders and I take on too much...I think it's an awful thing to have because you never rest...it's strung around your neck, a bit like an albatross'. One case which illustrates this danger quite dramatically is that of Dorothy. A theme which runs throughout her interviews is that of a lifelong, unrequited quest for freedom. When asked what freedom would mean for her, she answers, 'That those people [the ones for whom she provides furniture, sets up hostels, or who are otherwise in need], didn't have those problems.' As long as they exist with their problems, she will feel the compulsion to do what she can to lessen their burden. Yet, as she writes in a letter to me, 'Spending so much time and participating in absolute Poverty and Degradation and being at one with these people, treating them with Dignity and Respect takes its toll on you.' In an interview, she comments: 'It takes so much out of me. It dominates my life...But you can't half do it. You can't decide "well, this person will have it, and this won't"' Dorothy says she does not go out looking for problems to solve, that 'poverty is on...[her] doorstep', and no doubt, living in the North-East of England, where unemployment is high, this is true. Yet others living in the same economically deprived area do not 'see' the problems in the way that she does; responding to need does not dominate their lives.

The one time Dorothy did experience freedom in her life was when she and her husband rented a cottage in the Yorkshire Dales. She describes this experience: 'It shut all the people out and it was beautiful country, quiet, and it was isolated. You could get inside yourself, and oh it was a marvellous feeling.' Her husband felt frustrated because Dorothy would not accompany him to explore the area. 'She might have a small walk and that would be it', he protests. But Dorothy explains, 'I was so happy to have no obligations to anybody...That was freedom.' Minimal interaction with her environment allowed her to rest, if only temporarily. Yet when, in our interview, I suggested that perhaps she could create a similar space for herself in her own environment by disconnecting the phone or resisting communication and interaction in other ways, she strongly rejected the idea. She knows she is surrounded by others in great need, and that she has the skill to alleviate some of it.

Dedicating herself so fully to the service of others necessarily entails a denial of some of her own needs; still, through her work, she fulfils another aspect of herself, as she calls it, her 'inner self', which desires to be constructive and useful. 'I feel it's important', she explains, 'to make some contribution to life, to improve life for other people, that you don't live for yourself'.

Dorothy reflects that her dream of freedom in an isolated country cottage

is a myth...because I'm quite sure in realization that I wouldn't be happy with nothing to do, only think about myself...I don't think I could live without feeling there was some usefulness there.

Thus the question of 'needing to be needed' is not completely straight-forward – where poverty and unemployment exist, Dorothy feels she must contribute what she can. When her husband suggests that 'families are necessary to her more than families need her', she responds, 'I don't believe that. I don't. If those families were alright, I could forget them.' But that 'if' is a major qualifier, for such families are not alright, and therefore she can't forget them. Dorothy makes the distinction between needing to be needed and being 'conscious of being needed'.

The situation described here illuminates an interesting aspect of the data. Earlier I stated that respondents' self-descriptions were marked by a particularly social orientation, and that, further, this was not an indication that they did not have a well-developed sense of self, but rather that this very sense was itself social. In the passages cited above, Dorothy is so acutely attuned to the needs of others around her that she must be physically isolated from them before she can psychologically remove herself from their problems. Her husband suggests that in responding to the needs of others she is also responding to her own needs. While she flatly rejects this suggestion, she does feel that it is important to make a contribution to life, and not to live for oneself. In helping to meet the needs of others, she is showing herself to be a living embodiment of the principles which she believes are important – even while this might not be a conscious motivation of hers. She knows that she wouldn't be happy with nothing to do, simply because she could not be the kind of person she wants to be. The distinction which she makes between needing to be needed and being conscious of being needed is an important one; given the fact of the existence of poverty and unemployment, she feels compelled to act in such a way as to alleviate the circumstances of others. Thus the environment around her and her feelings regarding it combine to create in her a sense of responsibility.

Rose comments on this aspect of self-fulfilment in helping others:

I remember taking psychology classes, and people saying this question of altruism, you know. And I remember them saying that nobody does anything absolutely altruistically. In the long run one satisfies [one's] self. Now that's conscience again, that's me...You see, I'm satisfying me, I'm not just being good for others...That's the reason that eggs most people on.

She speaks of satisfying herself, because through her actions she is given the opportunity to show herself to be the kind of person she wants to be. Eileen speaks of the self-interest that is part of 'being good', as Rose terms it. She believes there is a close and almost conscious association between the work one does and how one feels about oneself.

There's an awful lot of self-interest in it, if one is very honest. Because...it gives you a feeling of identity, and I often think all the work I do is very important to my ego, there's no doubt about it.

The language used by Eileen here, that of ego and identity, is foreign not only to the speech patterns of Dorothy, but to the very way in which she thinks. Indeed, most of the respondents would not have expressed this thought in this way, even were they to share its sentiments. Nonetheless, all of the respondents do seem to derive a strong sense of satisfaction from the work they have done. Not only have some of their efforts met with successful results, but they feel they have spent their time in a worthy way. They feel good about themselves and about the lives they have led.

Indeed, when participants were asked what, if any, benefits they have derived from their political work, their responses reflected a strong sense of personal satisfaction: 'satisfaction of mind' (Walter), 'living a positive life' (Jack), 'peace of mind' (Dorothy), feeling more complete, and emotional fulfilment were among the answers provided. Other statements addressed the positive feelings which result from putting beliefs into action: 'I think it's a kindly byline of the Creator to enable you to feel happier about being active for the causes which you think are right' (Edward); 'What I believe in, I've tried to do something about' (Walter); and 'a certain pleasure that one was trying to do something about the things which seemed appallingly wrong' (Mary).

Whether satisfaction is the result of meeting a need to be needed, or of working for something which one believes in, the fact remains that all of the participants have a very positive self-image which reveals itself most poignantly when they discuss their political work. While direct questions on self-description yield answers which are very modest and often hesitating, comments concerning their political activism radiate strong, positive self-images. Frida, a mother of four, describes how her activism was itself an expression of care for her children: 'It seemed to me that it was in...the children's interest that I should keep it up. I mean work for peace, you're working for them.' Thus, Frida did not feel torn between her political work and her responsibility to her children, as she saw them as related to each other; her activism was also an important part of her being a mother. Her political work was not isolated from, but rather an integral part of the other aspects of her life. This is true of all the respondents.

Of his political beliefs, Jack states categorically, 'They are me and I'm them.' His political activism is more than merely something which he does. It has become his way of being him. Walter reflects, 'It just became my life, anyway', and later adds, 'My political attitudes, they are me, aren't they? They can't be separated.' Rose echoes this, saying her political ideas are 'of first importance to me. Of course that motivates everything I do.' Indeed, she goes on to say that it would be 'not possible' for her to think of herself without her politics. 'Once you're involved', Elizabeth states, '...it becomes part of your blood'.

Perhaps one of the reasons why respondents tend to experience the end of their lives as a time of continued purposefulness is that old age has not stripped them of their perception of themselves as political activists, which has been dominant throughout their adult lives. One can imagine that the onslaught of old age has different psychological implications for those whose sense of self is primarily dependent upon physical capability. Although amazing stories do exist – such as Beethoven continuing to compose music, despite his loss of hearing – often physical demise prohibits individuals from doing those things with which they associate their essential selves. Is one still a painter, if after having lost one's sight, one no longer paints? What happens to the identity of a sportsperson who can no longer physically perform? Or that of an aging model? The situation for the respondents of this study is different; for them, old age does not challenge but enhances their social identity. Respondents continue to regard their political commitment as one of the major sources of meaning in their lives. The following statements reflect the importance which activists ascribe to their political commitment:

If you are committed, it becomes part of yourself, and stopping being committed would be sort of tearing yourself apart. I can't picture how I would feel if I stopped being interested in socialism...I would lose face with myself and a lot of other people if I gave up now (Edward).

I'd have been an empty life without socialism...If you...give up and become inward, then you've just wasted the previous years that you've given (Jack).

It gives you a motive for going on living. It is very strong. It is survival (Eileen).

If I didn't feel like going on, doing what I'm doing, activating people and encouraging them to struggle, I think I'd become so depressed at home (Rose).

I think if I had to give up, I should be more or less dead on my feet, if I can't take an active part in some movement that's important... I would like, as long as I possibly can, to have contact with a movement, to keep on the move... rather than just sit and everything goes on past you outside. I think as long as you can keep feeling you're part of a great movement... it's something to keep you alive (Frida).

You ought to see these around here, the old people, it's an old people's estate this, and they're dead, but they won't lie down. I don't want that. I don't want to lie down. I've never lain down (Louie).

This series of quotations expresses two themes: (1) participants derive a sense of purpose and meaning in their lives from their political commitment, and (2) were they to 'give up' now, not only would their future seem empty ('depressed at home', 'dead on my feet', and laying down), but their past, too, would be stripped of its meaning (they would 'lose face' and feel they had 'wasted the previous years'). Continued commitment and activism function as a link across time, as a constant and fundamental expression by the respondents of who they are, have been, and will be; it is the way they have come to live their lives.

8   Growing into socialism

The best way to overcome it [fear of death] ... is to make your interests gradually wider and more impersonal, until bit by bit the walls of the ego recede, and your life becomes increasingly merged in the universal life. An individual human experience should be like a river – small at first, narrowly contained within its banks, and rushing passionately past boulders and over waterfalls. Gradually the river grows wider, the banks recede, the waters flow more quietly, and in the end, without any visible break, they become merged in the sea, and painlessly lose their individual beings. The man who, in old age, can see his life in this way, will not suffer from the fear of death, since the things he cares for will continue.

Bertrand Russell (quoted in Seckel 1986: 33)

One of the major limitations of developmental psychology which we identified in the opening pages of this book is its definition of what is and what is not growth. We examined one paradigm of life-span developmental theory, Levinson's *Seasons of a Man's Life*, which stated that at the end of the life cycle, development meant an individual 'reaching his ultimate involvement with the self' (1978: 38–39). While this might be an accurate description of the culmination of the life course in an individualistic society, Levinson's presentation of his theory extends into the realm of prescription, confounding what is with what ought to be. However, for the respondents in this study, development has taken a form exactly opposite to that which Levinson suggests; in the course of their lives, participants have become increasingly oriented toward their social environment, and away from themselves and their immediate needs.

One of the definitions of development listed in the *Penguin Dictionary of Psychology* is:

a progressive change leading to higher levels of differentiation and organization. Here the connotation is one of positive progress, increases in effectiveness of function, maturity, richness and complexity (Reber 1985: 1940).

The words which I would like to emphasize here are 'progressive change' and 'complexity'. Development in the lives of the respondents has not been marked by a radical reorganization of their belief systems. They have not 'outgrown', but grown into the very principles which they endorsed as young adults. The development in their lives, thus, can be best described as change within constancy; their growth can be charted by an examination of the ways in which their political concepts have become more complex through years of experience.

In response to the question 'How would you describe changes in yourself that have happened through the years?', Eileen queries, 'Well, has one changes? You're presupposing that one changes.' She elaborates on this:

basically, one is the same in... the way one sees life... sometimes I think, 'Oh God, I'm stuck with the same philosophy', then I think 'Fine, I still believe it. Nothing has taken away my belief in this.'

Eileen, who quotes Einstein, saying, 'the only constant is change', sees in herself a progressive change, represented in a deepening of her understanding of Marxism, but not a change which involves a rejection of the political ideas she embraced many years ago.

If you have a philosophy like mine that is a political one... it obviously gets modified, but I think your basic beliefs stay the same... I still believe in progress, I still have my Marxism.

Eileen describes how she sees change in her own life. She recalls going to see the Walt Disney film *Fantasia*, and listening to a Bach fugue, which corresponded to her perception of life.

That it was, the interchanging and the movements, and how changes occur. What I was telling you about my own life, that it heaps up and suddenly it moves into something else and it weaves intricately and it gets lost and it gets stronger and finally there's a change... it was the music, it was the clarity of Bach, and the order, and the symmetry.

Thus, Eileen identifies change in her life, but of an evolutionary nature. One understanding grows out of another – earlier perspectives are enhanced, not replaced.

Jack Lindsay identifies a common theme throughout his writing:

my enduring interest at all phases has been in the nature of development, in the ways in which change and forward movement occur with a leap into new levels: conflict and contradiction driven to the decisive point, then bring about either breakdown or the liberation into a qualitatively new dimension. The concern with such things, the effort to test out generalizations in field after field, in situation after situation, and to grasp yet more finely and fully how fundamental change occurs is what I call Marxism; and it has been the restless movement of my Marxism... that has driven me on (Lindsay 1982: 809).

Jack's description of fundamental change and forward movement can as easily be applied to psychological development as to the many varied fields which he researched. Elsewhere he comments: 'To the extent that one grasps the principles of dialectics can one begin to understand development in any sphere' (Chaplin 1983: iv).

Edwards says of himself: 'I develop in understanding, but basically I don't think I've changed all that much.' However, he also states that 'if one doesn't change, one is dead' and identifying the areas of changes in his own life, he adds:

I've a more realistic way of trying to work for socialism than I had earlier on. I think I've got a deeper understanding of the meaning of Christianity...I think they're the same values [as held earlier in life] but I hope I've grown in understanding how to work for them.

Edward, then, identifies change in himself insofar as he has grown in his understanding. But the tenets of his most basic beliefs have remained relatively unaltered.

Christopher describes what he sees as being his political growth:

I said just now that I believed politically speaking...I'd arrived...I *don't* mean that I've arrived at some sort of plateau or summit of knowledge and understanding from which no further advance is possible. That's an absurd notion, it's something not given to humans...I simply mean that I think my *general orientation* is right, that I have before me the possibility of travelling intelligently...All we can do, as humans, is travel, and if I say 'I've arrived' I only mean I've arrived at...'a path with heart'...a path which one can follow with the consent of all one's being.

Christopher's development is a dynamic one, and one which involves the whole of himself. It is not a casting off of a past self, but rather the expansion of a present one.

Elizabeth sees change as 'inevitable', but again the change is of an evolutionary rather than a radical nature. She qualifies her use of the word change, saying that with age you become 'much more open to a real understanding of the world...comparatively...it's looking back and seeing your, I wouldn't say changed attitudes, but more developed attitudes'. The distinction between changed and developed attitudes is a useful one. Mary does not feel that she has changed since the time she became politically aware, saying she still 'work[s] to the same principle or fail[s] to the same principles.' She observes about herself that

even at seventy-five (or not quite), I get some of the reactions which I don't think are good which are just the same as when I was eight or nine. And I always thought that when you grew up, you'd be perfect, you know. It's interesting that that doesn't happen.

Frida expresses a similar feeling, approaching that of surprise, when upon self-examination she does not identify change in herself.

I think... I'm a kind of a dinosaur, because I believe in what I believed in thirty years ago, or fifty years ago. You know, it seems extraordinary.

The role of experience is perceived to be very important. As Jack surmises, 'to get to eighty years without experience would be useless. It would be a waste of eighty years', and Rose also speaks of 'getting wiser through experience'. When Walter is asked if his commitment has changed in time, he responds:

Life of experience has taught me a lot, I'm pleased to say. But it hasn't changed me. No. The things I learned in 1934 on the hunger march... I hold fast to this day... I was never the same after that hunger march. I could never go back to being just the same person.

Respondents' engagement with the social and political issues of their times has not resulted in an alteration of their fundamental political beliefs. However, through their long-term political involvement, the beliefs themselves have become, in most cases, more complex, accommodating to information acquired by the activists as they encounter various situations. Thus, through their experiences, individuals grow into their ideas.

In contrast to a linear progression of development, the growth of these individuals would more accurately be depicted in the form of a spiral. Again, the emphasis here is on retaining a basic set of beliefs throughout the life course, but with those beliefs growing in depth and complexity with time and experience. Eileen uses this image when speaking about the direction her life has taken:

You don't come back, it isn't the wheel has come full circle. You come in a spiral. This is the Marxist theory of progress... Life doesn't go back to where it began, it comes up a bit further, and that's where you see progress.

Life's experiences are thus interpreted not only when they happen, but re-examined time and again through an ever-expanding lens.

It is only through the passage of time that one derives a sense of who one is in relation to who one has been. Elizabeth describes the experience of looking back over her life, the years giving her a perspective which would have been impossible to acquire while actually living through those times.

when you look back, you see the path or the paths that you've taken. The path would obviously not be so clear when you're groping up and finding it, would it? I mean it's rather like going up a mountain, you're sort of looking that way and that track and it looks too steep and you're going round another one.

Whereas when you're high up you can look back and see and it sort of stands out much more clearly, things you didn't realize at the time.

Thus, the questions of change and development arise invariably in the course of a life review. In Chapter 3, we mentioned that reconstructed memory reflects an individual's current understanding of a past event, illuminating a continuous flow of perceived meaning across experience and time. An example of this is Jack's retrospective understanding of the General Strike, which he recalls in the following way:

I got me first lesson in political divisions, and the cunning they used. When I went over to the Bank of England and there was all armoured tanks around there. And every solider I spoke to, they was always Scotch or Irish or Welsh. There was no Cockney. And then I was told the Cockneys was in Glasgow. So there could be no loyalties evoked from it ... years afterwards when I was reading it [*The Fall of the Roman Empire* which outlined the theory of divide and conquer] it took me back to my experiences when I was talking to the soldiers guarding the Bank of England.

Development happens as a result of interaction, not only between the individual and the current environment, but also between the individual and past environments, that is, through the reinterpretation and reprocessing of past lived experiences. In this way, individuals grow not only through encountering new experiences, but also through revisiting old experiences, and thus making them new.

Encountering challenges to socialism

Cognitive development, it has been argued, is a dynamic process which involves the tension between 'holding on' and 'letting go' (Kegan 1982; Koholberg 1981, 1984; Piaget 1977). Development is not, Kegan declares, 'a matter of differentiation alone, but of differentiation and reintegration' (1982: 67). One of the most essential tenets of Piaget's theory of cognitive development is that individuals adapt to their environment through a combination of assimilation and accommodation. Where possible, individuals process information regarding the external world through assimilation to existing cognitive structures. When those structures are not adequate to incorporate information (and if the stimulus persists over an extended period of time) they are altered, and as a result become increasingly complex, as they accommodate to the information. Cognitive development comprises hierarchical integration, whereby higher stages reintegrate, rather than negate, structures found at lower stages (Kohlberg 1984: 14).

While we are not specifically concerned with the cognitive development of the respondents, this dualistic orientation to development is helpful to our present discussion regarding the ways in which respondents deal with information which might potentially threaten their beliefs. Clearly all of the respondents have managed in one way or another to retain their political convictions. Most of them have achieved this through adopting a belief system which is flexible enough to accommodate new information. There is, however, also evidence of situations in which individuals, finding themselves unable to assimilate information, instead deny the information itself rather than alter their original views.

Earlier, we saw that respondents became radicalized in a particular historical context in which political issues appeared to be relatively straightforward. Ed expresses a view common amongst the respondents:

It seems to me that the issues were very clear, there was none of this complications of everything being grey. Everything was black and white. To my mind it was fascism against anti-fascism. It was Hitler against the Soviet Union.

Since that time, the international situation has changed considerably. During the period immediately following the Second World War, socialists and communists in the West might be said to have experienced a 'siege mentality'; so constant and virulent were the Western criticisms of all things communist and/or Soviet, that sympathizers may have regarded any and all criticism of the Soviet Union as capitalist propaganda.

Thus, a particularly challenging period of history for committed socialists was in the late 1950s, when revelations about the Soviet Union caused many sympathizers to re-evaluate certain aspects of their political beliefs. Two major international events occurred in 1956 which provoked many committed socialists to re-examine their views about the Soviet Union. The first was the Twentieth Party Congress in February 1956, in which Khrushchev denounced Stalin and his methods and revealed facts about the persecutions which had taken place in the Soviet Union under Stalin for more than twenty years. This famous speech was followed several months later by the Hungarian National Rising, in which Soviet tanks went into Hungary to uphold a pro-Soviet government, and proceeded to execute leaders of the uprising.

The combination of these events precipitated a re-evaluation by most of the participants of their beliefs in the practical application of their political ideas. Although many people became very disillusioned, not only with the Communist Party but also with socialism in general, and turned away from belief in left-wing politics, clearly this was not the case for any of the participants in this study. Most of the respondents in this study found Krushchev's speech very disturbing, posing the most significant challenge to their commitment to socialism that many would ever encounter. Heinemann (1976), writing of this period, states:

It is hard to convey now the degree of shock and horror with which the CPSU critique was received among British Communists. It was soon obvious that support for the CPSU and the Soviet Government could never again be as simple and instinctive as before (p. 43).

Eric Hobsbawm, Britain's leading Marxist historian, describes the effect of these events on Communist Party members as

a certain weakening of the old belief that, as Catholics used to say, 'Outside the church there is no salvation,' you have to be in the Communist Party or else there's nothing. Once upon a time we believed this and perhaps 1956 indicated that even those of us who stayed in, no longer believed it in quite the same old way (*Guardian*, 20 October 1986).

The examples I shall discuss here are of the respondents who closely reassessed their attitudes toward socialism and its relationship to the Soviet Union; this critical period strengthened their commitment as it deepened their understanding of their own political ideas.

Although Edward had never joined the Communist Party, he had always been very sympathetic to it, and in the 1930s had spoken on many a street corner on its behalf. Up until the 1950s, he thought 'they ought to have brought down paradise from heaven when the Russian Revolution occurred'. He describes himself at that time as 'too pro-Stalin', and with Khrushchev's speech

we had to rethink quite a lot of things...we weren't critical enough...I didn't have to rethink everything, but only some things...I suppose I continued to believe in the Soviet Union, but much more critically than before.

As Edward had not been a Party member, his new and more critical approach did not involve shifting party allegiances. But as he said earlier, experiences such as these gave him a more enhanced analytical outlook, and consequently a 'better understanding of how to work for socialism'.

Mary was a member of the Communist Party during the 1950s, and her reaction to Khrushchev's speech was clearly from the perspective of a Party member.

I'd always accepted that some of the things that happened in Russia were not at all what I would approve of. But I had felt that their whole basis...was so important that I was willing to go along with it. But when it came to the point that even after a great many disclosures...that the official party felt it was dangerous to admit that any single thing was wrong, I felt that they would have no influence.

Still a committed socialist, Mary left the Party because she no longer thought it could be a politically effective organization if it did not allow for discussion of controversial issues. She had to draw a distinction between her commitment to socialism and her commitment to the Communist Party; forsaking the latter did not weaken the former.

Ed was also a member of the Party in the fifties, and had been so for some thirty years. Like Mary, the revelations caused him to rethink his position as a Party member, but unlike her, he was able to resolve his tensions while remaining in the Party. His first reaction to reading Khrushchev's speech was:

a load of lies, don't believe it. A few days later it became clear that it was not a load of lies, that it was true. It took me two to four weeks, and it was the most difficult experience I've ever had in my life. I started to think about it and try and understand what had happened and how it affected me.

Ed did not see any political purpose in leaving the Party. It was not his commitment to socialism which he began to question, nor even his commitment to the Party, but rather his attitude toward the Soviet Union.

There was no question of leaving as far as I was concerned...from the point of view of conviction, I didn't see that you were going to put anything right. What was wrong was in the Soviet Union, they'd have to put it right...the only thing that would make me leave the Communist Party was if Marxism...were shown to be false.[1]

Describing the alterations that these events produced in him, Ed explains, 'Prior to 1956, I had a very idealised conception of the Soviet Union...Partly through their propaganda, partly because of our great belief in socialism...we did tend to idealise it very, very much.'

Edward, Mary and Ed, all in slightly different ways, became more sophisticated in their political outlooks as a result of inner questioning which was precipitated by the events of 1956. In each of these three cases, the individuals retained their basic political commitment. However, they no longer viewed the Soviet Union as 'heaven on earth', (in Edward and Ed's cases), nor the Party as undoubtedly the only place for a committed socialist (in the case of Mary). The result was that their understanding of socialism became more complex.

The combined effect of the Twentieth Party Congress and the Hungarian National Rising on these three committed socialists offers a convenient but not unique illustration of the ways in which individuals can develop while not changing their fundamental beliefs. Their political conviction is retained through the dynamic process of holding on (to their fundamental belief in socialism) and letting go (of those aspects of their beliefs which external events, in their view, have proven to be inadequate).

The experiences of accommodation reported here are similar to those of most of the other participants. However, there are three contrasting incidents, in which there does not appear to be much evidence of respondents accommodating their beliefs to incorporate new, and challenging information. In the examples which follow, events which may have been expected to have caused respondents at the very least a moment for pause, were instead quickly processed through their previously established perspective and seemingly rationalized. Each of the instances involves a lifetime Communist Party member in some way defending the Soviet Union. For these respondents, allegiance to the Soviet Union was and continues to be an important tenet of their commitment. Louie explains that 'anybody attacking...the Soviet Union at all, I will defend it, while ever I can...I regard that as an insult to attack the Soviet Union'.

The question of sustained commitment is somewhat different for lifetime CP members than for the others, because the former have a more immediately identifiable structure, i.e. the Party, and even country, to which the commitment is attached. Some of the lifetime CP members felt that a negative statement about the Soviet Union, implicit or explicit, was a direct affront to their political convictions; thus, they either outrightly denied the factual basis of the criticism, or offered what appears to be a rationalization for the event under discussion. Each of the examples provide evidence of the speaker's struggle to resist any challenge to their belief system; defending the actions of the Soviet Union, and by implication reaffirming their political convictions, is of primary importance.

Jack's description of his reaction to the Soviet–Nazi Pact of 1939 reveals a strong desire to see the Soviet Union in a positive light.

I got shook by it at first. Until I met leading cadres, and read more on it, and went to some political groups, and we discussed the whole issue. And then of course the clarity of it came out...I learned the ABC of dialectics and the materialism and the politics and I see how correct it was...the trade pact...was also offered to us, which wasn't accepted, so they offered it to Nazi Germany in order to buy time...It was British imperialism that prevented...the pact of the four nations.

This statement contains a swift and radical shift in Jack's thinking. Initially he was 'shook by it' because an indictment against the Soviet Union would have been an indictment against his political beliefs. However, by explaining this pact in terms of British imperialism, his beliefs remain intact.

A few days prior to one of my visits to Rose – in December 1986 – she had received some Polish guests. When we met, our conversation turned to the political tension in Poland. The root of the problem, Rose explained to me, was not in any denial of rights on the part of the government, but was to be found in an essential greediness of the people.

They're terrific eaters of meat, and there wasn't enough meat. When you think in terms of the people in this country who are now turning to vegetarianism and how many people don't eat meat from a principled point of view, then the issue was terrible to think that this was what they were struggling about, not getting chunks of meat. There was a lot of greed in the thing. These are the little things that mount up ... and that's why they had the trouble in Poland.

Rather than confront the possibility that the Polish people may have legitimate grounds on which to protest, and by implication criticize the Soviet Union, Rose instead avoids the issue altogether by discussing the virtues of vegetarianism. In so doing, she has cognitively reorganized, one might say 'digested', a potential challenge to her political beliefs. During the same conversation, Rose gives her view of the Soviet invasion of Hungary: 'so he stepped in to help the Hungarian government. Now Hungary is a good country today, people are doing well there, and living better ... I had no argument within myself about that.' If Rose does have any criticisms of the Soviet Union, she does not communicate them to me.

Louie, too, fiercely defends every action of the Soviet Union. Her reaction to the events of the late 1950s sharply contrasts with the reactions of Edward, Mary and Ed cited earlier. She says that she read all about Hungary and, later, Czechoslovakia. 'I knew all about it ... I didn't believe any of it ... It was all provocation.' Describing her feelings toward Khrushchev and his speech at the Twentieth Party Congress in 1956, she states:

I didn't support him altogether. Just a little. I agreed with Stalin. I agreed with Stalin. We'll never get socialism through the ballot box ... He's killed millions, they're only just finding out that he's killed a million. At time he never killed a million. It's all a tale. Propaganda is very powerful you know.

Louie's message seems to be that Khrushchev himself was bending to Western propaganda, that Stalin had not killed millions, and that even if he had, he would have been morally (not to mention politically) justified, because socialism won't come through the ballot box. Effectively, Louie has covered all of her bases; when she can cognitively reorganize interpretation of historical events to both acknowledge and justify their existence, she has done so. Failing that, she employs a strategy of complete denial; thus, the invasion of Hungary quite simply never happened.

These three instances stand out amongst the data. Because Jack, Rose and Louie all bind their commitment to socialism very closely to their belief in the Soviet Union, their interpretation of any of that country's actions must be favourable, if it is not to be fundamentally threatening to their belief system. Interestingly, only Jack experienced any form of discomfort, reflected by his statement that he 'got shook'. Neither Rose nor Louie appear to have experienced any form of anxiety over the events they describe. All of the respondents have retained their belief in socialism, and most of them have adjusted and readjusted aspects of this belief in order to incorporate an increasingly greater diversity of experience. Thus, they grow not by abandoning their socialism, but through acquiring a deeper understanding of it. Through such expericnes as these, to use Eileen's phrase, '[life] comes up a bit further, and that's where you see progress'.

'You can't argue with an earthquake': the 1989 revolutions

None of us were to know at the time of the interviews that one of the most dramatic challenges to socialism in modern times was soon to come. Between August and December 1989 there were anti-communist 'revolutions' in Poland, Hungary, East Germany, Bulgaria, Czecho-slovakia and Romania. These months contained many memorable moments, the opening up of the Berlin Wall and the execution of Nicolae and Elena Ceauşescu on Christmas Day being amongst the most dramatic. Even as I write, it is not possible to have a perspective on these momentous changes. Gwyn Prins in his Introduction to *Spring in Winter: The 1989 Revolutions* asks the rhetorical question, 'What is an historical turning point? How do we know when we meet one?' (1990: 2). The only thing which does seem certain is that these are times of historically important change.

The revolutions in Eastern Europe were greeted in the West with much enthusiasm. The interpretation of these events by Western media was as superficial as it was monomaniacal: capitalism had triumphed over socialism. As the decade came to a close, so had the life of socialism, Mrs Thatcher proclaimed. Indeed the pervasiveness of this viewpoint was quite startling, even to some seasoned political observers. However, there were some dissenting voices. Laurence Harris, Professor of Economics at the Open University, cautioned: 'The West makes a great mistake in identifying the rejection of old Communist regimes with a desire for capitalism' (*Guardian*, 4 January 1990). Jan Urban, one of the leaders of Civic Forum in Czechoslovkia, came to speak at the Cambridge University lecture series 'Understanding the Revolutions in

Eastern Europe'. At the end of his speech, I asked what, if anything, he saw as being the role of socialism in his country's future. To this he replied that while the Czechoslovakian people might be wary of any labels, particularly socialism and communism, nonetheless those things which they were working for, others might identify as socialist; while there was much they wished to borrow from the West, they did not want to import 'carelessness with people' (Prins 1990: 9).

What, then, did the participants of this study make of these changes? I wrote to each of them, enquiring whether the revolutions had had an effect upon their perception of, and commitment to, socialism. Their responses came in different shapes and sizes, ranging from short notes to one 'personal testimony' of more than fifteen pages. Many expressed their gratitude for the opportunity to put into words the many thoughts which had been provoked in the previous months, and to try to make sense of it all. While there was a wide range in reactions, most of the respondents felt quite similarily to one another. Indeed, several wanted to know what the others had written, and later when I shared some of the material with them, they seemed to feel heartened by reading the words of like-minded others.

Janet is the most exhilarated of all the respondents. She writes to me with unqualified joy:

How exciting and how heartening to all good socialists have been the events of the last few months...How lucky one has been to be able to follow them day by day...It is the ideas and beliefs of socialists which have inspired the people of Eastern Europe to take to the streets and to demand the exit of the communists and their ideas. Never has socialism and its defenders been so creative and effective as we have seen them and heard them in the last few weeks...If you pass this way come in and we shall toast the future in champagne which is ready and waiting.

Janet is perhaps the least left wing of all of the respondents. Crucial to her construction of events is the hard distinction she makes between socialists and communists. Janet sees in these events cause for celebration; far from challenging her commitment to socialism, they seem to vindicate it.

Louie does not see things the same way. She is perhaps the most hard-line left winger of the group, and she is also the most depressed about the events. She writes:

Certainly it is all a huge setback for Socialism but nothing, that is smaller than the might of the working class, can hold Socialism from reaching its goal.

Louie says that those who are 'so much against Socialism and Communists...will find their awakening when they see Fascism raising its ugly head'. In contrast to Janet, socialism (an ideology) and communists (the people) are grouped together in Louie's construction. Despite how dispirited Louie is, however, she does not despair of the future of socialism. Rather, she says: 'I think we shall have to wait and see these things have to slowly work themselves out. I still have faith in the Working Class...[and] am still fighting for Peace and Socialism.'

The thoughts of Janet and Louie represent the two ends of the spectrum: Janet seeing greater times being heralded in, Louie holding on to her beliefs despite what she identifies as a huge setback. The other respondents occupy more of a middle ground in their reactions. I am reminded here of a comment made by Eric Hobsbawm, in response to the question of whether he welcomed what was happening in Eastern Europe and the Soviet Union: 'It is of course deeply moving. "Welcoming" seems to be an irrelevant word. You cannot argue with an earthquake' (*Independent on Sunday*, 4 February 1990).

This reflects the sentiments expressed by many of the respondents, who recognize that momentous changes are happening around them: they neither welcome them, nor fundamentally despair of them. That is not at issue. Rose comments, 'I feel that we are too near historically to estimate matters and the happenings are in so much fluidity to pass judgment that I don't feel capable of explaining it to myself or to anyone else.' Eileen describes herself as 'constantly rethinking' and says she is 'trying to work through all that is going on – can't tell you yet what I think. I get nauseated by the media pundits and the politicians burying socialism...' Dorothy says, 'It is difficult to have a firm view as the situation changes...It is impossible to see what the long-term implications will be.' It is difficult to gauge one's reactions to what is happening, as it is time which will reveal the effects of what we are now living through.

Respondents' descriptions of the recent changes fall broadly into three, sometimes overlapping, categories. First, some respondents look to the history of communism in Eastern Europe for an explanation of the current situation. Second, respondents make East/West comparisons, offering an alternative interpretation of life in capitalist democracies from that put forth in the Western media. Third, respondents adopt a wide perspective on history, and warn against the dangers of short-term analysis.

Hobsbawm describes how 'Communism was never established in Eastern Europe' because it never came from the people; it was a foreign import, imposed from above, something which never really took root. This he contrasts with the Soviet Union, which 'is the legitimate government, the successor of the tsar, and has been ever since 1917'

(*Independent on Sunday*, 4 February 1990). Edward, too, offers an historical synopsis, referring to 'post-war Eastern Europe, where socialism was imposed by the Red Army, with the additional disadvantage that it was a foreign importation'. Frida writes that 'communism has never had a chance to prove itself', and protests that

we should not blame Communism for the evils of Ceaucescu or Stalin any more than we blame Christianity for the Inquisition, or for Cromwell's crimes, or the Crusades... Can you imagine turning your back on the Ninth Symphony just because it has been badly performed? Well, I can't! What is great and good and beautiful does not turn out to be paltry and rotten because the wrong people got hold of it and misinterpreted it! Communism has not yet had an adequate performance, and we'll have to work for it long and hard before this can happen.

Frida does not deny the severity of the abuses which characterized communist rule in various Eastern Bloc countries. What she does challenge, however, is that these abuses are inherent in communism.

That the communism in Eastern Europe was not 'real' communism is something suggested by several respondents – it was not a people's movement, and was only supported by the state apparatus. However, respondents also reject the implicit, and sometimes explicit, message perpetrated by the Western media and elsewhere, that life in capitalist democracies is far superior to that in the Eastern Bloc countries. Walter writes:

[Young people in Eastern Europe] cry out for Freedom and Democracy, but living under the Thatcher administration which refuses to sign the EEC Charter giving the people legal rights at work, I could also join them in the same demands. I wonder how long the British people will wait before they too join in this political enthusiasm. How much more will they take?

Frida, too, makes comparisons between East and West. The Western media 'in its strident anti-communist comments crows about the poverty, pollution, deprivation in Eastern Europe as if these ills did not exist in the capitalist West'. She continues:

No mention is made of the East's good features: state-subsidized welfare, full employment, promotion of the peace movement, and of culture and sport; not a word about the absence of commercialism, crude advertising (no sex or violence for private profit!) crime, drugs, unemployment.

Respondents question not only the comparative quality of life in the West, but the very process by which wealth is accumulated. Ed refers to the commercialism of the West, and what it is built on: 'If only the people in Eastern Europe understood that the so-called prosperity of the West depends on the starvation and death of hundreds of thousands of children in the so-called Third World things might be different.' But it is not only the labour of poorer nations which has been the building stones for Western opulence, but also the labour of Western democracies' poorer citizens. Louie reminds us of this when she writes: 'People will always remember Capitalism and its policy of living on the backs of the working class. Capitalism have nothing to be prowed of look at the wars they have caused how many millions they have led to their death.' Indeed, a critique of Western capitalism runs throughout her letter.

Respondents look to history not only to explain the past, and thus the present, but also the future. Later in this chapter we shall see how respondents have always adopted a long-term view of history, and regard the effectiveness of their political actions by this yardstick. This perspective has been particularly important in their assessment of more recent events. Trevor remarks:

if it's the death of socialism... that would make totally meaningless the whole of the historical process, and for me it's intolerable that Thatcher should talk in that sense, it always has been. She doesn't really know anything. She's got so little historical sense anyhow, she doesn't understand what socialism means at all. And it's exceedingly arrogant and offensive.

Christopher, too, writes that he inclines 'toward the LONG HAUL view of things, perhaps even the eternal haul'.

Perhaps it is for this reason that respondents do not seem to feel that they have been proven 'wrong'. Frida writes:

You ask whether my 'commitment'... has been shaken by last year's events in Europe and China? My answer is unhesitatingly No! To me, the achievement of your research is in showing that your subjects' commitment was *not* skin-deep: how could it have endured into their 8th decade if it were not deeply ingrained and well propped up by reason, experience and historical truth.

Walter, too, reconfirms his socialist commitment, while acknowleging the effect of recent events:

The big events have taken place since our first discussions, but although I have been shocked at times, astounded at others, I would not wish to alter anything I have already stated to you, and significantly you do not even ask me to do so.

Ed states emphatically:

Scientific Socialism remains valid. The most important is the dialectic. All the old shibboleths are in the melting pot. The enemy is dogmatism. Marx said 'Doubt everything.'

Eileen, too, sees no reason to reject her Marxism, which she sees as being, above all,

a tool which has enabled me to make some sense of the world and to see some positive way through. It has taught me that the world can be changed once people realise their own power – first through individual understanding, then through collective action: in other words, we make our own history and must accept that responsibility. Marxism has also taught me that existence...is the source of and fashions our thinking and our ideas...Nothing that has happened has changed these basic beliefs for me.

We can see then that recent upheavals have not caused respondents to reject their belief in socialism.

Harris sees reason for hope in the revolutions of 1989:

What is relevant is that now in 1989, it is clear that East European and Soviet socialism are able to examine their histories openly – both the crime and the progress – and that they have a tremendous momentum for developing a new socialist politics. The opening up of political life in the socialist countries is the greatest reason to believe socialism could be entering a new, hopeful, and more democractic era (*Guardian*, 4 January 1990).

Edward agrees, regarding the happenings as 'signs of the welcome capacity of socialism to reform and purify itself', describing socialism as a 'more enduring creed' than capitalism 'because it can more easily practise repentence, to which they give the name perestroika'.

While it seems slightly premature to judge how respondents shall make sense ultimately of these events, initial impressions indicate that although the revolutions did not cause respondents to reject their commitment to socialism, most did feel some sort of sadness or unease with the course of events. Eileen reprimands herself quite severely: 'I am disturbed at my political naivete, misjudgement and far too unquestioning spirit, if not romanticism...I am shocked and angry at my innocence.' Eileen is the only respondent who expresses such feelings about herself; in other respondents, the source of anger, where it exists, is a different one. Frida's main reaction was 'a surge of indignation at the East-European countries being conned into Western capitalist ways'. Dorothy, too, is 'appalled at how easily people were bought and spent the cash they were given on glitter'. Rose describes herself as 'emotionally upset by events, but [I] carry on with trying to better our lot under Thatcherism with regard to pensioners, the health service, Poll Tax which keep me from going round the bend'.

In no instance did the Eastern European revolutions cause respondents to reject their commitment to socialism. While only Janet seemed to welcome the changes without hesitation, all of the others still found reason to continue to believe in the future of socialism. It seems to be, as Frida suggests, that the commitment of the respondents is not skin-deep, but rather it is complex and flexible enough to accommodate new information without being put substantially at risk. Respondents do not embrace what James Galbraith calls 'Simplistic Ideology' which 'pictures a starkly bi-polar world' (*Guardian*, 26 January 1990), but rather attempt to make sense of the present political situation through their understanding of history. It is this perspective which allows them to retain the faith of their convictions.

The heart and mind of political purpose

How do respondents view the relationship between the workings of their heart and mind? Does one tend to lead, and the other follow? Do they ever come into conflict? Indeed, do respondents even perceive a clear distinction between their emotions and their intellect? When Rose describes political commitment, she explains

You have to have it here and here – in your head and in your heart. Because those people who are intellectually in the movement only, they very seldom stick it out. Those people who are only there emotionally can't work it out... Your mind ought to work it out, but you should never turn down this feeling of the heart, this emotion, for people, and for things.

When Eileen tries to identify the primary motivator behind her activism, she refers to 'seeing clearly what's got to be done... It is an intellect, it's head, it's not emotions.' But neither does she deny the importance of emotions, as she refers to the necessary 'quantities of both'. 'I think one should be caring... certainly if you're doing... any political work.' Elizabeth, too, refers to a necessary balance: 'You've got to use your brain as much as you can to understand, but it's got to be balanced with a compassion and a caring for the world, where the heart is involved.'

Jack believes that all emotions are the result of political understanding. He rejects the notion that the heart motivates individuals in their lives. Rather, it is the brain which functions as the sole source of understanding. Motivation of the heart hints at a sentimentality which he flatly rejects.[2] Walter, too, feels uneasy with making a distinction between cognition and affect.

I don't want to make that split. I'm unable to make that split. I'm unable to cope with the phrase 'motivation of the heart' which you're using. It's not something that I would use at all.

If the term 'feelings' were to replace the objectionable phrase, Walter says that the question would make more sense to him, but that still he could not make that distinction. He would not want to separate his feelings from his intellectual understanding, 'nor do I think it's possible'.

Most respondents did feel that intellect and emotion were separate, but that they must be held in balance with each other. Mary's decisions are guided by 'a complete mixture of both ... the intellectual analysis and not very intellectual ... I suppose caring is emotion, isn't it?' Christopher does not recall a time when he consciously experienced a split between his intellect and his emotions. For him, movement is gradual, and motivations can only be analysed in retrospect.

I'd drifted along the river, and suddenly there I was, somewhere else. I'd try to figure out why I was somewhere else, and what was the nature of the river that had carried me there, rather than having a tremendous shoot out of ... mind versus emotion.

At the time of his early radicalization, he recalls that 'the intellectual and the emotional were very much running parallel and hand-in-hand'. For Edward, it is often through prayer that 'the emotional and the intellectual link up'. When he is reading, he feels 'it's sometimes very useful to stop and just meditate on whatever subject has arisen in this book and let it sink in, and become more part of my emotional make-up. That's the sort of way I pray.'

For all of the participants, politics is not only an appreciation of abstract principles of justice, but an enactment of a responsibility to others, both known and unknown. Their hearts and minds do not clash, but rather converge with each other. Political engagement, then, is not intellectual understanding alone, but entails personal involvement. Such emotional connection, however, is not based upon a romantic sentimentality, but upon a sense of responsibility for, and connection with others. The marked resonance between respondents' cognitive and affective assessments of their experiences, and of their lives in general, is not surprising, as they are guided in their actions by a clear sense of purpose. It is most likely this that accounts for the strong correlation between respondents' beliefs and actions discussed earlier.

Ed, when asked if he had ever been confronted with a moral conflict, responded:

Never. The most serious thing that's ever happened to me was the Twentieth Congress of the CPSU. But I didn't regard it as a moral issue. I regarded it as a political issue. I regarded it as a need to deepen my understanding of the world and see what had gone wrong and why and that the reason it had gone wrong was a departure from correct communist theory.

The Twentieth Party Congress did not pose a moral problem for Ed, because he was not re-evaluating his belief in socialism, but rather reviewing the more political question of how best to put that belief into practice. Jack's political convictions have guided his actions:

I've never had a moral dilemma. I know what's morally right and what's morally wrong. I've never had a dilemma about it. You see I make everything black and white...grey is a dirty colour anyway. But everything to me is black and white, there's right and there's wrong...Always clear what to do, once I understood.

Walter feels similarly. When asked if he had ever had a moral conflict, he responds 'No, I don't think I've had a conflict like that. My working days of course were a battle on trade union issues...[But] I was never torn with a personal conflict.' Again, the distinction is made between personal and political conflict. Generally speaking, all of the respondents have led lives full of political conflict of one sort or another.

Dorothy flatly rejects the idea of moral conflict in her life. When asked how she decides between competing claims, she responds:

It depends what you feel is right...Not what's right for you, but what's morally right...I think I know instinctively what's right...[from] experiences...I don't think I ever have a dilemma...I just know...I've certainly never dithered over anything. I make my mind up, and I think I make it up right.

She is very confident about the correctness of her instincts, which she continually stresses come from her life's experience.

While generally respondents report that they have not experienced moral conflict in their lives, there are three exceptions to this. In these cases, respondents felt that although one particular course of action was more consistent with their political beliefs than another, were they to follow that course, they might not be acting in the best interests of others close to them – in every case, their children. In two of the three instances, the conflict concerned educating children; in the third case, the difficulty focused on resolving demands of conflicting roles. The only respondents who did identify moral conflict in their lives were middle class. Three of the middle-class activists had never faced a moral conflict, while the other three had.

Edward and Eileen both struggled with the question of whether to send their children to private schools. While both of them made similar decisions, i.e. to send them there for a short time, neither of them felt completely comfortable with this choice. Edward comments, 'Sometimes you have to make decisions which are the least bad in the circumstances.' Describing the dilemma as he and his wife perceived it, he explains:

When our children were growing up, there was quite a good argument for letting them go to private school where they would get a higher proportion of teachers to the children and a better education and a better chance in life. On the other hand, the whole system of elitism in schooling is contrary to the socialist faith. Should one sacrifice...one's children to one's beliefs? Or should one put one's children's immediate advantage first?

Although they did send the children to a private school for several years, he says he felt 'very relieved' when they came back to the state system. Edward, himself educated at Harrow, thought that his children would receive a better education in the private school system, yet he was sharply aware that sending them there ran contrary to his political beliefs. For him, the conflict consisted of a choice between sacrificing his politics or his children's long-term welfare. Given that he perceived the private sphere of education to be superior to the state sphere, it was difficult for him to ask others, particularly his own children, to 'suffer'; interestingly, Edward has never confronted a similar conflict involving himself. For instance, when deciding what sort of parish he would like to work for, he was always quick to opt for disadvantaged neighbour-hoods. This was an easier decision to make, however, for if any sacrifice, either material or professional, was being made, it was by him, and not by his children.

Eileen faced a similar dilemma. Returning to England from ten years of living in Canada, she and her husband thought that their children would benefit greatly by being placed in private education. They were, she explained, two years behind in their studies, and would not have been able to pass their eleven-plus examination (see note 2 to Chapter 4).

It was sheep and goats... I do feel guilty, from the point of view of the socialism, yes. I'm bound to... I think that was a moral conflict. Yes, it was... I willingly acquiesced, because I saw no alternative. They had to catch up with those two years.

Feeling that there was no alternative, she sent her children to private school for two years. Edward and Eileen made similar decisions regarding their children's education; given the inequality of the prevailing system, they believed their children would receive their best chance in life by attending private school. Still, both were very aware that the same options were not open to everyone, and for this reason, their decisions did not sit comfortably with them.

Elizabeth's moral dilemma concerned a decision whether or not to attend a demonstration at Holy Loch, where there was a strong chance that she would be arrested and sent to prison, and thus be leaving her young son at home with his father to look after him. She says she was torn between

a responsibility to your family, you've brought them into the world, and it was your right to see that they were looked after and cared for and so on. On the other hand, you also had a duty to the world in general, hadn't you, and to the destruction and the poverty... And you don't want to force your children into a certain situation.

Elizabeth's description of being torn between activist and mother, and being forced to decide how she will allocate her use of a particular period of time, is in some ways reminiscent of Christopher's tension described earlier, in which he feels himself caught between 'the studio and the street'. The difference, however, is that Elizabeth's dilemma involves an immutable decision, whereas for Christopher, the situation is ongoing. Moreover, Elizabeth feels she is asking a sacrifice of her child when she engages in political action; Christopher must sacrifice one part of himself for another.

Elizabeth resolved her dilemma by discussing the situation with her son, explaining what the consequences of her actions might be, and ultimately receiving his approval for her to go. Thus, in the end she resolved her conflict by consulting the very person whom she thought her actions would affect. Elizabeth's son was still a child, and some might argue, therefore, that he did not know to what he was agreeing. Still, his approval, informed or otherwise, was important to her. At the demonstration, Elizabeth was arrested and, as a consequence, she spent three weeks in a maximum-security prison.

Before going to Holy Loch, she had a dream which dramatically illustrated the situation:

I dreamed there was a tray and my hands were underneath holding the tray and I was doing a lot, what with the family and the famine relief and one thing and another. I was doing a lot, and more and more things were piled on this tray, and I said 'Oh Lord, don't put on anymore, I can't hold it.' And then I looked under the tray. It wasn't my hands that were holding it, it was sort of symbolic hands, large thick hands that you get on Henry Moore sculptures. And I knew that it wasn't really me, that what I was doing was right, one was upheld in another dimension somehow... It was right, and it was go ahead.

Elizabeth's dream gave her reassurance that she was capable of more than she thought; she did not need to choose between being a caring, responsible mother, and being a committed political activist.[3] Ultimately she felt she was being upheld by something greater than herself.

While the content of the dilemma was quite different to that experienced by Edward and Eileen, one feature is common among the three. In each situation, the participant was torn between his or her role as a parent, putting the child's immediate needs first, and his or her role as a committed socialist activist. Elizabeth's dilemma, for instance, was not about whether or not she should break the law; about this aspect of her proposed action she was clear. Rather, for her the question was whether it was fair to her young child not to have his mother around for a few weeks, because she had been arrested and was serving a prison sentence. In some sense she felt that her son was paying the price for having a politically active mother. This is similar to the feelings expressed by both Edward and Eileen regarding their dilemmas of where to educate their children; was it fair, because of their politics, for them to ask sacrifices of their children?[4]

The dilemmas identified here are exceptions in a series of life stories which were generally characterized by a high degree of certainty and a remarkable lack of personal moral conflict. Indeed, in all of the fifteen lives combined (totalling over one thousand years of lived experience), there were only three identifiable, singular moral conflicts which they reported. Middle-class respondents were more likely to experience personal moral conflict that the working-class activists, particularly when the tension between their own socio-economic status and the object of their activism was heightened. Edward comments:

> I was brought up bourgeois and so the choice of some form of private school would be the sort of choice which would impinge on me probably more than it would have on some of the other ones [working class respondents] you've been talking about.

Thus when they confront real-life decisions whose outcomes will ultimately affect others close to them, conditions for experiencing moral conflict are optimal. Such situations highlight the most vulnerable aspect of their social identity, as they try to rise above the interests of their class, denouncing privilege and yet at the same time having access to material benefits if they so desire them. It is easier for them to decline such benefits for themselves than for their children. The dilemma of whether or not to send one's children to private school is one which would be less likely to confront working-class individuals.

With the exceptions noted above, it is generally true for all of the participants that the arena for conflict has been clearly defined in their lives: the primacy of political and social struggles over individual needs and idiosyncrasies dictates that intra-individual moral conflict will be minimal, while individual–society confrontation will be high. Now let us see how this sense of certainty, and its concomitant optimism, extend to individuals' perceptions of the long-term results of their actions.

Beyond a lifetime: optimism and long-term activism

We have seen that these lifetime socialist activists have experienced relatively little inner conflict regarding major decisions they have made or actions they have performed in their lives. But the respondents are certain not only about their own actions: they are fully confident of the ultimate success of socialism. This is based primarily upon their view of the movement of history, as alluded to earlier; while not unrealistic in their appraisal of the immediate results of their individual efforts to effect social change, they are very optimistic about the long-term outcome. Ed explains that

one thing that you need to sustain commitment is a knowledge of revolutionary theory. You need to have done a fair amount of reading and studying and have a deep conviction, a conviction that's based on an understanding of the historical processes and theoretical conceptions.

The respondents have witnessed significant change within their life-times, and though Britain is further from becoming a fully socialist state than it appeared to be in the 1930s and late 1940s, they still remain confident that the direction of the overall movement of history is on their side. It is this unshakeable belief, perhaps more than any other single factor, which accounts for the longevity of their commitment. Many of them are in their ninth decade of life and no longer think they will see a socialist Britain within their lifetime. Still, this does not diminish their commitment, believing as they do that others will one day reap the benefits of their work.

Speaking of the events of 1989, Frida says, 'Yes, I'm as convinced as ever that socialism will come, but desperately sorry that it has to wait perhaps even beyond my children and grand-children's time.' She then reads aloud to me a passage from the writings of William Morris:

But if to any of you I have seemed to speak hopelessly, my words have been lacking in art; and you must remember that hopelessness would have locked my mouth, not opened it. I am, indeed, hopeful, but can I give a date to the accomplishement of any hope, and say that it will happen in my life or yours? But I will say at least, Courage! for things wonderful, unhoped for, glorious, have happened even in this short while I have been alive (1934: 537).

Christopher, too, shares this view:

I can't be proved wrong because I don't attach a time-quotient to my foreshadowings: I don't use phrases like 'by the end of the century' or 'in a hundred years' time' – so I, or more likely my ghost, can always say 'wait a bit, you'll see, it's on the way'.

Rose says of herself that at times she feels 'disappointed, but not disheartened. I still hope.'

Hope and patience are very important for sustaining belief and commitment. When Trevor met with some of the anti-apartheid activists who had been jailed for twenty-seven years, he was struck by their magnanimity.

One of them said in reply to 'Did you you never get bitter ... the waste of time and all that, with your life?' and he said 'We soon saw that bitterness was a luxury we couldn't afford, that we must concentrate on hope and for the future and we mustn't let ourselves get caught into the emotional drain of bitterness.

They would not be side-tracked; they were sustained by the conviction of their beliefs.

Edward speaks of his feelings regarding the popularity of Thatcherism:

[What sustains me]...is the belief that this is a temporary hiccup, and not something that's going to be indelibly implanted on the human race. That the human race will overcome this present triumph of wickedness, as I would think of it, triumph of greed.

This feeling is shared by other respondents. As Eileen surmises:

If you take a long-term view of history...then you know things come back. They will get better...If you're optimistic in spite of [surrounding events], I think you're rather naive and foolish and you've not got to underestimate the difficulties.

Here Eileen distinguishes between blind optimism which refuses to allow for potentially discrepant evidence, and that which is founded upon an informed long-term view of history. She speaks about her 'certitude about the political process and the march forward of humanity', which, she says 'is not a linear progression...it's full of pitfalls, and ups and downs, but it works round in the spiral we've talked of so often'.

Frida echoes similar sentiments:

I just think it is the only answer. I think really it's as simple as that...to advance towards socialism is the only way we're going to make the world a fit place to live in...it's bound to come out right in the end, that's the way history is.

Later, she tells of coming to her radical point of view by studying history: 'It seemed to me perfectly clear what history taught us.' For Rose,

the materialist conception of history explains it...there's never been anything that I was convinced about that hasn't turned out to be what it is. I've never been disillusioned....[What keeps you going?] Just the feeling that I'm right, I think.

In my interview with Jack Lindsay, he describes how it was through his efforts to understand the ancient world that he came to understand the politics of the twentieth century. Thus, he said, his 'was not a simple conversion, but came out of the whole of me.' He elaborates on this elsewhere:

I had been so obsessed by the ancient world that I had paid little attention to what was happening in my own...Now, looking with renewed interest at the contemporary situation, I grew aware of what Hitler's rise portended, the conflict between fascism and humanism was cleaving Western society and exposing much of its basic structures... In turning thus to the world about me, I felt the need to understand the terms on which the struggles were being waged, and for the first time I read Marx. The effect was powerful (Chaplin 1983: iv).

When Walter was asked what keeps him going when he feels discouraged, he responds: 'The arrogant attitude that I'm right, I suppose... Because whether I'm right or wrong, the facts are there, the facts are out there in the streets... Nothing is proving it's wrong to me.' Trevor, who has dedicated his life to abolishing apartheid in South Africa, says, 'What keeps me going is that I know that the African people will win. I mean there's no question, they're going to win alright.' Jack shares the sentiment of assured victory: 'the picture is on our side, we're going to win. It's Marxism, the change has got to come.' Later he adds:

it's inevitable that there will be a socialist world... I'm talking about scientific socialism. The whole basis of it is inevitable... You see, it's not faith with me. I'm a Marxist, I'm a materialist, I know that it will happen.

Repeatedly throughout our interviews, Jack offers the example of the Soviet Union, whose revolution was realized through 'one step backward, two steps forward'. Emphasizing that the movement of history is in a positive direction, Jack states, 'There's never been good old days.' Mary, too, mentions her irritation with the myth of golden olden days. 'One of things which makes me annoyed... is when people say, "Ah, what wonderful Victorian times"... I mean the improvement since those times is really absolutely colossal.' But Mary's enthusiasm is infused with much realism. She says, 'I only pray the world is going slightly more humanitarian and not slightly more fascist.' As further evidence that her general optimism is realistically grounded, she documents the changes she has witnessed in her lifetime. 'I've seen of course during my life immense improvement in education for poorer children and to some extent housing.'

Christopher, too, is convinced that civilization must be moving in a positive direction, but this belief is based less on an adherence to historical materialism, and more on spirituality. He relates his vision in the following way:

I think there has to be some kind of scenario which we are part of, and it would seem to me most unartistic if this scenario, having reached the twentieth century, and opened up so many possibilities, were permitted by the great director to blow itself up... I don't think it... is likely to move in the direction of total disaster or self-destruction because that would be such bad art, and the director doesn't seem to be a bad artist.

Arriving at their beliefs from a variety of perspectives, all of the respondents agree that the long-term view of history is on their side. Edward demonstrates the connection between his religious and political beliefs: 'if God does exist, he works in history, that's how he makes it'. He feels that 'tak[ing] a broad sweep of history...is the best way to maintain some optimism'. Indeed, the characteristic of optimism is included in the majority of self-descriptions. Some of the phrases used are: 'super-optimist' (Dorothy), 'hopeless optimist' (Rose), 'optimistic by temperament' (Christopher), 'blessed' with optimism (Eileen), 'always an optimist' (Jack) and 'it's my nature to be optimistic' (Mary). Many of the respondents say that one of their attractions to Marxism is its fundamental optimism. Whether these individuals are optimistic because of their belief in an optimistic philosophy, or that they are drawn to such a philosophy because of their own inherent nature is a question which must remain open to conjecture. Eileen questions: 'Why do we go towards optimistic philosophies? Why do I pick on dialectical materialism which is a hopeful philosophy?' Whichever came first, the optimistic disposition or the belief in an optimistic philosophy, it is clear that the two reinforce each other. It is important to note that it is the 'scientific' nature of Marxism – its dialectical and historical materialism – which indicates the inevitability of change. For respondents, that is more significant than its optimism, which is a mere corollary.

When Trevor is asked if he believes that history inevitably moves toward socialism, he responds, 'I don't know that I would put it quite like that. I think inevitability is a difficult word to use, because you can then become fatalistic, and you can cease acting.' His distinction points to the possibility, as well as the necessity, of taking action, without which there can be no assurances of outcomes. Interviewed after Mandela's release from prison, he emphasizes the importance of the continuation of the active struggle against apartheid. He mentions a speech made by Julius Nyerere of Tanzania:

the theme of the speech was [that] apartheid is like a great wall and on top of the wall is a crack...now the governments in the West are saying 'Look, that wall is going to fall down. We don't need to do any more, just sit back and wait for it to fall.' He said 'Don't you believe it. Get out that pick-axe and bring the wall down and start negotiating.'

It is when individuals gather together and collectively embark on a goal-directed course of action that they can influence the environment in which they live. Through performing these modest actions collectively, individuals help to shape the course of history; this is what many of the respondents identify as the optimism of Marxism.

Dorothy describes the way in which she has tried to exercise control over her environment, despite any obstacles:

I can't face defeat anywhere...it was said so often that I believed it, that you always had to overcome everything. You had to be the master of your fate, really. You had to decide, and you didn't let other circumstances enter into it. You had to overcome all those things.

Dorothy believes that she has it within herself to make an impact upon her environment, no matter that the circumstances into which she was born were rather difficult. Her's is a very practical outlook; by examining the situation realistically, and then making a decision to overcome, she can help to influence future outcomes. The language which she employs here reveals a determination to be empowered. All of the respondents believe that they can help to shape the direction of history, if only through the performance of their small and limited actions.

Several participants make the analogy between planting seeds and being politically active. Rose says:

I know I'll never turn the world around now by myself...You don't know where you're dropping a seed...the seed will grow, it's not the one individual, if you can convince an individual and she convinces another, this is the only way that you'll succeed.

Jack would agree with Rose's description, and it is from the knowledge that the seeds will grow that he derives his patience to wait for the results.

You must not give up, you must keep pegging away...it's just like the farmer who sows the seeds, and one year you get a bad crop, or he might not get a crop at all, but he doesn't give up his farmland, he doesn't give up being a farmer. He still continues to sow the seeds and the next year he probably gets a much more bountiful harvest. So it's the same in the world of politics. You're sowing a seed, you're germinating socialist philosophy.

Mary believes in the importance of small actions, even while she is very realistic about the probability of successful immediate results. For her, the issues are so important, and she knows that if there is no form of sustained, organized, public resistance, things will not change. One must, therefore, act, but in the full knowledge that the results might not be successful.

As an activist, I believe that the difference it makes is very slight, but I think it does from time to time make some difference, and therefore because the issues are so important, it's worthwhile...I'm a great sceptic; I don't think for one moment that it suddenly moves mountains or any such thing.

Remember, too, that it was Mary who spoke of the advances in education and housing which she had seen in her own lifetime; she is fully aware of the difference that concerted action can make, and yet she is hesitant to be overly exuberant in her expectations. Dorothy is also modest in her appraisal of the effects of her political actions. She says she 'cannot be part of burying' socialism, and that 'you've to stand by it whilst ever it is breathing'. She feels very strongly that she must add her contribution, while recognizing that there are no immediate guarantees.

Dorothy has concentrated her efforts on local issues, where she feels it is easier to make a significant difference. Her interviews abound with phrases such as the following: 'I can't face defeat. I won't let defeat beat me', 'you can overcome if you are determined', 'you're not going to let anything stand in the way', 'I don't fight losing battles', and 'not having anything that I've worked for...going flop'. Her self-perception is that of a person who is clearly determined, competent, and successful in achieving what she sets out to do. She has focused her efforts where she sees the greatest urgency, i.e. helping those in need. In so doing, she has also placed herself in a situation where her actions are more likely to meet with tangible and more immediate results, and indeed the various organizations she has established and has been involved with have been successful. Clearly, though, in so many years of activity it is unlikely that there were no defeats. In the course of our interviews, Dorothy told of trying to get public access to restricted footpaths in the area. When asked if this, too, had been successful, she responded: 'They were just not interested...it fell on deaf ears, I didn't get it.' While Dorothy admits here that they did not get the access they sought, this small incident does not seem to challenge her perception of never having been defeated, which seems to be very important to her.

The other respondents are similar to Dorothy in this respect. Because their time-scale is so long-term, believing as they do that history will move in a progressive direction, they rarely, if ever, perceive themselves as encountering defeat. The incident of the footpaths cited above was slightly different, in that it was a particular and time-specific issue. However, if in several years' time the decision to keep them closed were to be rescinded, would that then be a victory for Dorothy? One example of such a time lag is the Spanish Civil War. Frida, who actually went to Spain, recalls, 'You never thought for a moment the Spanish could possibly lose. This was the awful thing afterwards.' Walter shared these feelings:

Do you know, it never occurred to me, certainly when I went to Spain, that I might be joining the losing side. I never even for one moment thought of losing the war, right till I was captured...a good soldier, of course, weighs up the possibilities and he doesn't fight unless he's certain of winning, but perhaps I'm not a good soldier.

Still, Walter felt that the defeat of fascism in the Second World War was a delayed partial victory for the cause for which he had fought. Fifty years later, forty years of which had seen a Franco rule over Spain, Walter returned to Spain, to the scene of battlefields such as Jarama. This he describes as a 'tremendous, tremendous, experience'. Perhaps he had not been a poor soldier in his calculations after all, though victory was long in coming.

Elizabeth comments that 'things that sometimes appear to be a failure aren't always, you make contacts there and there's a growing point here, and something comes out of it'. Her point directs the reader to the process of change over time. She further suggests that 'it doesn't matter even if it was a failure'. Jack's reference to the Russian Revolution as being 'one step backward, two steps forward' allows for setbacks within a general progression. Ed, too, emphasizes the need for a

very big perspective if you're going to sustain it... the history of the movement has been built as much on defeats as successes... but it's been the way forward, it's the struggle that people have learned.

Regarding the relationship between age and the propensity to work for the betterment of society, Laslett writes:

It could be claimed... that many more duties of older people go forward in time than is the case in those who are young. This follows from the fact that they owe less to their own individual futures – now comparatively short – and more to the future of others – all others... In this the elderly of any society can be said to be *trustees* of the future (1989: 196).

Respondents' reflections on their own aging seem to lend evidence to this claim. Eileen believes that with age, immediate and observable success becomes less important. Without a long-term perspective, it is easy to feel depressed and defeated. Eileen has seen this in the modern peace movement:

They got too depressed, and they felt it was the end of the world... I had to say, 'Look, it's not the end of the world. We have to go on struggling. You haven't to give up'... People are depressed and they see no results, but I think it's the old people who keep going. I think age brings that perspective.

With age, activists develop a wider perspective on their contribution to political struggle. Many of the things for which they are fighting, they know they will not see in their own lifetimes. While this knowledge may have been with them for many years, now, as they near the end of their life cycles, it becomes imbued with personal significance.

As we have seen, all of the respondents view their lives as being intricately bound to the movement of history, a history which in their small way they have all tried to help shape. This contrasts with the findings of Sharon Kaufman (1986), whose respondents, sixty middle-class elderly American men and women, 'did not talk about their lives in relation to social trends or the times in which they have lived. They did not place themselves in a broader historical context' (p. 22). Kaufman's respondents 'do [not] view themselves as makers of history' (p. 83), and she suggests that 'Perhaps only great men and women can consciously construct their accounts to explain relationships between personal development and historical processes' (p. 86). The respondents of this study would not perceive themselves as being particularly great or extraordinary, and yet they would identify their personal development in terms of its relation to wider historical processes; participants see themselves as makers of history, not as individuals, but as members of political organizations. Because of their belief in historical materialism, they retain their optimism regarding the long-term results of their political activism. Their lives continue to have a very pronounced sense of purpose, and their spirits will not be defeated.

Several of the respondents have, through their political work, lived quite close to death. Eileen says that death is very important to activists 'Because they do disregard death really. Because, you know, it's part of life.' They disregard death, not in that it is insignificant, but that the possibility of dying will not impinge on their political activities. At the height of Jack's trade union work on the docks, he received phone calls and letters threatening his life and that of his family. Describing his reactions to these, he says he was 'a bit upset, but I shook it off. I always said to myself, "part of the political struggle." You can't go into battle without getting hurt.' Frida, however, differs from Jack on this point: 'I'm committed, but I'm not martyr material and I wouldn't want anyone to be hurt because of my views... I wouldn't risk my children's life and limb to make a moral protest.' Christopher, too, questions how he would behave in a situation where holding his beliefs would exact a particularly high price:

One doesn't know how one would actually behave in moments of stress, just as one thinks one ought to oppose militarism, and fascism, how would one have behaved if they had been in occupied France? Would one have joined the resistance? If one joined it, would one have been brave? If one had been captured and tortured, given away one's comrades? One doesn't know till one tries.

Neither Frida nor Christopher entertain romantic ideas about their commitment. They do not know how it would hold up under certain kinds of tests; what is certain is that it has held up very well under the conditions of their actual lives. Two of the respondents suffered the loss of someone very close to them as a result of the fighting in the Spanish Civil War: Christopher lost his brother John, and Walter lost one of his closest friends. Their motivation to continue the struggle was heightened by a sense of responsibility to others who were absent. Walter explains, 'there's a debt we owe to those who died'.

Other respondents have also suffered losses. Mary's husband, who had inspired her to join the Communist Party, died during the Second World War; in fact it was as a direct result of his becoming a communist and thus renouncing pacifism that he had joined the army. One of the people who had a strong influence on Edward's radicalization died in an accident. Not only did he experience this as a loss of a close personal friend, but 'It was a loss to the movement, too. I felt a big sort of responsibility to try and follow his work so far as I could.' In the case of Trevor, he feels he has a responsibility to those who have been silenced by the South African state, people with whom he has worked and who have been in prison since the Treason Trial, more than a quarter of a century ago. He also describes activists' attitude toward death. Recalling the words of a woman who had gone to see her son before his execution in South Africa, he says:

'He said to me "Don't cry mother. If you cry you're crying for yourself." He said "You sing."' That was her entire message. That sort of spirit makes you know that people are not going to be defeated.

Because of their advanced age, many of the respondents have been widowed. Of the fifteen respondents, all of the women have now survived their husbands. Trevor was never married, Jack lost his wife during the course of our interviews, but the spouses of all the other male respondents are still living. Many of their closest friends have also died. Rose lost her husband nearly ten years before we met. She says:

I'm not concerned what happens to me after I die and that's it...you get people who say you live in the hereafter. Well you do, you'll live in the hereafter in the person that loves you. My husband lives in me forever, we loved one another and I've loved him, and because I think in terms of what would Peter have done about this...he's living in the hereafter.

Dorothy lost her husband shortly before the changes in Eastern Europe began. Their routine had been to sit at the end of the day and read the paper.

I have found myself, particularly since the uprising in Europe, reading something and turning to the other chair with an exclamation and no-one there to share ideas. I have always had an intense interest in what happens in other parts of the world. It is not sufficient to read about it, you have to live it by talking about it and getting another opinion.

Frida sums up the effect of losing those close to oneself:

That's a great loss, not being able to talk to them. Well not because, not necessarily because you talk to them as individuals, but because they are for the movement and you get a lot of support from that... It's difficult to be committed unless you've got some back-up.

Thus, all of the respondents have dealt with death quite intimately, and many in their work have felt a responsibility to those who have died. The cause is greater than any one life. Indeed, this attitude is expressed quite poignantly in their discussion of their own lives. While they would like to see the eventual results of their actions, that they will not is not altogether shattering, and is certainly no reason to discontinue those efforts. Edward says, 'I know from the outset that the efforts would have some result, but it might well not be soon, or even in my lifetime.' The confidence that all actions will ultimately have some effect is motivation enough to sustain him in his efforts.

In one of our interviews, Jack reflects:

when I depart from this world, in my departure I know that I've left my mark. I know that... I've not led a negative life... I wanted to be a real person, a real mensch... It's what's said after you're gone by those who you've left and departed [that matters].

Jack died in June 1989. Ironically, the day he died the dockers were in the midst of a major industrial dispute. I learned of Jack's death as I watched the news on television that night, the reporters making the connection between the industrial struggle and the loss of one of the dockers' greatest leaders. *The Morning Star*, a Communist Party daily newspaper, was filled with tributes to him for weeks following his death. Typical of these were: 'We thought you were immortal, your example certainly is', 'We mourn the death of an outstanding leader of the dockers, a trade unionist and fighter for his class', and 'Militant Fighter for Peace and Socialism: A Giant.' Jack had left his mark.

Trevor reflects upon his own aging: 'I've become more revolutionary every year I've lived. And certainly now, because life is so much shorter. I mean I want to get apartheid dead before I'm dead. There's no time to do that.' Even while there might not be time to do that, he is relentless in his involvements, no matter that he may never live to see the results of his endeavours. In life, the cause has been bigger than him. Now, it expands its boundary beyond his lifetime. He is but one particle of a large movement which extends across places and through time.

While the participants are not despondent that they will not see their ultimate goal realized, they, like Trevor, lament this fact. Louie had the strongest reply when asked if she ever had moments of discouragement:

'Rome wasn't built in a day.' Still, she feels 'disgusted. To think that we nearly had it, we nearly had a new system of society and we've lost it, somewhere along the way, from 1936 to now.' To this, she then adds, 'Nothing can stop it. It will have to come.' Rose says that when she was younger, she had 'great hopes that we would finally have socialism in my time [laughter]. I'm disappointed that we haven't. Frida, too, says that she is 'sad because I shan't see it in my lifetime'. Dorothy, in one of her letters, reflects:

All I can say is I seriously thought and hoped I would see a Socialist Society in my lifetime, but it is not to be so all one can do is put it into practice as far as one can in your relationships and never be afraid to speak out where there is injustice. We are still working very hard.

At the time of writing this letter, Dorothy was eighty-five.

None of the respondents gave any evidence of 'reaching his ultimate involvement with the self'. Indeed, it is precisely the large perspective not only of their own lives, but of the movement of history, which sustains them in their work. They continue to fight for causes the results of which they themselves will probably never see. Working for socialism has been the core of their lives, and continues to be so. During their lives, participants have grown in their understanding of socialism, while retaining their commitment to its fundamental principles. Once having become politicized, they experienced virtually no moral conflicts which deterred them from the ongoing purpose of their lives' work. While they became radicalized at a time when the domestic and international political scene appeared to be very simple and straightforward, they have developed a complexity in their political thought which can accommodate challenges to their beliefs. Thus, their commitment has been constant but dynamic. Although they have watched the movement of political tides, socialism rising and falling in popularity, none of them are in any way doubtful what the ultimate end result will be. That in itself is motivation enough to continue the struggle.

Conclusion: aging and sustained purpose

> The knowledge of life... which we grown-ups have to pass on to the younger generation will not be expressed thus: 'Reality will soon give way before your ideals,' but 'Grow into your ideals, so that life may never rob you of them.'
>
> Albert Schweitzer (1925: 102)

It was more than ten years ago that I first wondered why the many elderly people I saw at demonstrations were excluded from the 'received wisdom' of what aging is and should be. Eventually, these vague notions became articulated in more sophisticated academic language. Throughout this time, however, my guiding interest has been the question: does growing up necessarily mean growing out of our ideals? The message of this book can be simply summarized in the one-word answer: No. Psychological development and the commitment to work for social change are not antithetical. Indeed, in the lives of these fifteen people, these two processes have been one and the same.

Western psychology, not surprisingly, tends to reflect the values of Western capitalist ideology. Nowhere is this more true than in its theories of aging; much of the literature describes the later stages of life as a time of disengagement, disillusion, alienation and hopelessness. In Levinson's words, it is a time of 'preparing for... death... liv[ing] in its shadow, and at its call' (1978: 38–39). If this is an accurate description of how some people experience the end of their lives, we as a society must ask why this is so. Mental health in old age can and should mean more than the mere absence of depression and illness. Particularly given changing demography, it is now more important than ever that society regard its elder citizens, and that they regard themselves, not as a social problem but as a vital resource. Perhaps they would not 'live at death's call' if they felt that they still had important work in this life. Those who are advanced in their years are also advanced in their experience.

For the old to experience their lives as having meaning and purpose is important not only to them, and to ourselves as individuals, but also to ourselves as a society. As Simone de Beauvoir reminds us:

the meaning or the lack of meaning that old age takes on in any given society puts that whole society to the test, since it is this that reveals the meaning or the lack of meaning of the entirety of the life leading to that old age (1970: 16).

Old age is the culmination, the final chapter, of life. By denying that phase of life its due integrity, everyone suffers, for integrity is denied to the whole of the life cycle.

It is not only, nor even primarily, of academic interest to me that there exist positive models of successful aging. I am always inspired to see people who have tried throughout their lives to improve the world, particularly when these efforts are conducted in an environment which offers little reward for such dedication, and which instead marginalizes and seeks to alienate those who engage in these struggles. Through my involvement with this project I have become increasingly aware of just how many unsung heroes and heroines there are, often in the most unexpected places. One needs only to open one's eyes to see they are there.

Ultimately, then, what can be said of these fifteen lives, apart from that they have been lived in this particular way? These men and women have been and are still fully involved with living, knowing that even after they die, the fights in which they have been engaged will persist. Unlike many others of their age who feel they no longer belong to society, they continue to have a strong purpose in life, a reason for living. They have sustained their commitment to socialism, and their commitment, in turn, has sustained them.

Notes

1 DEFYING THE STEREOTYPE

1 While I had originally intended the sample to be racially mixed, my initial enquiries led me to think that, perhaps due to – among other things – the erratic British immigration quotas for non-whites, locating potential non-white respondents who met the other criteria might be rather problematic. Ramden (1987) in his very thorough book *The Making of the Black Working Class in Britain* documents the history of the black intelligentsia in Britain. He writes that in spite of

> seemingly liberal influences [of British Marxism and socialism on Labour Party and Independent Labour Party politics] entry of black Africans, West Indians and Asians into Britain was difficult... If 'reds' were feared, Blacks who ventured outside the colonial elementary school–based education system for higher education and training in the Metropole were particularly marked... most of those who found their way into Britain during this period [the inter-war years] were from colonial middle classes (p. 144).

Nonetheless, there was a pronounced black intelligentsia in Britain which consisted of such people as George Padamore, C. L. R. James and R. P. Dutt. In 1933, the Third International disbanded the International Trade Union of Negro Workers, and later during the Italian–Ethiopian War, the Soviet Union traded in war materials with Italy; thus the black alliance with European communists was brought into serious question (Ramden 1987: 144). By the late 1950s, 'the black radical intelligentsia had... left Britain. They returned to the colonies to educate, organise and involve the masses' (p. 186). Since that time, there has been a large influx of blacks into Britain; however, these immigrants would be too young and would not have lived in Britain long enough to be eligible participants for the present study.

2 Throughout this book, when italics are used in quotations this reflects how they appear in the original.

3 There are two correct spellings of aging: aging and ageing. In my writing I use the former, and the latter only appears in this book when it is so spelled by another author who is being quoted.

4 Because of the often ambiguous use of the masculine third person, readers might fail to be alerted to the fact that Levinson's book is indeed about men's lives. Levinson makes no effort to correct this potential misunderstanding, as

he appears to communicate to his readers that his is a theory about the lives of humans; in fact, this is the way that the theory has been understood within psychology. He is not unique in this regard. Gilligan argues that the main psychological theorists (Freud, Piaget, Erikson and Kohlberg) have based their theories on all-male samples. 'Implicitly adopting the male life as the norm, they have tried to fashion women out of a masculine cloth' (1979: 432).

3 ON THE SUBJECT OF SUBJECTIVITY

1 Readers are invited to consult my doctoral dissertation for a more detailed account of the method I used.
2 This question was borrowed from the work of Carol Gilligan.
3 See p. 150 and Note 2 on Chapter 7 for two respondents' comments regarding this issue.
4 The particular quality of relationship which I enjoyed with the respondents was influenced by the fact that I admired them and their work, and they knew it. This is obviously not the case in many research situations. Lifton (1986), in his study on Nazi doctors, poignantly describes the difference between his relationships with concentration-camp survivors and the Nazi doctors. Similarly, Sparks (1989) relates his experience of conducting research in maximum-security prisons. But it is integrity and not empathy or warmth which is essential to the establishment of trust between researcher and researched.

4 PERSONAL STORIES

1 More than fifty years later, Walter has saved the many local newspaper accounts of this arrest and the subsequent 'political trial'.
2 The eleven-plus examination is a test taken by British primary-school children to determine whether they merit an academic education in a grammar school or a more vocationally oriented course in a secondary modern or technical school. The eleven-plus declined with the spread of comprehensive schools in the 1960s and 1970s, and its use is now limited to areas where there are still selective secondary schools.
3 To distinguish Edmund Frow from Edward Charles, I shall refer to the former as 'Ed', a name by which he is commonly known. Similarly, to distinguish Jack Lindsay from Jack Dash, I shall refer to the former by his full name.
4 Regarding the relationship between socialists and the Labour Party, Winter writes: 'Socialists have held divergent views about the Labour Party throughout its seventy-year history. But despite constant arguments about policy, most have learned to live with it, and within it. Some have struck out on their own, but without much success. For better or for worse, the party had become by 1918 what it is today: the political home of the overwhelming majority of the British socialist movement' (1974: 270–271).

5 A NATION IN TURMOIL: BRITAIN BETWEEN THE WARS

1 Even while I myself use the Pankhursts as an example of the early British suffragettes, it is nonetheless rather regrettable that it is almost exclusively they, and other middle- and upper-middle-class women, such as Millicent Garrett Fawcett, who tend to be mentioned in the history of women's struggles in the early part of the twentieth century. The cotton workers in Lancashire, amongst many others, are often missing from such retellings. See, for instance, Liddington and Norris (1978) for a broader picture.

2 There are, however, some exceptions to this. Rowbotham writes that in the 1920s 'Socialist feminism was a minority tradition within the left. It was nonetheless there' (1977: 21). Two outstanding examples of socialist feminists at this time were Stella Browne and Dora Russell.

3 German National Socialism was not the first voice of anti-Semitism in Europe in the twentieth century. The French Third Republic, for instance, had earlier been the home of much anti-Jewish propaganda. There was throughout much of Western Europe a belief in an international Jewish conspiracy, devoted to the destruction of the Western world. The 'evidence' for this belief was a spurious document, *Protocols of the Learned Elders of Zion*, produced in France under the Second Empire, and which contained 'instructions of the Jewish "Elders" to the Jewish people... for the complete disruption of Christian civilisation' (Griffiths 1983: 60). This anti-Semitism was then at least partially furthered by the Russian Revolution, as several of the Bolshevik leaders were Jews (e.g. Trotsky and Zinoviev). Thus 'the idea of a Jewish Bolshevik conspiracy gained wide acceptance in the western world' (*ibid.*). While British anti-Semitism was not as pronounced as its European counterparts, 'parlour anti-Semitism' was very common (p. 65), and in the early 1930s much of the negative reporting on Germany was attributed to the fact that Jews controlled the British press (p. 70).

4 Trotsky's description of fellow-travellers is also interesting: 'They do not grasp the Revolution as a whole and the communist ideal is foreign to them. They are more or less inclined to look hopefully at the present over the head of the worker. They are not the artists of the proletarian revolution, but her artist 'fellow-travellers.' ...As regards a 'fellow-traveller', the question always comes up – how far will he go?' (cited in Caute 1973: 1).
Trotsky's question seems well founded: many of those who professed themselves to be communists or communist sympathizers later renounced these affiliations. See, for instance, Crossman (1949) *The God That Failed.*

5 All told, Franco received approximately 300,000 soldiers from foreign countries: 150,000 from Italy, 50,000 from Germany (of whom Hitler decorated 26,113 for 'meritous conduct'), and some 100,000 from North Africa (see Note 6 below). This dwarfs the number of foreign volunteers for the republican side in the International Brigades, which amounted to no more than 35,000 from fifty-four countries (Green 1970: 324).

6 Walter wrote to me, clarifying some of these figures: 'You have quoted figures, always a dangerous thing to do because of the impossibility of getting accurate details either then or now. In the International Brigade Association,

we would claim 2,010 went from this country at least, and possibly a few more. Of these, 526 died, mostly on the battlefield, but some from Typhoid and some shot as prisoners by the fascists... We believe that around 42,000 joined the International Brigades... of which 20,000 were killed, missing or totally disabled. Your figures of German and Italian involvement may be about right, but I find an estimate of 100,000 Moors rather high. We believe nearer 40,000 with 15,000 losses to be more accurate – but is it important? Perhaps not.'

6 RADICALIZATION: COMING TO COMMITMENT

1 Jack often commented that the love of theatre ran in his blood, his mother having been an actress and his father responsible for stage lighting. Jack describes his ambitions as a young child: 'I always wanted to go into the theatre like my mother... I suppose being a public orator is something like theatre, because whether you're aware of it or not... if you're a good orator, it's acting. It don't mean that you're false, but your whole presentation when you want to warm people up, it's like when you're delivering your lines.' Here, one is reminded once again of Goffman's work on the presentation of selves as performers. Jack is very conscious that he is playing a certain role, but it is a role which he believes in, and he is therefore not 'false'.

2 Unlike Dorothy and Rose, Janet's family were financially well-off. Nonetheless, when her mother died, the responsibility for her father fell solely to her, the only daughter, and not to her two brothers. 'It was at once clear that I must give up all idea of becoming either a consultant physician or a general practitioner as I had wished and planned... To become either I should need to take several resident hospital appointments, but it was obvious that I must be free to come home...' (quoted in Caldecott 1984: 112). This situation lasted less than five years, up until the time her father remarried.

3 Eileen tells the story of how it was that her mother was denied the opportunity to continue her education. Her mother was a twin, and the parents had to choose which daughter would train as a teacher and which would stay at home. '"Our Mattie" they called her, "our Mattie will stay at home. Mary can go and be a teacher." Now the other twin was not bright... my mother was intellectually much stronger, and I think she never got over that... My aunt brought up home to Yorkshire every holiday her friends from teaching, they were all unmarried... and they were very wonderful teachers from London with red hair, beautiful beads and clothes, they sang, they were talented. And my mother took their breakfast trays up in the morning... But they became her friends and she sewed clothes for them and I can just think what must have gone on underneath it all.'

4 Upon reading this passage in my thesis, Walter wrote to me: 'I suppose I was rather ambiguous on an issue I would claim to be very clear about... they [middle-class International Brigaders] were too influential back home and they had capabilities that the working class could not afford to lose in the blood bath of the Ebro Offensive... Finally, on this point, I would claim to have the support of no less a person than Harry Pollitt [General Secretary of

the CPGB], who, on one of his visits to the Battalion in Spain, told [the person under question] that he should go home, and [he] refused, typically.'

5 This is notwithstanding the fact that people who are in positions of control (due to class, race, or gender) might in fact experience themselves as being such, and for good reason.

7 POLITICAL CONVICTION AND THE SOCIAL SELF

1 In this book, I do not address the important role that physical capability has played in respondents' long-term engagement. With the exception of Louie, all of the respondents have enjoyed reasonably good health throughout their lives. Louie has a bad neck, and tells me that she has been in constant pain for twenty-five years. Our interview was at 10 a.m. and already by that time she had taken ten pills for medication. She feels that many people use infirmity and illness as an excuse for not taking action. 'You see, all they're for is their illness. I says none of you has got as much illness as I've got.' Still, the physical strength that persistent activism requires is considerable, and most respondents at some point in our interviews acknowledge the importance of the energy they have. Moreover, they feel that physical capability brings with it a certain responsibility. Jack explains: 'I have an ability... to speak and talk and that's my responsibility and I should use it.'

2 Other respondents made similar comments to me, explaining that in preparing for an interview they would see a pattern to events in their lives which they had not previously observed. Perhaps the most notable among these was Eileen's revelation: 'I realised that – this only hit me when I was thinking about it, preparing for you – my training in industrial relations and particularly through [my husband], and working with him... it's bridge-building. And in my peace work that's exactly what I tried to do. And I realise it's been – I never realised it till two days ago – it's been a total continuity of philosophy'.

8 GROWING INTO SOCIALISM

1 It's interesting to note here that when Ed made this comment he was no longer a member of the Party, although he had not abandoned his belief in Marxism. After having been a Party member for over sixty years, Ed left the Party about one year before our interview together. He explains this by saying that his wife had been expelled for refusing to cancel a meeting called to discuss Eurocommunism. 'I relinquished my membership as we always work together.' He further expanded on this in a letter to me: 'A far more fundamental issue is involved for both of us. That is the complete abandonment of Scientific Socialism as formulated by Marx and Engels by the CPGB leadership... neither of us are dogmatists and are acutely aware of the fact that the ideas and policy of yesterday are inapplicable today. However, the fundamental theory remain[s] valid although it too must be developed and not ossified.'

While there is not room in this thesis to discuss the current divide in the CPGB, it is nonetheless interesting to note that in this particular situation, Ed's words, quoted in the main text, do not reflect his actions.

2 See pp. 60–1, for Jack's feelings on this subject.
3 This contrasts with the experience of Frida, cited on p. 171, who feels that through her activism, she is ultimately expressing responsibility for her children's future.
4 Virtually all of the children of all the respondents, not only of these three, are, as adults, very politically active and appear to be quite proud of the commitment their parents have so consistently displayed through the years.

Bibliography

Abercrombie, Nicholas, Stephen Hill and Bryan S. Turner (1988). *Dictionary of Sociology*, 2nd edn. Harmondsworth: Penguin.

Adorno, T. W., Else Frenkel-Brunswik, Daniel J. Levinson and R. Nevitt Sanford (1950). *The Authoritarian Personality*. New York: Harper & Row.

Allport, F. H. (1924). *Social Psychology*. New York: Houghton Miflin.

(1962). 'A Structuronomic Conception of Behaviour: Individual and Collective', *Journal of Abnormal and Social Psychology* 64: 3–30.

Allport, G. W. (1968). 'The Historical Background of Modern Social Psychology', in Lindzey and Aronson (1968).

Anderson, Orin (1984). 'Introducing Jack Lindsay', in B. Smith (1984).

Andrews, Molly (1989). 'Lifetimes of Commitment: A Study of Socialist Activists', Ph.D dissertation, University of Cambridge.

Arber, Sara and Jay Ginn (1990). 'The Invisibility of Age: Gender and Class in Later Life', paper presented at the BSA Annual Conference. Mimeo.

Armstrong, Pat, and Hugh Armstrong (1983). 'Beyond Sexless Class and Classless Sex: Towards Feminist Marxism', *Studies in Political Economy* 10 (Winter 1983).

Baddeley, Alan (1989). 'The Psychology of Remembering and Forgetting', in T. Butler (1989a).

Baltes, Paul B., and Orville G. Brim, Jr, eds. (1979). *Life-Span Development and Behaviour*, Vol. 2. London: Academic Press.

eds. (1980). *Life-Span Development and Behavior*, Vol. 3. New York: Academic Press.

Barber, James (1990). 'The Promise of Political Psychology', *Political Psychology*, Vol. 11, No. 1: 173–183.

Bar-Tal, Daniel, and Yoram Bar-Tal (1988). 'A New Perspective for Social Psychology', in Bar-Tal and Kruglanski (1988).

Bar-Tal, Daniel, and Arie W. Kruglanski, eds. (1988). *The Social Psychology of Knowledge*. Cambridge: Cambridge University Press.

Bartlett, Sir Frederic C. (1932). *Remembering: A Study in Experimental and Social Psychology*. Cambridge: Cambridge University Press.

BBC, 18 March 1990. 'Everyman: Nelson Mandela in his own Words'.

Beall, Jo, Shireen Hassim and Alison Todes (1989). '"A Bit on the Side"? Gender Struggles in the Politics of Transformation of South Africa', *Feminist Review* 33 (Autumn 1989): 30–56.

Becker, Howard S. (1963). *Outsiders: Studies in the Sociology of Deviance*. New York: Free Press.

(1976). *Sociological Work: Method and Substance*. Chicago: Aldine Publishing Co.

Becker, Howard S., and Blanche Geer (1979). 'Participant Observation and Interviewing: A Comparison', in Filstead (1970).

Bell, Colin, and Helen Roberts, eds. (1984). *Social Researching: Politics, Problems, Practice*. London: Routledge.

Benn, Tony, ed. (1984). *Writings on the Wall: A Radical and Socialist Anthology 1215–1984*. London: Faber & Faber.

Berger, Peter, and Thomas Luckmann (1966). *The Social Construction of Reality: A Treatise in the Sociology of Knowledge*. Harmondsworth: Penguin.

Berkowitz, L. (1972). 'Frustrations, Comparisons, and Other Sources of Emotion Arousal as Contributors to Social Unrest', *Journal of Social Issues* 28: 77–91.

Bertaux, D., ed. (1991). *Biography and Society: The Life History Approach in the Social Sciences*. Beverly Hills, CA: Sage.

Bhavnani, Kum Kum (1990). 'What's Power Got to Do With It?: Empowerment and Social Research', in Parker and Shotter (1990).

Bhavnani, Kum, Kum and Coulson, M. (1986). 'Transforming Socialist-Feminism: The Challenge of Rascism', *Feminist Review* 23 (Summer 1986): 81–92.

Blake, Frances (1986). *The Irish Civil War 1922–1923 and What it Still Means for the Irish People*. London: Information on Ireland.

Blythe, Ronald (1979). *The View in Winter: Reflections on Old Age*. Harmondsworth: Penguin.

Bornat, Joanna, Chris Phillipson and Sue Ward (1985). *A Manifesto for Old Age*. London: Pluto Press.

Branson, Noreen (1975). *Britain in the Nineteen Twenties*. London: Weidenfeld & Nicolson.

Branson, Noreen, and Margot Heinemann (1971). *Britain in the Nineteen Thirties*. London: Weidenfeld & Nicolson.

Brenner, Johanna (1989). 'Feminism's Revolutionary Promise: Finding Hope in Hard Times', *Socialist Register* 245–263.

Brewer, William F. (1986). 'What is Autobiographical Memory?', in Rubin (1986).

Briggs, A., and J. Saville, eds. (1977). *Essays in Labour History 1818–1939*. London: Croom Helm.

Briggs, Charles L. (1986). *Learning How to Ask: A Sociolinguistic Appraisal of the Role of the Interview in Social Science Research*. Cambridge: Cambridge University Press.

Bromley, D. B. (1966). *The Psychology of Human Ageing*. Harmondsworth: Penguin.

(1988). *Human Ageing: An Introduction to Gerontology*, 3rd edn. Harmondsworth: Penguin.

Broughton, John M. (1985). 'The Genesis of Moral Domination', in Modgil and Modgil (1985).

ed. (1987a). *Critical Theories of Psychological Development*. London: Plenum Press.

(1987b). 'An Introduction to Critical Developmental Psychology', in Broughton (1987a).

Brown, Maurice F. (1985). 'Autobiography and Memory: The Case of Lillian Hellman', *Biography* 8.1 (Winter 1985): 1–11.

Brown, Norman, Steven K. Shevell and Lance J. Rips. (1986) 'Public Memories and their Personal Content' in Rubin (1986).

Brunt, Rosalind (1989). 'The Politics of Identity', in Hall and Jacques (1989).

Burgess, Robert G., ed. (1982). *Field Research: A Sourcebook and Field Manual*. London: Allen & Unwin.

(1984). *In the Field: An Introduction to Field Research*. London: Allen & Unwin.

Burke, Peter (1989). 'History as Social Memory', in T. Butler (1989a).

Buss, Allan R. (1979). 'Dialectics, History, and Development: The Historical Roots of the Individual-Society Dialectic', in Baltes and Brim (1979).

Butler, R. (1975). *Why Survive: Being Old in America*. New York: Harper & Row.

Butler, Thomas, ed. (1989a). *Memory: History, Culture and the Mind*. Oxford: Basil Blackwell.

(1989b). 'Memory: A Mixed Blessing', in Butler (1989a).

Buxton, Neil K., and Derek H. Aldcroft, eds. (1979). *British Industry Between the Wars: Instability and Industrial Development 1919–1939*. London: Scolar Press.

Caldecott, Leonie (1984). *Women of Our Century*. London: BBC.

Campbell, Bee (1987). *The Iron Ladies: Why Women Vote Tory*. London: Virago.

Caradon, Lord, C. Coulson, and T. Huddleston (1967). *Three Views on Commitment Delivered to an Oxfam Youth Discussion in 1966*. London: Longman.

Carmines, Edward G., and Richard A. Zellar (1979). *Reliability and Validity Assessment*. London: Sage.

Carr, E. H. (1961). *What Is History?* Harmondsworth: Penguin.

Caute, David (1973). *The Fellow-Travellers: A Postscript to the Enlightenment*. London: Weidenfeld & Nicolson.

(1988). *Sixty-eight: The Year of the Barricades*. London: Hamish Hamilton.

Centre for Contemporary Culture Studies (1982). *Making Histories: Studies in History-writing and Politics*. London: Hutchinson.

Chaplin, Harry, ed. (1983). *Jack Lindsay: A Catalogue of First Editions Extensively Annotated by the Author, Together with Letters, Manuscripts, and Association Items*. Sydney: The Wentworth Press.

Clark, J., M. Heinemann, D. Margolies and C. Snee, eds. (1979). *Culture and Crisis in Britain in the Thirties*. London: Lawrence Wishart.

Cliff, Tony, and Donny Gluckstein (1986). *Marxism and the Trade Union Struggle: The General Strike of 1926*. London: Bookmarks.

Cohen, Stanley (1972). *Folk Devils and Moral Panics: The Creation of the Mods and Rockers*. London: Sociology and the Modern World.

Cohn-Bendit, Dany (1986). *Nous l'avons tant aimée, la Revolution*. Paris: Editions Bernard Barrault.

Coleman, Peter G. (1986). *Ageing and Reminiscence Processes : Social and Clinical Implications*. Chichester: John Wiley & Sons.

Condor, Susan (1989). '"Biting into the Future"': Social Change and the Social Identity of Women', in Skevington and Baker (1989).

Cook, Judith, ed. (1979). *Apprentices of Freedom*. London: Quartet Books.

Cottle, Thomas J. (1982). 'The Life Study: On Mutual Recognition and Subjective Inquiry', in Burgess (1982).

Crossman, Richard (1949). *The God That Failed*. New York: Bantam Books.

Cumming, Elaine, and William E. Henry (1961). *Growing Old : The Process of Disengagement*. New York: Basic Books.

Cunningham, Valentine, ed. (1986). *Spanish Front : Writers on the Civil War*. Oxford: Oxford University Press.

Dash, Jack (1987). *Good Morning, Brothers!* London: London Borough of Tower Hamlets.

Datan, Nancy, and Leon H. Ginsberg, eds. (1975). *Life-Span Developmental Psychology : Normative Life Crises*. London: Academic Press.

Davies, A. (1980). *Skills, Outlook and Passions : Psychoanalytic Contribution to the Study of Politics*. Cambridge: Cambridge University Press.

Davies, Graham M., and Donald M. Thomson. (1988). *Memory in Context : Context in Memory*. Chichester: John Wiley & Sons.

de Beauvoir, Simone (1970). *Old Age*. Harmondsworth: Penguin.

DeWaele, J. P., and R. Harre (1979). 'Autobiography as a Psychological Method', in Ginsburg (1979).

Dill, Bonnie Thornton (1983). 'Race, Class and Gender: Prospects for an All-Inclusive Sisterhood', *Feminist Studies* 9(1): 131–156.

(1987). 'The Dialectics of Black Womanhood', in Harding (1987a).

Draper, Hal, and Anne G. Lipow (1976). 'Marxist Women versus Bourgeois Feminism', *Socialist Register* 179–226.

Ebbinghaus, H. (1885/1964). *On Memory*. Trans. H. A. Ruger and C. E. Bussenius. New York: Dover.

Elbers, Ed (1987). 'Critical Psychology and the Development of Motivation as Historical Process', in Broughton (1987a).

Elder, Glen H., Jr (1981). 'History and the Life Course', in Bertaux (1981).

Ellwood, Sheelagh (1988). 'Oral History and Spanish Fascism', *Oral History* 16.2 (Autumn 1988): 57–66.

Erikson, Erik (1963). *Childhood and Society*. Harmondsworth: Penguin.

Erikson, Erik, Joan Erikson and Helen Kivnick (1986). *Vital Involvement in Old Age*. London: W. W. Norton.

Eyesenck, H. J. (1954). *Psychology of Politics*. London: Routledge.

Farley, Margaret (1986). *Personal Commitments : Beginning, Keeping, Changing*. San Francisco: Harper & Row.

Filstead, William J., ed. (1970). *Qualitative Methodology : Firsthand Involvement with the Social World*. Chicago: Markham Publishing Co.

Finch, Janet (1984). '"It's Great to Have Someone to Talk to"': The Ethics and Politics of Interviewing Women', in Bell and Roberts (1984).

Florey, R. A. (1980). *The General Strike of 1926 : The Economic, Political and Social Causes of that Class War*. London: John Calder.

Ford, Janet, and Ruth Sinclair (1987). *Sixty Years On: Women Talk about Old Age*. London: The Women's Press.

Frank, Geyla (1985). 'Becoming the Other: Empathy and Biographical Interpretation', *Biography* 8.3 (Summer 1985): 189–210.

Fraser, Ronald (1979). *Blood of Spain: The Experience of Civil War, 1836–1939*. London: Allen Lane.

Freeman, Mark (1984). 'History, Narrative, and Life-Span Developmental Knowledge', *Human Development* 27: 1–19.

Freire, Paulo (1972). *Pedagogy of the Oppressed*. Harmondsworth: Penguin.

Freud, S. (1920/1979). 'The Psychogenesis of a Case of Homosexuality in a Woman', in *Case Histories*, Vol. 2. Harmondsworth: Penguin.

Frisch, Michael H. (1981). 'The Memory of History', *Radical History Review* 25: 9–23.

Galbraith, J. K. (1990). 'Why the Right is Wrong', *Guardian*, 26 January 1990.

Geiger, Susan, N. G. (1986). 'Women's Life Histories: Method and Content', *Signs: Journal of Women in Culture and Society* 11.2: 334–351.

Gergen, K. J. (1980). 'The Emerging Crisis in Life-Span Developmental Psychology', in Baltes and Brim (1980).

Gilligan, Carol (1979). 'Women's Place in Man's Life Cycle', *Harvard Educational Review* 49.4: 431–446.

(1982). *In a Different Voice: Psychological Theory and Women's Development*. Cambridge, MA: Harvard University Press.

(1985). Methods course taught at the Harvard Graduate School of Education, Cambridge, MA, Spring 1985.

Ginsburg, Gerald Phillip, ed. (1979). *Emerging Strategies in Social Psychological Research*. Chichester: John Wiley & Sons.

Gioseffi, Daniela, ed. (1988). *Women on War: Essential Voices for the Nuclear Age*. New York: Touchstone Books.

Gittins, Diana (1979). 'Oral History, Reliability and Recollection', in Moss and Goldstein (1979).

Goffman, Erving (1959). *The Presentation of Self in Everyday Life*. Harmondsworth: Penguin.

Green, N. (1970). 'The Communist Party and the War in Spain', *Marxism Today* 14.10. (October 1970): 316–324.

Grele, R. ed. (1985). *Envelopes of Sound: The Art of Oral History*, 2nd edn. Chicago: Precedent Publishing Inc.

Griffin, Christine (1989). '"I'm not a Women's Libber, But..."' Feminism, Consciousness and Identity', in Skevington and Baker (1989).

Griffiths, Richard (1983). *Fellow Travellers of the Right: British Enthusiasts for Nazi Germany 1933–9*. London: Allen Lane.

Gurin, Patricia, and Hazel Marks (1989). 'Cognitive Consequences of Gender Identity', in Skevington and Baker (1989).

Hall, Stuart, and Martin Jacques, eds. (1989). *New Times: The Changing Face of Politics in the 1990s*. London: Lawrence & Wishart.

Hammersley, Martyn (1989). *The Dilemma of Qualitative Method: Herbert Blumer and the Chicago Tradition*. London: Routledge.

Hannington, Wal (1936/1977). *Unemployed Struggles 1919–1936: My Life and Struggles amongst the Unemployed*. London: Lawrence & Wishart.

Harding, Sandra, ed. (1987a). *Feminism and Methodology*. Milton Keynes: Open University Press.

(1987b). 'Introduction: Is There a Feminist Method?', in Harding (1987a).

Hareven, T. K. (1982). 'Life Course and Aging in Historical Perspective', in Hareven and Adams (1982).

Hareven, T. K., and Kathleen J. Adams, eds. (1982). *Ageing and Life Course Transitions: An Interdisciplinary Perspective*. London: Tavistock Publications.

Harris, Laurence (1990). 'Why I Remain a Small "c" communist', *Guardian*, 4 January 1990.

Heinemann, Margot (1976). '1956 and the Communist Party', *Socialist Register* 43–57.

Henderson, Lesley, ed. (1990). *Twentieth Century Romance and Historical Writers*, 2nd edn. London: St James Press.

Hermann, Margaret G., ed. (1986a). *Political Psychology: Contemporary Problems and Issues*. London: Jossey-Bass Publishers.

(1986b). 'Prologue: What is Political Psychology?', in Hermann (1986a).

Hessing, Dick J., Henk Elffers and Russell H. Weigel (1988). 'Exploring the Limits of Self-Reports and Reasoned Action: An Investigation of the Psychology of Tax Evasion Behaviour', *Journal of Personality and Social Psychology* 54.3: 405–413.

Hindley, Colin (1979). 'Problems of Interviewing in Obtaining Retrospective Information', in Moss and Goldstein (1979).

Hobsbawm, Eric (1986). 'The Age of Political Nervous Breakdown', *Guardian*, 20th October 1986.

(1990). 'Waking from History's Great Dream', *The Independent on Sunday*, 4 February 1990.

Hogg, Michael A., and Dominic Abrams (1988). *Social Identifications: A Social Psychology of Intergroup Relations and Group Processes*. London: Routledge.

Hoggart, Richard (1986). 'A Publishing Initiative that Shaped the Future', *The Observer*, 18 May 1986.

Honore, Deborah Duncan, ed. (1988). *Trevor Huddleston: Essays on His Life and Work*. Oxford: Oxford University Press.

Hood, Sidney (1943). *The Hero in History: A Study in Limitation and Possibility*. Boston: Beacon Press.

Huddleston, Trevor (1990). *Father Huddleston's Picture Book*. London: Kliptown Books.

Inglis, Fred (1982). *Radical Earnestness: English Social Theory 1880–1980*. Oxford: Martin Robertson.

Itzin, Catherine (1986). 'Media Images of Women: The Social Construction of Ageism and Sexism', in Wilkinson (1986).

James, William (1890). *The Principles of Psychology*, Vol. 1. New York: Macmillan.

Jay, Paul (1987). 'What's the Use? Critical Theory and the Study of Autobiography', *Biography* 10.1 (Winter 1987): 39–54.

Jeffreys, Margot, ed. (1989). *Growing Old in the Twentieth Century*. London: Routledge.

Jeffreys, Margot, and Pat Thane (1989). 'Introduction: An Aging Society and Aging People', in Jeffreys (1989).

Jennings, M. Kent, and Richard G. Niemi (1974). *The Political Character of Adolescence: The Influence of Families and Schools*. Princeton: Princeton University Press.

Johnson, Samuel (1969). *The Rambler*. New Haven: Yale University Press.

Jupp, James (1982). *The Radical Left in Britain 1931–1941*. London: Frank Cass & Co. Ltd.

Kaufman, Sharon (1986). *The Ageless Self: Sources of Meaning in Late Life*. New York: Meridian.

Kaufman, W., ed. (1956). *Existentialism from Dostoevsky to Sartre*. New York: Meridian.

Kegan, Robert (1982). *The Evolving Self: Problem and Process in Human Development*. Cambridge, MA: Harvard University Press.

Keniston, K. (1968). *Young Radicals*. New York: Harcourt Brace.

Kimble, Judy, and Elaine Unterhalter (1982). '"We Opened the Road for You, You Must Go Forward" ANC Women's Struggles, 1912–1982', *Feminist Review* 12 (October 1982): 11–35.

Kingsford, Peter (1982). *The Hunger Marches in Britain 1920–1936*. London: Lawrence & Wishart.

Klugmann, James (1979). 'The Crisis in the Thirties: A View from the Left', in Clark *et al.* (1979).

Kohlberg, Lawrence (1981). *Essays on Moral Development*, Vol. 1, *The Philosophy of Moral Development*. San Francisco: Harper & Row.

(1984). *Essays on Moral Development*, Vol. 2, *The Psychology of Moral Development*. San Francisco: Harper & Row.

Kohlberg, Lawrence, and Richard Shulik (1981). 'The Aging Person as Philosopher: Moral Development in the Adult Years'. Cambridge, MA: Center for Moral Education, Harvard Graduate School of Education. Mimeo.

Kohli, Martin (1981). 'Biography: Account, Text, Method', in Bertaux (1981).

Larkin, Philip (1974). 'The Old Fools', in *High Windows*. London: Faber & Faber.

Laslett, Peter (1989). *A Fresh Map of Life: The Emergence of the Third Age*. London: Weidenfeld & Nicolson.

Lasswell, H. D. (1930). *Psychopathology and Politics*. New York: Viking.

LeBon, G. (1896). *The Crowd: A Study of the Popular Mind*. London: Unwin.

Lenin, V. (1960). 'The Irish Rebellion of 1916', in *Collected Works XXII*. London: Lawrence & Wishart.

(1985 [1934]). *On the Emancipation of Women*. Moscow: Progress Publishers.

Levinson, Daniel J. (1978). *The Seasons of a Man's Life*. New York: Alfred A. Knopf.

Lewis, John (1970). *The Left Book Club: An Historical Record*. London: Victor Gollancz Ltd.

Lichtheim, George (1970). *A Short History of Socialism*. London: Weidenfeld & Nicolson.

Lichtman, Richard (1987). 'The Illusion of Maturation in an Age of Decline', in Broughton (1987).

Liddington, Jill, and Jill Norris (1978). *One Hand Tied Behind Us: The Rise of the Women's Suffrage Movement*. London: Virago.

Lifton, Robert Jay (1986). *The Nazi Doctors : Medical Killing and the Psychology of Genocide.* New York: Basic Books.

Lindsay, Jack (1982). *Life Rarely Tells: An Autobiography in Three Volumes.* Harmondsworth: Penguin.

Lindzey, G., and E. Aronson, eds. (1968). *The Handbook of Social Psychology,* 2nd edn, Vol. I. Reading, MA: Addison Wesley.

Louw-Potgieter, Joha (1986). 'The Social Identity of Dissident Afrikaners', Ph.D dissertation, University of Bristol.

Macintyre, Stuart Forbes (1975). 'Marxism in Britain 1917–1933', Ph.D dissertation, University of Cambridge.

MacKinnon, Catharine A. (1987). 'Feminism, Marxism, Method, and the State: Toward Feminist Jurisprudence', in Harding (1987a).

MacNeice, Louis (1979). *The Collected Poems of Louis MacNeice,* ed. E. R. Dodds. London: Faber & Faber.

Maley, William (1987). 'Ireland and the Origins of English Imperialism', paper presented to the Department of Social and Political Sciences, University of Cambridge, November 1987.

MARHO the Radical Historians Organization (1983). *Visions of History.* Manchester: Manchester University Press.

Marsh, Allan (1977). *Protest and Political Consciousness.* London: Sage.

Marshall, Judi (1986). 'Exploring the Experiences of Women Managers: Towards Rigour in Qualitative Method', in Wilkinson (1986).

Marshall, Victor, ed. (1987). *Later Life: Social Psychology of Aging.* London: Sage.

Martin, David E., and David Rubinstein, Eds. (1979). *Ideology and the Labour Movement: Essays Presented to John Saville.* London: Croom Helm.

Marwick, Arthur (1970). *Social Change in Britain 1920–1970.* London: Birbeck College.

Marx, Karl (1977). *Karl Marx Selected Writings,* ed. David McLellan. Oxford: Oxford University Press.

Mass Observations (1939/1986). *Britain.* London: Cressett Library.

(1943/1987). *The Pub and the People.* London: Cressett Library.

McCord, Phyllis Frus (1986). 'A Specter Viewed by a Specter: Autobiography in Biography', *Biography* 9.3: 219–228.

McCraken, Grant (1988). *The Long Interview.* London: Sage.

Meer, Fatima (1988). *Higher than Hope: A Biography of Nelson Mandela.* London: Hamish Hamilton.

Miliband, R. (1977). *Marxism and Politics.* Oxford University Press.

(1979). 'John Saville: A Presentation', in Martin and Rubinstein (1979).

Miliband, R., and J. Saville, eds. (1976). *Socialist Register,* Part I, *1956 and After.* London: Merlin.

Mishler, Eliot (1986). *The Research Interview: Narrative and Context.* Cambridge, MA: Harvard University Press.

Modgil, Sohan, and Celia Modgil, eds. (1985). *Lawrence Kohlberg: Consensus and Controversy.* London: The Falmer Press.

Morris, William (1934). *William Morris: Selected Writings,* ed. G. D. H. Cole. Bloomsbury: The Nonesuch Press.

Mosley, Sir Oswald Ernald (1932). *The Greater Britain.* London: BUF.

Moss, Louis, and H. Goldstein, eds. (1979). *The Recall Method in Social Surveys*. London: University of London Institute.

Mowat, Charles Loch (1955). *Britain Between the Wars 1918–1940*. London: Methuen.

Neisser, U., ed. (1982). *Memory Observed: Remembering in Natural Contexts*. San Francisco: Freeman.

Nesselroade, John R., and Hayne W. Reese, eds. (1973). *Life-Span Developmental Psychology: Methodological Issues*. New York: Academic Press.

New Reasoner, The (Summer 1957–Summer 1959), Vols. 1–10.

Newton, Kenneth (1969). *The Sociology of British Communism*. London: Allen Lane.

Nisbet, Dorothea E. (1984). 'Social Activism among the Ageing: An Empirical Study of its Attitudinal, Ideological and Personality Correlates', Ph.D dissertation, State University of New York, Buffalo.

Oakley, Ann (1981) 'Interviewing Women: A Contradiction in Terms', in Roberts (1981).

Outhwaite, W. (1975). *Understanding Social Life: The Method Called 'Verstehen'*. London: Allen & Unwin.

Palmer, Alan (1983). *Dictionary of Twentieth Century History 1900–1982*. Harmondsworth: Penguin.

Parker, Ian (1989). *The Crisis in Modern Social Psychology and How to End It*. London: Routledge.

Parker, Ian, and John Shotter, eds. (1990). *Deconstructing Social Psychology*. London: Routledge.

Passerini, Luisa (1987). *Fascism in Popular Memory: The Cultural Experience of the Turin Working Class*. Cambridge: Cambridge University Press.

Peele, Gillian, and Chris Cook, eds. (1975). *The Politics of Reappraisal 1918–1939*. London: Macmillan.

Pelling, Henry (1975). *The British Communist Party: A Historical Profile*. London: A & C Black.

Personal Narratives Group (1989). *Interpreting Women's Lives: Feminist Theory and Personal Narratives*. Indiana: Indiana University Press.

Petrov, Krink Vidakovik (1989). 'Memory and Oral Tradition', in Butler (1989a).

Phillipson, Chris (1982). *Capitalism and the Construction of Old Age*. London: Macmillan.

Piaget, Jean (1977). *The Essential Piaget*, ed. H. E. Gruber and J. J. Voneche. London: Routledge.

Pimlott, Ben (1977). *Labour and the Left in the 1930s*. London: Allen & Unwin.

Pope, Alexander (1896). *The Poetical Works*. New York: Thomas Y. Cromwell and Co.

Popular Memory Group (1982). 'Popular Memory: Theory, Politics, Method', in Centre for Contemporary Cultural Studies (1982).

Prins, Gwyn, ed. (1990). *Spring in Winter: The 1989 Revolutions*. Manchester: Manchester University Press.

Pugh, Martin (1980). 'Women's Suffrage in Britain 1867–1928'. London: The Historical Association Pamphlets.

Pugh, Patricia (1984). *Educate, Agitate, Organize : 100 Years of Fabian Socialism.* London: Methuen.

Ramazanoglu, Caroline (1989). *Feminism and the Contradictions of Oppression.* London: Routledge.

Ramden, Ron (1987). *The Making of the Black Working Class in Britain.* Aldershot, Hants.: Gower.

Reber, Arthur S. (1985). *The Penguin Dictionary of Psychology.* Harmondsworth: Penguin.

Reicher, S. (1987). 'Crowd Behaviour as Social Action', in Turner *et al.* (1987).

Reid, Betty (1979). 'The Left Book Club in the Thirties', in Clark *et al.* (1979).

Riegel, K. F. (1973). 'The Recall of Historical Events', *Behavioral Science* 18: 354–363.

(1976). *Psychology of Development and History.* New York: Plenum Press.

(1979). *Foundations of Dialectical Psychology.* London: Academic Press.

Riegel, K. F., and J. A. Meacham, eds. (1976). *The Developing Individual in a Changing World* (2 vols.). The Hague: Mouton.

Riessman, Catherine Kohler (1987). 'When Gender is Not Enough: Women Interviewing Women', *Gender and Society* 1.2 (June 1987): 172–207.

Roberts, Helen, ed. (1981). *Doing Feminist Research.* London: Routledge.

Robinson, John A. (1986). 'Autobiographical Memory: A Historical Prologue', in Rubin (1986).

Rokeach, M. (1960). *The Open and Closed Mind.* New York: Basic Books.

Rowbotham, Sheila (1973). *Hidden From History: 300 Years of Women's Oppression and the Fight against it.* London: Pluto Press.

(1977). *A New World for Women. Stella Browne: Socialist Feminist.* London: Pluto Press.

Rubin, David C., ed. (1986a). *Autobiographical Memory.* Cambridge: Cambridge University Press.

Rubin, David C., Scott E. Wetzler and Robert D. Nebes (1986b). 'Autobiographical Memory Across the Lifespan', in Rubin (1986a).

Runyan, William McKinley (1982). *Life Histories and Psychobiography: Explorations in Theory and Method.* Oxford: Oxford University Press.

Russell, Bertrand (1956/1986). 'Portraits from Memory', in *Bertrand Russell on God and Religion*, ed. A. Seckel. Buffalo, New York: Prometheus Books.

Russell, Diana (1989). *Lives of Courage: Women for a New South Africa.* London: Virago.

Russell, Dora (1925). *Hypatia : or Women and Knowledge.* London: Kegan Paul, Trench, Trubner & Co. Ltd.

Sartre, Jean Paul (1956). 'Existentialism is a Humanism', in W. Kaufman (1956).

Saville, John (1976). 'Twentieth Party Congress and the British Communist Party', *Socialist Register* 1–23.

(1977). 'May Day 1937', in Briggs and Saville (1977).

Schwartz, Howard, and Jerry Jacobs (1979). *Qualitative Sociology : A Method to the Madness.* London: Collier Macmillan.

Schweitzer, Albert (1925). *Memories of Childhood and Youth.* New York: Macmillan.

(1933). *Out of My Life and Thought: An Autobiography.* New York: Henry Holt & Co.

Sears, David O. (1987). 'Political Psychology', *Annual Review of Psychology* 38: 229–255.

Sears, Elizabeth (1986). *The Ages of Man: Medieval Interpretation of the Life Cycle*. Princeton: Princeton University Press.

Seckel, Al, ed. (1986). *Bertrand Russell on God and Religion*. Buffalo, NY: Prometheus Books.

Sherif, Carolyn Wood (1987). 'Bias in Psychology', in Harding (1987a).

Skevington, S., and D. Baker, eds. (1989). *The Social Identity of Women*. London: Sage.

Smith, Bernard, ed. (1984). *Culture and History: Essays Presented to Jack Lindsay*. Sydney, NSW: Hale & Iremonger.

Smith, M. B. (1977). 'A Dialectical Social Psychology: Comments on a Symposium', *Personality and Social Psychology Bulletin* 3: 719–724.

Sparks, J. R. (1989). 'Problems of Order in Maximum Security Prisons: Notes on a Research Process', unpublished paper, Institute of Criminology, University of Cambridge.

Spelman, Elizabeth (1988). *Inessential Woman: Problems of Exclusion in Feminist Thought*. Boston: Beacon Press.

Spender, Dale (1984). *Time and Tide Wait for No Man*. London: Pandora Press.

Sugarman, Leonie (1986). *Life-Span Development: Concepts, Theories and Interventions*. London: Methuen.

Tajfel, Henri, ed. (1978a). *Differentiation Between Social Groups: Studies in the Social Psychology of Intergroup Relations*. London: Academic Press.

(1978b). 'The Achievement of Group Differentiation', in Tajfel (1978a).

(1978c). 'Interindividual Behaviour and Intergroup Behaviour', in Tajfel (1978a).

(1978d). 'Social Categorization, Social Identity and Social Comparison', in Tajfel (1978a).

(1981). *Human Groups and Social Categories: Studies in Social Psychology*. Cambridge: Cambridge University Press.

ed. (1982). *Social Identity and Intergroup Relations*. Cambridge: Cambridge University Press.

ed. (1984). *The Social Dimension: European Developments in Social Psychology*, Vols. 1 and 2. Cambridge: Cambridge University Press.

Tajfel, Henri, M. G. Billig and R. P. Bundy (1971). 'Social Categorization and Intergroup Behaviour', *European Journal of Social Psychology* 1.2: 149–178.

Tanner, John, MIRC (Member of the Idle Rich Class) [Shaw, Bernard] (1905/1971). 'The Revolutionists' Handbook and Pocket Companion', in G. B. Shaw, *Collected Plays with their Prefaces*, Vol. 2. London: Max Reinhardt, The Bodley Head.

Thomae, Hans (1979). 'The Concept of Development and Life-Span Developmental Psychology', in Baltes and Brim (1979).

Thomas, Dylan (1974). 'Do Not Go Gently into that Good Night', in *Dylan Thomas: The Poems*, ed. Daniel Jones. London: Dent.

Thomas, William I., and Dorothy Swaine Thomas (1928). *The Child in America*. New York: Knopf.

Thompson, E. P. (1968). *The Making of the English Working Class*. Harmondsworth: Penguin.

Thompson, Paul, Catherine Itzin and Michele Abdenstern (1990). *I Don't Feel Old : The Experience of Later Life*. Oxford: Oxford University Press.

Turner, J. C. (1982). 'Towards a Cognitive Redefinition of the Social Group' in Tajfel (1982).

Turner, J. C., M. A. Hogg, P. J. Oakes, S. D. Reicher and M. S. Wetherell (1987). *Rediscovering the Social Group: A Self-Categorization Theory*. Oxford: Basil Blackwell.

Turner, J. C., and Penelope J. Oakes (1986). 'The Significance of the Social Identity Concept for Social Psychology with Reference to Individualism, Interactionism and Social Change', *British Journal of Social Psychology* 25: 237–252.

Victor, Christina (1989). 'Income Inequality in Later Life', in Jeffreys (1989).

Wallas, G. (1908/1921). *Human Nature in Politics*. New York: Alfred Knopf.

Webb, Sidney, and Beatrice Webb (1932). *Methods of Social Study*. London: Longman, Green & Co.

Wilde, William H., Joy Hooton and Barry Andrews (1985). *The Oxford Companion to Australian Literature*. Melbourne: Oxford University Press.

Wilkinson, Sue, ed. (1986). *Feminist Social Psychology: Developing Theory and Practice*. Milton Keynes: Open University Press.

Williams, Raymond (1983). *Keywords: A Vocabulary of Culture and Society*. London: Fontana Press.

Winter, J. M. (1974). *Socialism and the Challenge of War: Ideas and Politics in Britain, 1912–18*. London: Routledge.

    (1985). *The Great War and the British People*. London: Macmillan.

Zandy, Janet, ed. (1990). *Calling Home: Working Class Women's Writings*. New Brunswick: Rutgers University Press.

Index